RELIGIOUS EDUCATION IN A
PLURALIST SOCIETY

Woburn Education Series

General Series Editor: Professor Peter Gordon

For over 20 years this series on the history, development and policy of education, under the distinguished editorship of Peter Gordon, has been evolving into a comprehensive and balanced survey of important trends in teaching and educational policy. The series is intended to reflect the changing nature of education in present-day society. The books are divided into four sections – educational policy studies, educational practice, the history of education and social history – and reflect the continuing interest in this area.

For a full series listing, please visit our website: www.woburnpress.com

Educational Policy Studies
Education and Policy in England in the Twentieth Century
Peter Gordon, Richard Aldrich and Dennis Dean

A Significant Social Revolution: Cross-Cultural Aspects of the Evolution of Compulsory Education
edited by J.A. Mangan

The State and Higher Education
Brian Salter and Ted Tapper

Educational Reconstruction: The 1944 Education Act and the Twenty-first Century
Gary McCulloch

Fee-paying Schools and Educational Change in Britain: Between the State and the Marketplace
Ted Tapper

Going Comprehensive in England and Wales: A Study of Uneven Change
Alan C. Kerckhoff, Ken Fogelman, David Crook and David Reeder

Education Policy-making in England and Wales: The Crucible Years, 1895–1911
Neil Daglish

Her Majesty's Inspectorate of Schools since 1944: Standard Bearers or Turbulent Priests?
John E. Dunford

RELIGIOUS EDUCATION IN A PLURALIST SOCIETY

The Key Philosophical Issues

Peter R. Hobson

University of New England, Armidale, NSW, Australia

and

John S. Edwards

Catholic Education Office, Sydney, Australia

RoutledgeFalmer
Taylor & Francis Group

LONDON AND NEW YORK

First Published in 1999 in Great Britain by
WOBURN PRESS
Reprinted 2004
by RoutledgeFalmer
2 Park Square, Milton Park, Abingdon,
Oxon, OX14 4RN

Transferred to Digital Printing 2004

British Library Cataloguing in Publication Data
Hobson, Peter R. (Peter Ross)
Religious education in a pluralist society.
(The Woburn education series)
1. Religious education – Philosophy
I. Title II. Edwards, John S.
200.7'1
ISBN 0-7130-0218-2 (cloth)
ISBN 0-7130-4039-4 (paper)
ISSN 1462-2076

Library of Congress Cataloging in Publication Data
Hobson, Peter R.
Religious education in a pluralist society: the
key philosophical issues / Peter R. Hobson and
John S. Edwards.
    p. cm. – (Woburn education series, ISSN 1462-2076)
Includes bibliographical references and index.
ISBN 0-7130-0218-2 (cloth). – ISBN 0-7130-4039-4 (paper).
1. Religious education – Philosophy. 2. Critical
realism. 3. Liberalism. I. Edwards, John S., 1950–
II. Title. III. Series.
BV1464.H63   1999
291.7'5'01–dc21   98–35315
                                                       CIP

Contents

Acknowledgements   vii

Foreword by John Hull   ix

Introduction   xiii

PART I: The Legitimacy and Place of Religious Education in Schools

1   A Rationale for Religious Education in the Curriculum   3

2   Challenges to Religious Education in the Curriculum: 26
Scepticism, Exclusivism, Relativism, and Reductionism

PART II: Responses to Pluralism in the Teaching of Religious Education

3   The Implications of Religious Diversity for Religious   47
Education: The Case for Extended Pluralism

4   Critical Realism and the Role of Models in Religion   66

PART III: Ethical, Political, and Social Dimensions of Religious
Education

5   The Ethics of Belief Debate and its Implications for   85
Religious Education in a Liberal Democratic Society

6   The Rights of Parents, Children, and the State in   105
Religious Upbringing

PART IV: The Teaching of Religious Education: Case Studies and
Recommendations

7   Surveys of Religious Education Policies and Programmes   131
in the UK, the USA, and Australia

8   The Teaching of Religious Education: Recommendations   161
     and a Charter for the Teacher

     Glossary   173

     Further Reading   179

     Index   181

Acknowledgements

We gratefully acknowledge the assistance of the following colleagues: Peter Forrest, Erle Robinson, and Adrian Walsh – all of the Philosophy Department, University of New England, Australia – for helpful comments on various of the chapters; Kathleen Engebretson of the Australian Catholic University, Victoria, Australia for assistance with the Victoria section of Chapter 7 and Robert Jackson of the University of Warwick, UK for assistance with the UK section of Chapter 7.

Peter Hobson would also like to acknowledge with thanks the financial support received from the Faculty of Education, Health and Professional Studies of the University of New England in the form of an Internal Research Grant in 1997 which assisted in the completion of this book.

Some of the arguments in this book have appeared in journals in articles written by the present authors and we are grateful for permission to use material drawn from the following sources:

Hobson, P.R. and Edwards, J. (1997). 'The Pluralist Predicament in Studies of Religion', *Educational Philosophy and Theory*, Vol. 29, No. 2, pp. 33–50.

Hobson, P.R. (1995). 'What Does Religious Pluralism Mean for the Teaching of Religious Studies?', *Religious Education Journal of Australia*, Vol. 11, No. 3, pp. 22–5.

Hobson, P.R. and Edwards, J. (1995). 'The Ethics of Belief Debate and its Implications for Curriculum Developments in Religious Studies', *Curriculum Perspectives,* Vol. 15, No. 3, pp. 21–31.

Hobson, P.R. and Edwards, J. (1994). 'A Liberal Education Rationale for Studies of Religion Programs and its Application to Courses in Three Australian States', *Australian Journal of Education,* Vol. 38, No. 3, pp. 282–99.

Edwards, J. and Hobson, P.R. (1992). 'Recent Curriculum Reforms in NSW: What Place is there for Liberal Education?', *Curriculum Perspectives,* Vol. 12, No. 4, pp. 27–9.

Hobson, P.R. and Edwards, J. (1991). 'Religious Studies in the Secondary School Curriculum: A Suggested Model and a Response to Three Major

Philosophical Objections', *Educational Philosophy and Theory,* Vol. 23, No. 2, pp. 67–81.

Articles from *Curriculum Perspectives* are reproduced in part with permission of the Australian Curriculum Studies Association (Inc.). The article from *Australian Journal of Education* is reproduced in part with permission of the Australian Council for Educational Research Ltd.

Foreword

Almost every country in Europe today has some form of religious education in its state schools. France is a notable exception, but if French young people had been taught about Islam it is possible that the problem of integrating Muslim minorities would not be so great. Albania is also an exception, but in other countries of the former Soviet Union religious education has replaced the atheistic education sponsored by the Communist states. New religious-education provisions have appeared in England, Norway, and several other countries, and in almost every country there is a resurgence of religious-education curriculum development. These trends are not confined to Europe, but are also found in Australia and New Zealand, in post-apartheid South Africa, and in many other countries of Africa and Asia.

Several reasons for the interest in religious education may be suggested. First, it is increasingly evident that religious education shares the ideals of the Enlightenment. Religious education has to do with the development of reason in the area of religion, and religious-education teachers hope to help young people overcome superstition and bigotry. This educational religious education is far removed from the dogmatic instruction of former centuries.

Second, religious education has a vital part to play in education for spiritual, moral, and cultural values. The idea that the world has become a 'global village', popularised in the 1960s, has rapidly faded. We do not live in a harmonious and united world, made intimate by international communications; nor do we live in a developing world, where less developed countries are gradually catching up with the more highly developed ones. On the contrary, the iron curtain and the bamboo curtain have been replaced by the money-curtain. The wealthy two-sevenths of the world, enjoying the so-called 'hard' currencies, are surrounded by an invisible barrier that prevents the world beyond from entering. The barriers of space and time have been overcome by air transport and communication only to be replaced by the barriers created by the international currency markets. So gross is the disparity between the resources of the rich world and those of the poor world that we can go to them but they cannot visit us.

Beyond the money-curtain, which is more or less invisible to those of us who live within it, diseases almost eradicated 40 years ago are rampant once again. In Africa alone 10,000 children die every day from preventable conditions, which are unknown to those of us who live on this side of the money-curtain. This curtain lives not only in financial and economic realities; it lives in our imaginations, in our desires, and it thrives upon our fears and our self-deceptions. It is difficult to see how these forces can be resisted without a reaffirmation of the spiritual and moral values that lie at the heart of the world's religious traditions. However, this is not to say that only religious people can face these problems. The sad truth is that religion itself is a principal source of the illusions that sustain the money-curtain. It is the task of religious education in the West to awaken religious people, both adults and children, to this situation, and to enable Western citizens, whether personally religious or not, to gather new moral and spiritual courage through encounter with the central ideals of religious faith.

The third mission of religious education today is to make religious pluralism intelligible, and to help young people live lives of commitment and purpose in the midst of societies in which the variety of choice is sometimes overwhelming. Every Western country today lives more or less in the presence of religious pluralism. Christianity and Islam no longer face each other across continental borders but live side by side in European, American, and Australian cities. Whether they see the temples and mosques on the street corner, or on their television screens, children today know that there are many ways of living. The task of finding values by which to live is difficult, and it is easy for young people today to retreat into lives of indifferent selfishness. It is the task of modern religious eduation to develop the enthusiasm and optimism of young people, and to help them to shape their lives into patterns of meaning and purpose.

There is much evidence that this kind of modern, critical, spiritual, and pluralistic religious education is welcomed by many young people. In the 1998 public examinations in England, more than 190,000 young people enrolled for religious-education examinations, almost one-third of the entire cohort for the year.

Insofar as it is a legitimate heir to the Enlightenment, offering an image of a social and cultural life lived in peace and justice, religious education may be described as the Utopian Whisper in the ear of modern society. Peter Hobson and John Edwards provide an excellent rationale for modern religious education of this critical, descriptive, and value-oriented kind. Not only is their book a fine introduction to current trends in a number of Western democracies but, by setting out alternative policies with precision and clarity, they help the reader, whether teacher, parent, politician or administrator, sort out the controversial aspects of the subject and so work towards a wider consensus.

It gives me great pleasure to commend this book to everyone concerned with moral, spiritual, and religious values in schools, and to citizens seeking new paths for the future of democracy.

PROFESSOR JOHN M. HULL
University of Birmingham, England
October 1998

Introduction

Religious education in pluralist multi-faith societies such as the United Kingdom, the United States of America, and Australia has undergone radical change in the last 10 to 20 years. In the UK, where religious education has been a mandatory subject in schools since 1944, it has taken on a multi-faith, educational orientation since the 1970s. Despite some questioning by the Conservative Government in the early 1990s of the extent to which this should be taken, it remains the dominant orientation. Meanwhile, studies of religion remains an elective subject for senior school students and here the multi-faith orientation is largely accepted by all concerned.

In the USA, religious education has had a quite different history. Because of the clear separation of Church and State, denominationally based religious education is prohibited from being taught in state schools. However, education *about* religion is allowed and a number of states have developed programmes of a multi-faith nature in this area in recent years.

In Australia on the other hand, denominationally based religious education, while prohibited as part of the official curriculum of state schools, can be taught during school hours by visiting representatives of the local churches or religious groups. In addition to this is a major new development – studies of religion as an educational rather than faith-oriented study has recently been made available in all states up to matriculation level.

Overall then, the climate of change in religious education has involved a major shift towards multi-faith, educationally oriented programmes. This has meant significant changes to both the content and methodology of religious education courses and to the way they are conceived and taught in schools. Similarly, studies of religion as an academic subject at tertiary level has undergone major growth in all three countries in recent years.

This book examines some of the underlying issues surrounding this new orientation in religious education and is intended both for teachers of religion and tertiary students in education and religious studies as well as anyone else interested in the important issues it raises. We are using religious education in a generic sense to cover both studies of religion and education in faith programmes. We particularly focus on studies of religion programmes but many of our recommendations would also be applicable to those education in faith courses which strive to meet educational criteria. It is becoming increasingly clear from discussions in both popular and academic sources that this new approach to religious education represents an exciting area of topical interest in the current educational milieu and one where theory and practice strongly interact. Accordingly, the issues raised in this book have important implications for how religious education should be taught in schools and universities within pluralist, democratic societies.

One of the important implications for the teaching and study of religion is the need for a philosophical dimension, but such a dimension has generally been neglected both in terms of the content and methodology of such courses. Consequently, the issue of the truth status of religious statements has often not been given sufficient treatment but rather religion has been dealt with via phenomenological, sociological, or historical approaches. Valuable as they are, such methodologies do not confront the student with the more difficult but nevertheless crucial issues of the validity of religious belief systems. All religions make significant ontological claims, that is, they assert that the world is structured in a certain way, and no study of them is complete without assessing such claims.

This issue is made more critical by virtue of multiple competing truth claims of the various religions of which we are now more aware due to the nature of modern, pluralist societies. Such competing claims give rise to the problems of scepticism, exclusivism, and relativism. These claims are often dealt with in a descriptive way without any attempt to arrive at a satisfactory solution to the difficulties they raise, which by their very nature require a philosophical treatment.

Accordingly, this book attempts to provide the necessary philosophical underpinning which the study and teaching of religion in modern, pluralist societies require. We have explored and analysed the issues raised in a wide range of contemporary philosophical writing and drawn on those aspects of particular relevance to the understanding of religious issues. Moreover, we seek to present these in a way that is rigorous but at the same time accessible to persons without philosophical training. Of the various chapters in this book, Chapter 2 and the first half of Chapter 4 are the sections that readers without a philosophical background may find somewhat demanding. Such readers may wish to omit the more technical sections on a first reading and just focus on the major conclusions.

The two main branches of philosophy relevant to religious education are epistemology, and moral and political philosophy. Within these two areas the particular philosophical positions presented in this book are critical realism and liberalism respectively. Critical realism steers a mid-course between two extremes: on the one hand, naive realism or positivism which in the religious sphere is often expressed as literalism or fundamentalism, and on the other hand, instrumentalism or relativism which denies any possibility of objective knowledge.

Liberalism involves a commitment to the moral and intellectual freedom of the individual achieved through adherence to rational procedures, and, in the political sphere, to settling disputes by public debate and consensus rather than conflict. This in turn entails a commitment to the values of tolerance, respect for others, and equality of all citizens.

The two key ideas of critical realism and liberalism can be brought together through the overarching concept of epistemic liberalism which is developed in detail in Chapter 3. This is further developed in the political context in Chapter 6 in terms of the concept of comprehensive liberalism.

We believe that in the educational context these philosophical values are best reflected in a contemporary model of liberal education which stresses the three interconnected concepts of critical rationality, personal transcendence, and epistemological coherence. With regard to religious education in particular, this leads to a programme with the following characteristics: it will be genuinely open-ended, draw on a wide range of teaching methodologies (including the philosophical), assume a pluralist understanding of religion, reflect a critical realist epistemology, be sensitive to the issues of the ethics of belief, and stress children's educational rights (with appropriate consideration also given to the rights of parents and the State). These recommended features of religious education programmes will be developed in Parts I to III and then applied to an analysis of current religious education programmes in the UK, the USA, and Australia in Part IV of the present work. This final part concludes with a chapter drawing out the practical implications for the teaching of religious education of the philosophical and educational values argued for throughout the book and includes a charter for the teacher of religious education.

This book covers many areas of topical relevance. Foremost amongst these is the fact that we now live in multi-faith, pluralist societies where individuals interact on a daily basis with a wide range of conflicting belief systems leading to contentious issues such as the growth of fundamentalism, increasing religious intolerance and conflict, and fundamental differences of opinion on central moral problems influenced by religious beliefs such as birth control, abortion, and euthanasia. Moreover, the world has become a global village where all these issues are brought to our attention on a daily basis through the electronic and print media. Religious education programmes can no longer afford to ignore such topics.

Teachers as well as students are confronted by the complexity of these issues. Frequently, teachers have to wrestle with the problem of reconciling their own religious (or non-religious) commitments with the variety of perspectives they are expected to teach in multi-faith religious education. This especially comes to the fore when they find themselves required to deal with controversial ethical issues, such as the treatment of women and religious persecution, that may arise from the beliefs and practices of specific religions. Equally, students have to re-examine their own commitments with respect to these problems in the light of the range of points of view they encounter in such courses. The arguments presented in this book are designed to assist teachers and tertiary students to understand properly and grapple with these topics, and, as a consequence, will influence how school students encounter them in the classroom. For example, a major problem might arise from a clash of values between various groups in society due to different religious convictions and we present the case for resolving this in favour of core democratic values.

Attention to the topics raised in this volume is crucial not just for those with a professional interest in religious education but for everyone interested in contemporary educational and social issues.

We may conclude that the present time represents a watershed in the teaching of religion at both school and university levels due to the influence of living in pluralist societies. The growth and popularity of studies of religion programmes and multi-faith education in most western democracies is a manifestation of this trend. This book is an attempt to provide a theoretical and philosophical framework for dealing with these new developments in the study and teaching of religion.

PART I

The Legitimacy and Place of Religious Education in Schools

1

A Rationale for Religious Education in the Curriculum

A CONTEMPORARY MODEL OF LIBERAL EDUCATION AS THE BASIC JUSTIFICATION

If the study of religion is to meet genuinely educational criteria one must ask what are the underlying educational principles for teaching such a subject. While there are a number of possible justifications – such as promoting tolerance within the community, or helping students to understand the multi-faith and multicultural nature of society – we will argue that the principal educational justification for religious education is best situated within a liberal education model. It will be argued that there are three fundamental concepts underlying such a model: critical rationality, personal transcendence, and epistemological coherence – these will be elaborated in this chapter. A comprehensive theory incorporating these three concepts will be developed which draws upon the traditional theory as expounded by Charles Bailey, ideas gained from the new theory of holistic education, and our own analysis. We will argue throughout this book that the philosophy of liberal education as expounded here provides a critical framework against which to assess the place of religious education in today's society.

The concept of liberal education has a history going back to the Ancient Greeks, but has been interpreted in different ways depending on the social and historical context at the time.[1] The modern educational philosopher, R.S. Peters, suggests that liberal education has traditionally been put forward as a protest against education narrowly conceived to serve 'some extrinsic end such as the production of goods, obtaining a job, or manning a profession' (1966, p. 43). For Peters, liberal education involves a commitment to what is intrinsically worthwhile, to knowledge which has breadth or cognitive perspective, and to forms of education which are neither limited in their scope nor questionable in their methods. Although critics might argue that this is merely a prescription for the traditional school curriculum, Peters' justification opens up a broader perspective which educationists need to consider.

3

What is at issue is access to a world which knowledge unlocks. P.H. Hirst strengthens this view: 'A liberal education is, then, one that, determined in scope and content by knowledge itself, is thereby concerned with the development of mind' (1974, p. 41).

Access to different forms of knowledge develops the rational mind and provides students with key concepts and methods which enable them to interpret and interact with the richly articulated world past men and women have unfolded or created. But the type of knowledge Hirst employs is highly specific and consists of seven logically distinct forms (mathematics, physical sciences, human sciences, history, religion, literature and the fine arts, and philosophy) which correspond basically with the subjects of the traditional grammar school curriculum. Hirst, however, has difficulty in substantiating his claim of seven logically distinct forms and has been subject to a wide range of criticism on this point.[2] Nevertheless, the essential elements of liberal education are clear, in that knowledge and understanding are necessary for one's development as a person because description and explanation of an increasingly complex world of objects and persons are encapsulated within different forms of language and knowledge. Students need access to these if they are to realise their full potential as persons equipped to take part as free agents in such a world and to interact constructively with others in a pluralist, democratic society. Equally clearly, more is at stake within education than mere vocational training or furthering economic goals.

CHARLES BAILEY'S THEORY OF LIBERAL EDUCATION

Other philosophers who have developed this underlying theme of liberal education are R.F. Dearden (1968, 1984), A. O'Hear (1981, 1987), P. Phenix (1964), and J.P. White (1973, 1982). While all of these accounts contain something of value, none of them we believe is sufficiently comprehensive and coherent to stand on its own as a rationale for liberal education in the contemporary educational climate. The writer who comes closest to providing such a rationale is Charles Bailey (1984), in his book *Beyond the Present and the Particular*, although even in his case there are a number of criticisms that can be made of his work, as we shall see. Bailey's book offers a detailed analysis and criticism of three of the above writers – Hirst, Phenix, and White. He finds major faults with each of them and endeavours to set out a definition and justification for liberal education which draws upon their strengths while avoiding their weaknesses.

4

Bailey's model of education presents a cluster of tightly interlocking key concepts centred on the concept of a person. It is the coherence and objective value of these concepts which gives Bailey's model its great plausibility. We will examine his account in some detail as it highlights effectively some of the key educational values that will underlie our discussion of religious education throughout this book. While Bailey's theory was presented in 1984 it still remains the most comprehensive and coherent account of the traditional version of liberal education. We will, however, draw on some more recent writings where necessary to complement and critique Bailey's account and later in this chapter we will argue that his model needs to be supplemented by a more holistic understanding of human experience.

The cluster of five key concepts Bailey utilises is freedom, moral and intellectual autonomy, reason, justification, and knowledge – which are centrally focused on the concept of a person. While Bailey does not systematically show how all these concepts relate one to the other, it is possible to work out a model which indicates the main components necessary to an understanding of liberal education and how each of these concepts fits into it. This model rests on certain basic assumptions about the human condition, such as that objective knowledge is possible and that this can be acquired by the use of our powers of reason to reflect critically on the world of publicly available meanings into which each new generation is introduced. Our position here along with Bailey's thus stands in contrast to the tenets of postmodernism, and in this chapter we attempt to show how the basic assumptions of liberal education have an objective basis. A further defence of the possibility of objective knowledge is provided in Chapter 4, where we argue in favour of a critical realist position.

In considering how such a body of knowledge and understanding is built up, the five key principles apply in the following ways. Firstly, in regard to freedom, the following three questions need to be addressed: (i) what is the person freed from? (ii) what is the person freed for? (iii) what is the means by which this freedom is attained?

In relation to the first of these, Bailey's vision of liberal education is set against an understanding of the human condition wherein men and women have the capacity to 'open [their] minds to the countless imaginary possibilities of human agency set against different visions or understandings of the human situation' (1984, p. 117). Bailey contends, and quite plausibly in our view, that a person is not only born into, but may be entrapped by, the 'specific and limited circumstances of geography, economy, social class and personal encounter and relationship'

5

(1984, p. 21). This occurs because any given set of such factors entails only a limited number of possible horizons, which in turn are a subset of a far richer array of alternatives evident in human history and human imagination. This set of alternatives is opened up even further in the contemporary information age where the world has become a global village with multiple competing cultural, political, and religious perspectives. Accordingly, education should free persons from such limited perspectives and possibilities by letting them see that no single combination of factors uniquely defines the human condition nor exhausts its possibilities. Religious education, because of its concern for fundamental human issues, has much to offer in this area, but, as we shall argue in this book, needs to avoid the sort of entrapment discussed above.

The second question about freedom is what does liberal education free persons for? It frees persons to reflect upon the rich matrix of human possibility and allows them to choose accordingly. This freedom is expressed in the ideal of moral and intellectual autonomy – another of Bailey's key concepts.

The third question about freedom relates to the means of achieving it. Bailey is unequivocal on this: only reason can achieve it (1984, p. 24). In order to understand the logical relationship between reason and freedom we must look again at the two senses in which Bailey uses this term: 'free ... from' and 'free ... for'. Liberal education frees the person *from* the present and the particular, and frees him or her *for* moral and intellectual autonomy.

By autonomy, Bailey means 'self-government, not romantic anarchy' (1984, p. 22). We can to a significant extent control our destiny by understanding and rationally confronting the various forces acting upon us. In relation to reasons for believing and acting, the key point is: 'the reason must be my own. I must come to see for myself why it is right to believe this or do that' (1984, p. 25). The emphasis is not, however, on making rules for oneself, which has been criticised as an incoherent notion (Baier, 1973), but rather on being able to justify following the rules one does. In relation to religious education we may invoke the notion of religious autonomy and define it as a reasoned commitment to a personal philosophy of life with a justifiable position on the place of the transcendent realm within it.

The notion of autonomy as an educational goal has been questioned by some, such as Ruth Jonathon, who says 'overriding allegiance to the promotion of individual autonomy, though consistent with the emancipatory aim for individuals, is incompatible with the general aim of social emancipation for all' (1995, p. 105), because she sees education as a positional good 'where the emancipatory exchange value to those who have it depends in part on others having less of it' (1995, p. 98). However, we believe this is to see education too much in consumer or instrumentalist terms and the emancipatory values of liberal education do not necessarily have an exchange value as do consumer goods, but are generally available and relevant for all. It is utopian to expect that every child will achieve the same degree of emancipation, and unnecessary for this to be achievable in practice for liberal education to remain a valid educational goal. The debates about equality of opportunity versus equality of outcome and the related questions of meritocracy and élitism in education do indeed raise important issues. However, whatever the conclusions reached in this debate, liberal educational values remain relevant core goals for education in contemporary democratic, pluralist society.

Joseph Raz (1986) adds a useful perspective on the importance of autonomy by examining the different types of society in which it may be valued. He points out that the achievement of autonomy is not essential to personal well-being in tradition-directed societies, but in modern industrial and pluralist societies it is crucial:

> It is an ideal particularly suited to the conditions of the industrial age and its aftermath with their fast changing technologies and free movement of labour. They call for an ability to cope with changing technological, economic and social conditions, for an ability to adjust, to acquire new skills, to move from one sub-culture to another, to come to terms with new scientific and moral views. (1986, pp. 369–70)

He goes on to argue that autonomy is not just one goal among others in such a society; it is necessary for any individual to flourish in that society: 'For those of us who live in an autonomy supporting environment there is no choice but to be autonomous: there is no other way to prosper in such a society' (1986, p. 391).

Bernard Williams makes a similar point in discussing the growth of 'reflective consciousness' in modern western societies: 'the urge to reflective understanding of society and our activities goes deeper and is more widely spread in modern society than it has ever been before...' (1985, p. 163).

Raz and Williams thus bring out the central importance of the concept of autonomy for the sort of societies with which this book is concerned while pointing out that it is not necessarily a universal value.

In order to realise our autonomy it is necessary to transcend the restrictions of our socio-economic and cultural background. This also entails not being entrapped in too restricted or limited an understanding of one's personal religious tradition. Increasingly in our modern, multi-faith, pluralist societies children encounter a wide variety of competing religious beliefs both at school and in the society at large. This has led to widespread negative responses to this situation in the form of scepticism, exclusivism, and relativism. In this book we will be arguing that such negative responses are both unnecessary and unjustified. A detailed response to these three problems and the associated problem of reductionism is provided in Chapter 2 and further discussion takes place throughout the book.

To achieve autonomy we must first see the restrictions of our particular social and cultural environment as a possible barrier to personal freedom, as well as be aware of possible alternatives. Such awareness clearly depends on a person's capacity for critical reflection, the ability to set out the alternatives, to marshall the relevant facts, apportion value, justify the choice – in short, to think and reason. Reason, then, is a necessary condition for the freedom entailed in choosing one's life plan.

This means that if liberal education is concerned to develop freedom then it must be equally concerned to develop reason and the rational mind. This naturally leads on to the question: what conditions are necessary for developing reason or the rational mind? Bailey suggests two necessary conditions are justification and knowledge.

Bailey's emphasis on justification is perhaps one of his more important contributions to the liberal education debate. He suggests that our choice of beliefs and actions must reflect a rational decision, and not one based on 'force, threats, irrational emotional appeals, manipulatory conditioning or other influences below the level of consciousness' (1984, p. 11). While he admits a person can simply plump for one option as against another, he believes such a level of response falls 'short of our most commendable characteristic' (1984, p. 11), which Bailey maintains is a person's capacity for justification and that this valuation of justification is actually borne out in practice: 'All research, investigation, debate and decision making techniques would be pointless without their underlying assumption of the need for justification' (1984, p. 11).

In developing his case for the importance of justification, Bailey speaks of a need for care for reason and care for persons (1984, pp. 147ff.). 'Care for reason' centres on our valuation of justification and captures more plausibly what Peters had trouble conveying in his notion of commitment to the standards of a form of knowledge. Peters argued that 'all forms of thought and awareness have their own standards of appraisal. To be on the inside of them is both to understand and to care' (1966, p. 31). Bailey's justification requires the same commitment and care for standards but for a more feasible reason. While Peters' commitment suggests the dedication of an Oxford don, Bailey's is more in touch with the human condition: 'Justification is required as a feature of the attempt to make life rational, to make our activities and beliefs part of an intelligible and coherent whole, to understand what we are about' (1984, p. 12). This suggests that if it is important whether what we believe is true or false, or what we do is right or wrong, then justification matters – and so too the justificatory tests within given bodies of knowledge.

Bailey contends that accepting persons as reasoners and justifiers also gives rise to a moral perspective in the form of an attitude of respect and care for persons. We come to see persons as 'centres of rational purpose and intention ... worthy of being treated accordingly' (1984, p. 13). For Bailey this respect for others is shown by the need to justify our actions towards them: 'the treatment of persons by persons always calls for justification' (1984, p. 13).

In the case of religion, it is equally important to aim at developing justified beliefs and to pay attention to the distinctive tests for truth that apply in this realm. This goal is encapsulated in the notion of the epistemic community which stresses the four key principles of realism, fallibilism, rationalism, and respect for others and which is developed in the context of the ethics of belief debate in Chapter 5. It is argued there that it is essential in religious education for students to develop a commitment to basing their beliefs on thorough and sound evidence and this is presented as a fundamental tenet for the philosophy of religious education developed in this book.

The other necessary condition for developing reason is knowledge. Bailey here endorses the Hirstian argument that knowledge develops the rational mind. Echoing Hirst he says, 'to be rational is ... to become initiated into public bodies of knowledge in which statements gain meaning by their location within clusters of other statements related in publicly organised ways and tested for truth in publicly organised ways' (1984, p. 25). Clearly, in order to make sense of our world and of our socio-economic, cultural, and religious background we must first have 'those forms of knowledge and belief in which we make sense of our experience' (Hirst, 1974, p. 22).

The important question here is not whether knowledge is necessary for building a rational mind, but what type of knowledge is required. Bailey rejects Hirst's forms of knowledge argument and claims that a better basis for selecting curriculum content is to use the criteria of fundamentality and generality in relation to knowledge. The reason is that such knowledge will be 'more rather than less liberating', because fundamental knowledge provides the 'necessary foundation' (1984, p. 22) for one's belief structures.

This property of fundamentality is not a logical property of knowledge, nor does it emerge from some contentious logical analysis of the structure of knowledge as does Hirst's forms of knowledge, but derives from a value judgement as to which knowledge has 'perceived human significance of a general kind' (1984, p. 119). Nevertheless, this for Bailey is an objective judgement of practices seen as 'significant over long periods of time to large numbers of people', one of which is obviously religion. Bailey maintains, incidentally, that other attempts to develop more absolute criteria for choice of curriculum content ultimately break down into matters of judgement.

Bailey is on the right track when he argues that the areas of knowledge to be included in the school curriculum must ultimately depend on a value judgement rather than a dubious logical analysis of knowledge of the Hirstian kind. However, Bailey's value judgement on what areas of knowledge are important is too restrictive. His criterion is for knowledge which has 'perceived human significance of a general kind' demonstrated over an extended period of time. While this principle of selection is certainly valid for establishing what are the major areas of the curriculum, it fails to emphasise sufficiently those aspects of such subjects which lead a person to transcendence, empowerment, and autonomy.

A clear example of this transcending/empowering principle is found in Chapter 4 of this book. There it is argued that an essential component of religious education must be a treatment of the seminal role of models in both science and religion. The justification for this is that not to do so is to risk leading students to draw ill-founded conclusions about religious beliefs based on relativism, exclusivism, reductionism, or unfounded scepticism. In other words, the important role which religious or other world views can have in enriching a person's life may be vitiated through an inadequate understanding of their logical structure. Students are empowered by an adequate engagement with a personal philosophy of life as found in either a religious or non-religious belief system. What is needed then is not merely a value judgement of what has proven valuable over time, as Bailey contends, but a carefully orchestrated set of arguments showing the importance of a particular area of knowledge and its significance for empowering or emancipating students.

Some of the critics of liberal education argue that such an education is essentially conservative in that the type of knowledge favoured has usually been that of the 'Great Books' or the classic literature of the western world, featuring particularly western, white, male voices. However there is no reason why this has to be the case and liberal education, because of its philosophical rationale as presented here, is essentially one that broadens rather than narrows educational experiences. As Warren Nord argues:

> [a liberal education] has considerable liberating potential, even when the canon is relatively conservative, for it should not allow uncritical acceptance of tradition; it understands education as a 'great conversation' (to use Robert Hutchins' phrase), and even within the most conservative canons, the discussants do not agree. It forces critical thinking about major issues that often call tradition and the status quo into question. (1995, p. 88)

Another useful aspect of Bailey's account of liberal education lies in his discussion of intrinsic and instrumental value. Bailey argues that we involve students in fundamental knowledge 'because fundamental understanding of human experience is intrinsically worthwhile' (1984, p. 29). A consequence of this involvement is the instrumental value this knowledge has, because fundamental knowledge underpins a greater range of choices and decisions a student will make in life, and hence has greater liberating potential. Thus, Bailey is arguing for both the intrinsic and instrumental value of liberal education but insisting that the former is logically prior and that the instrumental value follows as a result of the development of intrinsically valuable mental capacities which happen to provide a firm basis for whatever we may wish to do with our life. This is an important contribution to the debate about liberal education which, in the past, has often set up an unproductive dichotomy between intrinsic and instrumental values in relation to education.

To conclude this discussion of Bailey's theory of liberal education and its relevance for the place of religious education in the curriculum, the major virtue in his overall model lies in its identification of the key elements that go to make up the description, justification, content, processes, and aims of liberal education. In this way we believe his account, with amplifications suggested above, is superior to those of some other writers who, as he says, tend to focus on one or two concepts involved in liberal education in isolation from the others. For instance, Hirst stressed knowledge and the development of mind, White, moral autonomy, and Dearden, intellectual autonomy. By using the overarching and unifying concept of personhood as his central principle, Bailey is better able to integrate these elements along with the other key goals that together contribute to the liberally educated person.

CONTRIBUTIONS OF THE HOLISTIC PARADIGM TO OUR UNDERSTANDING OF LIBERAL EDUCATION

While Bailey's account and the key concepts that flow from it are very powerful they are still very much in the traditional liberal education mould in stressing cognitive and discipline-based knowledge goals. Although these aspects of liberal education are very important, we would like to develop a broader, more contemporary understanding of the concept which brings out some other important dimensions. One of these is the holistic paradigm of education which stresses the emotional, social, creative, aesthetic, and spiritual as well as the rational components of human development. It is concerned with relationships and connections between all parts of our experience and aims to produce a fully rounded and balanced individual.

Holistic education emphasises particularly the second of the three goals of liberal education mentioned in the introductory paragraph of this chapter – personal transcendence. Although such a notion is implicit in Bailey's account, especially when he speaks of the need to transcend the restrictions of our socio-economic and cultural background, he is concerned primarily with the intellectual conditions for transcendence. The holistic viewpoint brings out the significance of the broader range of human qualities needed for full transcendence. Not only are we to be intellectually liberated, we also need to be emotionally, socially, and spiritually liberated so all elements of our person are functioning to their fullest potential.

If religious education is to meet the values of the holistic paradigm it needs to be conducted in a way that genuinely encourages enquiry and openness to new perspectives as indicated later in this chapter. For instance, religious education needs to deal with spirituality in a holistic way as a dimension of human experience not limited just to specifically religious beliefs. Anything that contributes to a sense of meaning and purpose in life or provides some broad metaphysical explanation could be deemed to be spiritual in this sense and would be a legitimate part of any religious education programme. Feelings of wonder, awe, and mystery about life and the universe can be felt by all and provide a valuable source of motivation for teachers of religious education dealing with children from a wide variety of backgrounds.

In essence, holism provides a new paradigm for education which builds upon and extends some hitherto neglected aspects of the liberal education tradition. As Ron Miller says:

> the holistic paradigm asserts that the materialistic world-view of the scientific-industrial age is a tragic narrowing of human possibilities. There is such greater depth to human experience, and such deeper meaning in existence than is allowed by the reductionistic and utilitarian tendencies of our culture. (1990, p. 61)

While science is not rejected in the holistic approach, the traditional mechanistic, positivist approaches to scientific knowledge are replaced by a view of science as a humanly constructed activity whose conclusions are to be seen as tentative and revisable. This new approach is linked to the theory of critical realism which will be discussed in Chapter 4.

In the social and economic context the holistic paradigm is the main alternative to the now dominant social conformist, economic rationalist model of education in the western world. Governments look on education primarily in utilitarian terms as a means of bringing about social cohesion and harmony along with economic competitiveness. While such goals are clearly important, there is a deeper meaning to education that is easily overlooked and regrettably is now in danger of being lost. It has already been suggested what this is and it can be encapsulated in the notion of personhood or what it means to be human in the fullest sense. This can only be achieved by a more broadly based assessment of the value of knowledge and understanding for the development of all our key faculties.

The model of liberal education in its broader form as informed by the holistic paradigm needs to be kept alive and continually re-asserted as a corrective to the current dominance of instrumental and utilitarian ways of thinking about education. It should also be pointed out that such a goal in fact contributes in a crucial way to the economic function of education in promoting the adaptability to change and flexibility of outlook which are necessary features of economic success in the contemporary world.

The stress on holism is particularly appropriate in today's multicultural, multi-faith, pluralist societies because it encourages an attitude of openness to new discoveries and experiences. Students today continually encounter a range of world views and, both for their own education and for the sake of social harmony, it is essential that they interact positively with these differing views rather than see them as threats to their own position. This does not mean they are obliged to look on all with equal favour but they should at least seek to understand and impartially evaluate them. In

13

regard to religion in particular we need to move beyond exclusivist notions of one religion being true and others false to a more pluralist position as we will argue in more detail in Chapter 3.

The holistic world view takes a global perspective – it stresses the interconnectedness of all humanity and the need to transcend national and cultural boundaries and develop a genuinely universal conception of what it means to be a person. Similarly, it involves an ecological commitment to the survival of all living things and the preservation of the earth's fragile environment. In this respect it rejects the anthropocentric and exploitative aspects of the advanced industrial world.

A number of contemporary religious or spiritual movements have made a more explicit recognition of this global perspective in their writings than others. Among these are the Baha'i faith, the Society of Friends (Quakers), the followers of Rudolf Steiner, and the 'Creation Theology' movement developed by Matthew Fox (1983). All of these are particularly in tune with the holistic paradigm and represent a source of fertile ideas for those coming from the traditional and well-established religions who are beginning to search for new perspectives more in tune with the human and physical crises facing the contemporary world.

Another aspect of the traditional model of liberal education that the holistic approach corrects is its stress on *individual* autonomy and its frequent neglect of social and political influences on how we as individuals develop. Individuals do not develop in a vacuum. They are partly a product of the particular influences on their upbringing which have a major impact on how they see the world. To overstress the individual's freedom as the main goal of education can also lead people to perceive their personal well-being as separate from the greater good of society. The holistic stress on the interconnectedness of all brings an important communitarian focus to liberal education that is missing in many of the traditional accounts.

A CONTEMPORARY MODEL OF LIBERAL EDUCATION

We have looked at the contributions of Bailey and the holistic educators to our understanding of liberal education, and it is now time to draw some of these threads and some notions of our own together into a broader model of liberal education suitable for contemporary society. As indicated in the introduction, the goals of liberal education may be summarised in terms of the three crucial concepts of critical rationality, personal transcendence, and epistemological coherence. Bailey's work highlights critical rationality and the cognitive dimensions of personal transcendence. The holistic paradigm serves especially to bring out a fuller understanding of personal transcendence. However, both have little to say about epistemological coherence, a concept which is important in assessing the relationship between subjects in the curriculum, such as the link between religion and science, which is particularly important for this book.

Let us now summarise the key features of these three concepts. Critical rationality may be understood as the ability to critically evaluate evidence and forms of justification in order to arrive at rationally acceptable conclusions. Critical rationality is a necessary condition for achieving moral, intellectual, and religious autonomy and is further developed in Chapter 5 in relation to the epistemic community and an ethics of belief. Critical rationality is important because the beliefs we hold will, in significant ways, affect our decisions and actions not only as they impact on our own lives but on the lives of others in our society. This problem is compounded in an electronic age where a surfeit of information can flow from a few keys typed at a computer keyboard or a casual review of the 'infotainment' on cable TV. There is an urgent need for students to develop skills in critically assessing information and evidence and for their developing sound principles as a prelude to their actions.

The second concept, that of personal transcendence, refers to the role of education in liberating people from the constraints of their immediate socio-economic and cultural environment towards being persons who have begun to explore the foundations for their own philosophy of life. The concept of transcendence is here being used in an epistemological sense to mean moving beyond a particular state of knowledge and awareness to a broader and deeper knowledge and perspective. It does not necessarily imply a commitment to a transcendent or spiritual realm, although this is certainly one significant possibility.

As Raz and Williams pointed out, the nature of modern society makes this goal of personal transcendence essential for flourishing in the sort of complex environment in which we live today. Traditional liberal education has tended to express this goal in terms of moral and intellectual autonomy, which provides a link to the first of our liberal education goals of critical rationality. But, as mentioned above, autonomy does not develop in a vacuum and needs the communitarian focus and global vision pointed out by the holistic educators to make it fully adequate to contemporary circumstances.

The notion of transcendence has particular importance in religious education: it implies liberating people from the constraints of their immediate socio-economic and cultural environment towards being persons who have begun to explore the foundations for their own philosophy of life. One particularly powerful cultural environment for many people is their religious upbringing. In the context of this book we would see personal transcendence as a move towards religious autonomy which we have defined above as a reasoned commitment to a personal philosophy of life with a justifiable position on the place of the transcendent realm within it.

The third concept of epistemological coherence has not as yet been explicitly discussed in much detail. It refers both to the consistency between different propositions within a subject, which may be referred to as *internal* coherence, as well as to the consistency between different subjects, which may be referred to as *external* coherence. This notion of epistemological coherence has not been adequately dealt with by Hirst or Bailey, two of the main philosophers of liberal education. Hirst's forms of knowledge thesis emphasises the logical interlinking of concepts within a form of knowledge (internal coherence) which he says 'form a network of possible relationships in which experience can be understood' (1974, p. 102). Nevertheless, he suggests that individual forms of knowledge are logically separate having their own 'distinctive logical structure' (1974, p. 102). Thus, Hirst fails to show how different forms interrelate with each other and how they achieve external coherence. The problem with logically distinct forms of knowledge is that it is logically possible for a proposition p in Form A to contradict proposition q in Form B. This situation is clearly untenable and gives rise, for example, to the possibility of students simultaneously holding a creation science account of the development of species in (some forms of) religious education and a contradictory evolutionary science account of the development of species in biology. Hirst needs to show how forms of knowledge interrelate and achieve external coherence.

Evers and Walker examine and reject Hirst's account of logically distinct forms and argue that 'knowledge is better viewed as a seamless web than as a partitioned set' (1983, p. 155). Within this view propositions stand alongside each other, from all domains of knowledge, and their consistency one with the other can be ascertained. While this approach is a significant improvement on Hirst, it fails to sufficiently spell out the logical structure of such a system of beliefs. A good example of such a logical structure is found in the logic of degrees of belief in Peter Forrest's *The Dynamics of Belief* (1986). This logic is briefly outlined in Chapter 2 where it is employed to help resolve the fallacy of tolerance – a problem emerging from holding conflicting belief sets.

As mentioned above, Bailey rejects Hirst's forms of knowledge thesis, which posits seven logically distinct sets of interrelated concepts, but accepts the notion that individual forms represent 'great assemblages of relationships already shared by the minds of many others and variously described as disciplines, forms of knowledge, realms of meaning, and so on' (1984, p. 65). The key question again is the external coherence between the different forms of knowledge, which Bailey does not address. But, as noted above, not to do so gives rise to possible inconsistency between what students learn in different areas of the curriculum. A clear example of this, given above, is the possible inconsistency between religion's and science's accounts of the evolution of species. The issue of the consistency of the logical structure of science and religion is dealt with in Chapter 4 on the place of models in both science and religion.

The issue of external coherence is not just confined to science and religion. Another example can be found in the relation between religion and ethics. Examples of the type of conflict which might arise between the two are dealt with in Chapter 5, where possible conflict between religious and liberal democratic values, as for instance on the issues of abortion, euthanasia, or the role of women, is examined.

We may conclude the first section of this chapter by reiterating that the broader contemporary model of liberal education as elaborated here provides a very adequate justification for the place of religious education in schools today. For the rest of this book, when speaking of educational values we will have in mind the sort of liberal education values as discussed here. We now need to move on to consider what sort of approaches and methodologies should be used in schools to achieve such a goal in religious education.

APPROACHES AND METHODOLOGIES FOR TEACHING RELIGIOUS EDUCATION

Two Conceptions of Religious Education

If religious education is to meet the goals of liberal education, what form should it take in schools? It is now generally accepted that religious education may be conceived in two distinct but interrelated ways, as education in faith or education in religion. The aim of the former is to bring about commitment to a particular faith and this may be done with varying attention to liberal educational values such as critical rationality and epistemological coherence. If these values are given an important place then it is appropriate to speak of education in faith rather than just

17

training in faith, or, more negatively, indoctrination in faith. To whatever extent such a programme is educationally influenced, the underlying aim nevertheless remains that of strengthening the student's belief in a particular religious tradition. This would involve participation in practices distinctive of that religion such as prayer and worship. On the other hand, in the model of education in religion, the prime aim is to bring about knowledge and understanding of religion as a sphere of human thought and action in general rather than commitment to any specific faith.

Education in religion is the form most appropriate for public schools but would also be relevant to church-related schools. Of the three countries we are concerned with in this book, the UK, the USA, and Australia, it is only in the last of these that direct education in faith can take place in state schools and here it must remain a voluntary subject. In all three countries, education in faith is a legitimate part of the curriculum in church-related schools. The nature of the provisions for religious education in the three countries will be examined in more detail in Chapter 7. In this book we are primarily concerned with education in religion and our recommendations about religious education should be understood as applying to that. However, we believe that many of our recommendations also have relevance for education in faith programmes and would serve to strengthen these because such recommendations can generally be adopted without in most cases sacrificing their other objectives.

Three Approaches to Teaching Religious Education Programmes

Three main approaches to the teaching of religious education can be identified.

Education for Commitment

The first of these is education for commitment which goes hand in hand with the education in faith, conception which has just been discussed. As indicated, while this may be appropriate for church schools it is not appropriate for religious education that aims to meet the goals of contemporary liberal education. Because of its goal of producing religious commitment to one faith, it fails to satisfy the condition of critical rationality and may fail the condition of epistemological coherence if the concern for commitment affects the way other subjects are taught. It may also fail the goal of personal transcendence if it does not promote moral and intellectual autonomy.

Education about Religion

In this interpretation the course makes no attempt to deal with issues of personal belief but simply aims to present a descriptive account of the major religions or world views. An example would be a course in Comparative Religion in which no attempt is made to assess the relative strengths or weaknesses of the various religions studied. While such a course would be worthwhile in itself and provide useful information for students preparing to live in a pluralist society, it is not really a course in religious education *per se*. It is more akin to a branch of Social Studies which may or may not be covered in other aspects of the curriculum. Methodologies in teaching such a course could be sociological, phenomenological, or historical. Either way it seems that there is an important element of children's educational development that is really not addressed, that is their need to develop a personal philosophy of life, a standpoint of their own on the question of religious truth, which is our second educational criterion for religious education – personal transcendence.

Open-ended Exploration of World Views or Philosophies of Life

In this third approach there are fewer restrictions on what can be covered in the course. The only major presupposition is that the quest for a philosophy to guide our life or the attempt to find solutions to ultimate questions is important and worthwhile and that the potential answer may be found in a realm that transcends the purely physical world. Such an answer could be a conventional religious view or it could utilise some alternative way of reaching religious understanding, for example, perhaps drawing on mystical experience, meditation techniques, altered states of consciousness, and so forth. The answer for some may come to lie in interpreting religious statements as mythic or poetic attempts to express important features of human experience rather than as stating literal truths about the world.

This approach (which we shall often refer to in the rest of this book as studies of religion or religious studies) therefore does not preclude at the outset the possibility that for some the answer may lie outside the purely religious domain in a secular philosophy such as humanism or existentialism. These or other secular philosophies may well be investigated to provide a contrast to a religious perspective. Whatever the preferred view, the final decision is left to the student's autonomous choice. The programme allows a genuinely open-ended critical exploration of all these possible alternatives and tries to present them all as honestly and rigorously as possible.

This third way of conceiving of religious education is in our view the best because it avoids the difficulties inherent in the previous two. Moreover, by allowing all relevant views to be fairly represented it is more likely to encourage students to reflect seriously on just where they stand with regard to these crucial questions. If they know in advance that nothing will be hidden and that no views are to be especially favoured, they will be more inclined to approach the course with real interest and personal concern. Because their autonomy is respected they are more likely to act autonomously and to try to work out for themselves a coherent world view. They will no longer treat religious education as a subject different in kind to other school subjects, but one that has genuine educational value and respectability.

Many children who are apathetic about religion may thus be stimulated to take an interest in the subject which they otherwise would not have developed. Churches which are concerned about losing adherents through such a programme taking the place of education in faith may find that they gain from it a significant number of genuinely interested inquirers and potential converts who otherwise may have ignored all established religion totally. In a discussion paper for Catholic educators, Crawford and Rossiter (1990) develop this point in some detail. They indicate evidence which shows that 'study of world religions seems to enhance young pupils' interest in knowing and studying their own religious tradition' (1990, p. 11).

A more detailed discussion of this third approach drawing on the philosophy of epistemic liberalism is developed in Chapter 3. This philosophy ties in very well with the approach and supplies the theoretical underpinning for teaching in a multi-faith context utilising an epistemological methodology we have entitled extended pluralism.

If we now consider the implications of this approach for the British, American, and Australian school contexts, the question arises as to what specific content is appropriate for a studies of religion course which will be relevant for such students. Obviously there will need to be a range of religions and religious issues covered but the question of just how many is a contentious one. Is it better to concentrate on one or two religions which students can then be expected to master in some depth or to cover a wider range with perhaps some loss of detailed understanding? The issue is complicated by the fact that the majority of students will already belong, because of family background, to one religious tradition, namely Christianity, and to a specific variant of that. Furthermore, to properly appreciate the place of religion in such societies would seem to entail that Christianity be at least one of the religions studied. However, Christianity should not become the prime focus of the programme or the other important educational goals of teaching studies of religion, mentioned above, may be lost. Moreover, with the growing number of non-Christian groups in such countries there is likely to be an increasing number of students from such backgrounds in both state and church schools and thus religious homogeneity can no longer be assumed.

It seems to us that the best response to this issue is to take a middle path between the two extremes of excessive narrowness and excessive breadth. This would allow Christianity to have an important place but require that students be exposed in some depth to at least two other religious traditions as well as having some introduction to secular alternatives to religion. While Christianity may justifiably be taught as one relevant model for western societies, it should not be taught as the model which ought necessarily to be preferred. Students from Christian backgrounds need to understand their own tradition, and thus be in a position to make a reasoned commitment to it, but should also feel free to commit themselves to another religious tradition or a non-religious one if that is their carefully chosen preference based on examination of some of the main alternatives. The advantage of having at least two other traditions examined in some depth is that this would seem to be the minimum needed to provide an adequate measure of comparison to Christianity. The advantage of having some examination of alternative responses (apart from traditional religious ones) to the ultimate questions is that students can then be said to have been exposed to the full range of possible responses to such questions. Without this their choices could not be described as falling within the liberal education criteria of critical rationality, personal transcendence, and epistemological coherence. These recommendations apply only to the core or prescribed aspects of religious studies courses. There should obviously be a much wider range of topics available in the optional elements.

The role of the teacher in such a model requires some discussion. Most teachers of religious education in the past have been members of a church or have possessed a definite faith commitment to one of the major religious traditions. This new programme could be taught by teachers from a wider range of backgrounds, the only necessary commitment being to the broad religious education of their pupils as outlined here. In other words, they would need to have a commitment to the importance of each individual developing a fulfilling life-stance or world view, that is, achieving personal transcendence, as well as a commitment to educational values such as critical rationality and epistemological coherence.

Teachers need not feel obliged to conceal their own religious views, as long as they are not presented as carrying any special validity or authority. It is better that their own views be brought into the open and assessed along with others, to avoid the danger of covert influence whereby pupils may be unconsciously or unduly influenced by the teacher's religious beliefs. A useful set of criteria for ensuring the educational authenticity of the course are the three set out by Harry Stopes-Roe (1978, pp. 149–54): objectivity, fairness, and balance. Objectivity applies when matters of personal belief are not presented as established fact and no views are given special favour over others. Fairness applies when all sides of the case are fully and accurately presented. Balance occurs when a broad range of views are considered and the major religions and their principal doctrines are given sufficiently detailed treatment. Perhaps no teachers or educational programmes could achieve these three goals in their entirety at all times but they establish a clear set of aims to guide teaching and curriculum construction if these are to be properly educational in this controversial area.

Methodologies for Studying Religious Education

A wide range of methodologies are available for studying religious education. Among the most popular are the phenomenological, sociological, historical, and theological approaches. In the phenomenological approach religions are studied from the point of view of the adherent and an attempt is made to get on the 'inside' of what it is like to follow that particular religion. Questions of truth are put on hold and awkward questions about the validity or otherwise of the beliefs being studied are avoided. Sociological approaches attempt to study objectively the role religion plays in human society. Likewise, historical approaches study its role in human history. All such approaches look at religion from an empirical, descriptive position. Theological approaches cover conceptual and doctrinal issues but largely from an insider's descriptive point of view. The fact that different religions make different truth claims is generally ignored in all these approaches and thus the philosophical problems caused by pluralism are never really confronted.

While such approaches to the study of religion may yield much interesting and useful information, there is often a sense of unease lurking in the background. Some students and teachers will feel this unease more than others, but eventually most will want to ask the question: which of these religions is the true one?; or which (if any) should I believe? They may even come to question the point of visiting various churches, synagogues, mosques, and such like and learning about the rituals, symbols, and practices of these different religions if such religions are mistaken in their basic beliefs. It is then that the cognitive predicament occasioned by pluralism can no longer be avoided.

It is here that the philosophical dimension needs to be employed whereby questions of truth and validity can be addressed. Most syllabuses in the UK, the USA, and Australia do not give sufficient emphasis to a philosophical methodology, partly because it is felt to be too demanding. We will argue in this book that at least at senior secondary school level such questions and issues can be fruitfully explored. Another important reason for the neglect of the philosophical dimension is that an examination of the validity of religious beliefs and moral acceptability of religious practices is felt to be too controversial. But once again we will argue that this need not be the case and if handled sensitively such an exploration can have valuable educational outcomes. The question of methodology is in fact a central concern of Chapters 3, 4, and 5. In Chapter 3 it is argued that there is a clear need for the teacher of religious studies to adopt the epistemological methodology of extended pluralism which allows him or her to impartially explore a wide range of competing views. Chapter 4 presents the philosophy of critical realism as a methodological basis for the teaching of religion which effectively counters the pluralist predicament. Chapter 5 advocates the use of an axiological methodology which focuses specifically on the question of the moral acceptability of holding various religious beliefs and the practices that flow from them. In Chapter 7 we examine religious education syllabuses and provisions in the three countries we are concerned with in this book to see how adequately they handle such philosophical issues.

Moreover, in terms of our liberal education model, none of the three criteria – critical rationality, personal transcendence, epistemological coherence – can be adequately achieved without some serious consideration being given to the philosophical dimension of religion: this necessarily requires the use of a philosophical methodology in the study of the subject.

This chapter has presented a rationale for religious education in the curriculum, seeing its main justification in terms of a contemporary model of liberal education. It has also discussed the approaches and methodologies that are appropriate to teaching the subject. In the next chapter we will examine some possible challenges to the place of religious education in the school curriculum.

NOTES

1. An historical overview of the concept with particular emphasis on Aristotle's influential discussion is contained in Bowen and Hobson (1987).
2. See the following for some of the main criticisms that have been made of Hirst's forms of knowledge thesis: Barrow (1976), Evers and Walker (1983), Phillips (1971), and White (1973).

REFERENCES

Baier, K. (1973). 'Moral Autonomy as an Aim of Education', in G. Langford and D.J. O'Connor (eds), *New Essays in Philosophy of Education,* London, Routledge & Kegan Paul.

Bailey, C. (1984). *Beyond the Present and the Particular,* London, Routledge & Kegan Paul.

Barrow, R. (1976). *Common Sense and the Curriculum,* London, Allen & Unwin.

Bowen, J. and Hobson, P.R. (1987). *Theories of Education: Studies of Significant Innovation in Western Educational Thought,* Brisbane, Jacaranda Wiley.

Crawford, M. and Rossiter, G. (1990). *The Prospect of a New Syllabus in Studies in Religion in N.S.W. Schools: Implications for Religious Education in Catholic Schools,* Sydney, Christian Brothers Province Resource Group.

Dearden, R.F. (1968). *The Philosophy of Primary Education,* London, Routledge & Kegan Paul.

Dearden, R.F. (1984). *Theory and Practice of Education,* London, Routledge & Kegan Paul.

Evers, C.W. and Walker, J.C. (1983). 'Knowledge, Partitioned Sets and Extensionality: a Refutation of the Forms of Knowledge Thesis', *Journal of Philosophy of Education,* 17, 2, 155–70.

Forrest, P. (1986). *The Dynamics of Belief,* Oxford, Blackwell.

Fox, M. (1983). *Original Blessing,* Santa Fe, CA, Bear & Co.

Hirst, P.H. (1974). *Knowledge and the Curriculum,* London, Routledge & Kegan Paul.

Jonathon, R. (1995). 'Liberal Philosophy of Education: A Paradigm Under Strain', *Journal of Philosophy of Education,* 29, 1.

Miller, R. (1990). *What Are Schools For? Holistic Education in American Culture,* Brandon, Vermont, Holistic Education Press.

Nord, W.A. (1995). *Religion and American Education,* Chapel Hill, University of North Carolina Press.

O'Hear, A. (1981). *Education, Society and Human Nature,* London, Routledge & Kegan Paul.

O'Hear, A. (1987). 'The Importance of Traditional Learning', *British Journal of Educational Studies,* 35, 2.

Peters, R.S. (1966). *Ethics and Education,* London, Allen & Unwin.

Phenix, P. (1964). *Realms of Meaning*, New York, McGraw-Hill.
Phillips, D.C. (1971). 'The Distinguishing Features of Forms of Knowledge', *Educational Philosophy and Theory*, 3, 2.
Raz, J. (1986). *The Morality of Freedom*, Oxford, Clarendon Press.
Stopes-Roe, H. (1978), 'Religious Education, A Humanist Insight', in W.O. Cole (ed.), *World Faiths in Education*, London, Allen & Unwin.
White, J.P. (1973). *Towards a Compulsory Curriculum*, London, Routledge & Kegan Paul.
White, J.P. (1982). *The Aims of Education Restated*, London, Routledge & Kegan Paul.
Williams, B. (1985). *Ethics and the Limits of Philosophy*, London, Fontana.

2

Challenges to Religious Education in the Curriculum:
Scepticism, Exclusivism, Relativism, and Reductionism

The contemporary model of liberal education developed in Chapter 1 provides a clear rationale for the place of religious education programmes in the school curriculum. However, there are a number of philosophical objections that may be mounted against such programmes which revolve around some fundamental questions within the philosophy of education. We shall consider four of the most important of such potential problems and argue that all can be overcome. These are the problems of scepticism, exclusivism, relativism, and reductionism.

SCEPTICISM ABOUT RELIGIOUS BELIEFS IN GENERAL

The first objection, that of scepticism, claims that religious beliefs do not constitute a legitimate domain of knowledge at all and therefore cannot provide the basis for an educationally valid curriculum area. Scepticism has a long history in philosophy going back to the time of the Greek philosophers, Socrates and Plato. It can take two forms, global or local. Global scepticism claims that no knowledge in any subject area is possible. In its modern rendition it is usually based on the problem of pluralism which occurs in all areas of knowledge. The problem of pluralism is that multiple competing truth claims raise difficulties for the justification of any one claim. Local scepticism claims that pluralism is a problem for some areas only, as for instance ethics and religion. Both types of scepticism raise difficulties for religious knowledge.

In his book *Pluralism* (1993), Nicholas Rescher examines two arguments for global scepticism, providing responses to each. The first argument involves the correct claim that a prime objective of pursuing knowledge is to seek truth and avoid error. In such a situation one is often confronted with conflicting truth claims, where there is difficulty in choosing the right claim over the many false claims. One way of seeking to avoid falling into error is to abstain from making a decision at all by remaining sceptical about all the claims and leaving the matter undecided.

However, Rescher maintains that this argument retreats too quickly to scepticism as a response to pluralism.

Rescher contends that the 'object of rational enquiry is not just to avoid error but to answer our questions, to secure *information* about the world' (1993, p. 82). This involves avoiding two errors or risks. The first is the risk of accepting a false claim when it should be rejected, the second is the risk of rejecting a true claim when it should be accepted. By rejecting all competing truth claims, the sceptic minimises the first risk – that of accepting a false claim – by maximising the second risk, that of rejecting a true claim. The optimal course of action is to minimise both risks by choosing a mid-course between accepting everything and rejecting everything. Of the sceptic's course of action of rejecting everything Rescher concludes, 'A sceptical policy of systematic avoidance is fundamentally *irrational*, because it blocks from the very outset any prospect of realising the inherent goals of the enterprise of factual inquiry' (1993, p. 86).

While Rescher is correct in judging the sceptic's retreat to scepticism as hasty and irrational he fails to outline an alternative for the sceptic to take. The problem still remains – how is anyone to choose between competing truth claims? This problem is a recurring theme throughout this book where various solutions are presented. The first solution is presented in the second section of this chapter which deals with the logic of degrees of belief.

The second argument for global scepticism examined by Rescher is that which involves the jump from the fact that simply because others think differently from ourselves this is a reason for us to abandon our own thinking. He suggests there is an error of perspective here: pluralism is a feature of the collective group, not a feature of the individual. That is, while a community can entertain pluralism the individual cannot. Individuals have to make a decision in favour of one world view as a standard by which to order their life. We make a similar point in Chapter 3 where it is argued that while religious education programmes should remain open to a range of world views, ultimately the individual student will need to make a choice between these for him or herself. Rescher maintains, 'To refuse to discriminate – be it by accepting everything or by accepting nothing – is to avert controversy only by refusing to enter the forum of discussion' (1993, p. 95). In this regard we agree with Rescher and will argue in Chapter 5, when dealing with the ethics of belief, that we have certain epistemic responsibilities to enter into dialogue in defence of our beliefs.

Now, while the above responds to the global form of scepticism it does not answer the problem of local scepticism or scepticism related to particular areas of knowledge such as religion. It would seem possible to be sceptical about religion while remaining non-sceptical about other domains of knowledge, such as science or history. The justification for this usually rests on arguments to the effect that religious propositions cannot be empirically or logically verified and rest on unproven axioms or assumptions. A prominent modern philosopher of education who has adopted this stance is Paul Hirst. He maintains, 'If in fact, as seems to be the case at present, there are no agreed public tests whereby true and false can be distinguished in religious claims, then we can hardly maintain that we have a domain of religious knowledge and truth' (1985, p. 12).

The response to this particular form of scepticism will be in two parts. The first will be to reject the sceptic's claim that religious propositions cannot be empirically or logically tested. This is not to argue that they will necessarily be found to be true but for the lesser claim that there is a method for testing the truth or falsity of religious propositions. As this criticism of the sceptic is similar to that of the relativist it will be dealt with in the third section of this chapter when looking at the problem of relativism. The second line of attack will be to reject the sceptic's argument that religious propositions are invalid because they rest on unproven axioms or assumptions. Whereas the first response relates to the testability of religious propositions, the second relates to their inherent acceptability.

Turning to the second problem, that of the unfounded assumptions underlying religion, we will argue that the only epistemological assumption needed to allow religious studies programmes to proceed is the belief in the possibility of a transcendent realm, in whatever way that may be interpreted. To deny this would be to assert that no realm over and above the empirical world as experienced through the senses exists. Such a claim would seem to be at least equally open to question, and hardly strong enough grounds to deny validity to the search for and consideration of alternative explanations of human existence as found in the great religious traditions or in other non-materialist views.

A promising line of argument that develops the above response is one that points to the fact that all domains of knowledge or understanding rest on certain basic assumptions or axioms and that questions may be raised regarding the provability of all such axioms, not just those in the religious realm. One such approach is that of Ron Laura and Michael Leahy who introduce the concept of 'epistemic primitives' which they say are 'the most deeply entrenched beliefs in any conceptual system' and 'which express our fundamental suppositions about the nature of our world'

(1989, p. 255). Examples they cite are the uniformity of nature in science, 'God exists' in theology, and the belief that diseases have physical causes in pathology. Laura and Leahy argue that such primitives are resistant to falsification in all belief systems as they are 'not testable against the kind of evidence they licence as relevant within those systems' (1989, p. 257). To reject them is equivalent to giving up engaging in the discipline.

Hick (1989, Part 2) makes a similar point when he contends that the universe is religiously ambiguous and that a religious interpretation is just as epistemically valid as a naturalistic one. The religious believer posits the epistemic primitive, 'God exists in the universe', while the naturalist posits the epistemic primitive, 'The universe is a self-maintaining system.'

While the Laura and Leahy argument identifies a valid property of all belief systems, be they science or religion, there are some qualifications which must be made. The first one is apparent from the examples already quoted – at what level of belief structures do epistemic primitives apply? The Laura and Leahy examples include science and also a subcategory of science, pathology, with the epistemic primitives in science being of a much more general level. The question is, how far can a branch of knowledge be broken up into subdisciplines and still have epistemic primitives, and are these primitives comparable to those in the more fundamental and comprehensive domains? If a line is not drawn somewhere as to what beliefs are epistemically primitive then it would leave open the possibility of enlarging one's set of epistemic primitives to include the whole set of beliefs, at which point it would become logically impossible to adjudicate between conflicting beliefs because epistemic primitives are immune to such comparisons.

The second qualification regards the interrelationships between primitives in different domains. Are they to be deemed conceptually discrete or could an epistemic primitive in one domain have logical links with one in another? For instance, the law of causality (every event has a cause) would seem to be a primitive in science but could it also help to justify epistemic primitives in other realms? For example, the religious epistemic primitive, 'God exists', could be seen as a deduction from the causal principle applied to the realm of religion. One of the positions argued for in this book is that of liberal education's criterion of epistemological coherence developed in Chapter 1. This criterion rejects the notion that each area of knowledge is conceptually and methodologically discrete to the extent that there can be no inter-domain comparisons and tests. This point is demonstrated more fully in Chapter 4 which suggests there is an overlap of approach between religion and science and that there exists a similarity in how models are used and tested in the two domains.

Thirdly, are all epistemic primitives to be regarded as equally valid? Laura and Leahy imply that they are but gloss over major difficulties and fail to specify any criteria for judging the relative merits of various primitives. One relevant consideration here could relate to the degree of specificity of the epistemic primitive. More general ones would seem to involve a less demanding epistemological commitment than those of a more specific nature. For example, belief in the principle of causality while not itself unquestionable would have a stronger claim to acceptance than 'all diseases have physical causes' (the possibility of psychological causes immediately springs to mind). Similarly, and more importantly for the present topic, belief in the possibility of a transcendent realm clearly has a stronger claim than 'God exists' as an epistemic primitive in the realm of religion. This would, therefore, be a better epistemic primitive to underlie a religious studies programme both in that it can be accepted by a much wider cross-section of people (whereas the other is only open to monotheists) and gives adequate legitimacy to such a programme.

Another relevant consideration in judging the adequacy of epistemic primitives would seem to be the extent to which they are regularly confirmed in experience. Not all possible primitives would be equal in this regard – consider, for example, the epistemic primitives in alchemy and chemistry. In today's world few would accept the basic premises of alchemy as a means of transmuting lead into gold as against modern chemistry's alternative explanations as to how this might proceed. In the Laura and Leahy examples, it could be argued that 'God exists' is not as clearly confirmed in experience as, say, the principle of causality. On the other hand, a belief in materialism does not seem to have a stronger claim in this regard than a belief in the possibility of a transcendent realm, so the latter remains a viable epistemic primitive for the religious realm.

None the less, the introduction of epistemic primitives has been an important device in showing how all areas of knowledge rest on unproven assumptions. We may conclude our response to the first possible philosophical objection to a religious studies programme (that is, that the religious realm in general lacks epistemological validity) by reiterating that both the local and global forms of scepticism can be met. The global form has been successfully countered by the use of Rescher's arguments, and the two aspects of the local form – the testability and acceptability of religious propositions – can be adequately addressed. Arguments in regard to the testability of religious propositions will be dealt with in the third section. Arguments in relation to the acceptability of religious propositions have been met by drawing on Laura and Leahy's concept of epistemic primitives.

THE EXCLUSIVIST NATURE OF RELIGIOUS BELIEF SYSTEMS

Now that it has been established against the sceptics that religion in the broad sense provides an educationally valid avenue of study, we need to look at some other philosophical problems that arise when we wish to study a range of different religions and world views. The first of these is the problem of exclusivism which points to the fact that virtually all religions claim to represent the whole truth and that therefore once you accept one of them you are obliged to regard all the others as false. Not to recognise this has been called the 'fallacy of tolerance' by Peter Gardner which he describes as 'the fallacy of refraining from concluding that beliefs held by others are wrong or that certain people are mistaken when such conclusions are a logical consequence of one's position' (1988, p. 93). Keith Ward raises a similar point when looking at possible inferences that can be drawn from the diversity of world religions: 'A believing member of any one tradition is compelled to regard all other traditions as holding false beliefs and therefore as not leading to salvation' (1990, p. 1). The fallacy of tolerance is to refuse to draw the conclusion in the following inferential schema:

Either p or (not-p)

p

Therefore, not (not-p)

As we have stated above, many of the teachers of religious studies will have a commitment to one or other of the views they will be presenting and would thus seem to be placed in the position of knowingly teaching what they hold to be false.

Once again, however, we believe that this objection can be met. We will begin with some general points about the nature of religious belief before going on to develop a more detailed epistemological response utilising the notion of degrees of belief. The fallacy of tolerance tends to take too hard and fast a definition of what it is to hold a religious belief and fails to recognise the complexity of such beliefs and the possible interconnections between the different religious traditions. Religious beliefs are not static, they develop and change over time and if people are rational and open-minded they should always be open to new insights. If one takes a liberal view of religion, one may come to accept that no one religion necessarily contains all the truth and that there may be something to learn from the others. Perhaps a full understanding of such a complex domain entails incorporating a number of perspectives. The analogy of observing a statue is a good one here – no one vantage point reveals all its details. Looking at it from a number of different angles reveals a more complete and accurate picture.

It may even be held that one can have equally valid experiences of the divine in different religious traditions. As Ward states, this could mean '(as in the often quoted wave-particle duality of light) that competent observers must agree that both of two descriptions of an object can be true, in different conditions of observation' (1990, p. 17). But this should not be taken to mean that every interpretation of religious experience is equally valid, but rather the lesser claim that different interpretations may be equally valid in respect of some similar, core set of religious experiences.

How far one can accept this broader view of religious understanding will depend on the extent to which one is prepared to take a more fluid, open-ended view of religion, in contrast to a more traditional dogmatic interpretation. But whatever view is taken, it is worth noting that a teacher committed to one belief can still accept that others may take a different view and are just as entitled to hold and defend their beliefs. By entering into arguments with others we are able to test the validity of our own beliefs – a point made by the nineteenth-century philosopher J.S. Mill (1962 [1859], p. 180). This is also consistent with Rescher's view discussed in the previous section that an individual has an obligation 'to enter the forum of discussion'. So while such a teacher is committed to a particular view, it is not necessary to stress the falsity of other views, merely to acknowledge that they are different to one's own. These points are developed in more detail in the next chapter where we introduce the notion of 'extended pluralism' as an appropriate epistemological methodology for religious studies programmes.

We may conclude this part of the discussion by noting that the fallacy of tolerance assumes a rather limited view of the nature of religious belief and that if the complexity and richness of religious traditions are taken into account, a religious studies programme can be conceived which greatly lessens the force of such a fallacy.

A more direct attack on the fallacy of tolerance is however possible and this involves questioning the epistemological assumptions upon which it rests. An attempt in this direction has been made, again by Laura and Leahy in the same article to which reference has already been made. They allude to the 'corrigibility' of beliefs, by which they mean that an individual can reverse the true/false status accorded to a proposition if at some later time that person has reason to believe differently (1989, p. 262). But the possibility of reversing the truth value of religious propositions at some later stage does not avoid committing Gardner's fallacy of tolerance now, for one is still obliged to deem propositions that conflict with one's present preferred set as false. What needs to be done is not to argue that one can hold either one set of beliefs now or an opposed set at some later time, but to examine under what circumstances it may be rational to maintain a set of conflicting or inconsistent beliefs concurrently. The logic of the latter situation is different and emerges from looking at the logic of belief structures themselves. Hirst is one who suggests this line of approach, arguing that, 'in many areas, beliefs and values may not be rationally assessable as true or false but rather as more or less defensible, and in some cases several equal rationally-acceptable answers may exist' (1985, p. 12).

Another writer who introduces this form of argument is Terry McLaughlin, who criticises Gardner for holding beliefs in an 'all or nothing way' (1990, p. 116), that is, beliefs are either true or false and that is all there is to it. Quoting Anthony Quinton, he suggests there are 'continuously variable degrees of belief and not just the decision between believing a proposition, believing its contradictory and suspending judgement' (Quinton, 1985, p. 47, quoted in McLaughlin, 1990, p. 116). The range of belief varies with the differing strengths of evidence and justification supporting a proposition. McLaughlin rightly judges that this allows 'a range of possible responses to a conflicting belief beyond the response of judging it false' (1990, p. 116). The question to emerge here is whether Gardner's fallacy of tolerance can survive the rejection of bivalence which posits a strict dichotomy between true and false beliefs. In other words, does the fallacy of tolerance logically depend on a false dichotomy? McLaughlin, however, does not develop the argument using degrees of belief but prefers a related argument employing 'open-mindedness'(1990, p. 116). Our contention is that the degrees of belief argument is more elegant and powerful: accordingly, we will develop it in more detail here.

Two authors who explore the logic of belief structures and degrees of belief are the Australian philosophers Brian Ellis (1979) and Peter Forrest (1986). In a logic of degrees of belief, propositions are not simply held to be true or false but are given an epistemic confidence level according to the evidence or justification supporting them. Propositions believed with certainty are given an epistemic value of 1, contracertain propositions (which represent disbelief) a value of 0, and agnostic propositions a value of ½. Furthermore, propositions believed with less than certainty but greater than agnosticism have a value between ½ and 1, while those believed with greater than contracertainty but less than agnosticism have a value between 0 and ½. What is being measured is not the truth or falsity of a proposition, but the relative degree of confidence with which that belief is held (Forrest, 1986, pp. 21–7). More importantly, it is again not the truth or falsity but the rationality of holding beliefs which is given epistemic priority. This shift from truth/falsity to rationality represents a quantum leap in the debate. Ellis remarks that the standard view is to accept that knowledge is a function of the truth claims of beliefs, and that while this seems plausible he suggests:

> (in) general, however, the opposite seems to be the case. We can recognise a rational system of beliefs, or an irrational one, even where we cannot adequately specify truth conditions for the sentences in question. We do not even have to believe the sentences involved are objectively true or false. Consequently, it is at least as plausible to maintain that knowledge of rationality precedes that of truth conditions. (1979, pp. vii–viii)

This shift gains in plausibility if we observe that what is being looked at is the rationality or logic of a belief system as a whole rather than isolated beliefs, in which case it seems preferable to speak about the rationality rather than truth or falsity of the system.

The important point, for this book, is that it would seem that Gardner's fallacy of tolerance does not readily apply within such a logic of belief systems. An example may help to bring this out. Let us consider the following artificially simple case where Alfred and Betty are to place bets on a race which they have videotaped. They do not know which horse won, but do know only one horse won. The racing guide gives the following odds for a win: horse Alpha at 3–7 on (30 per cent chance), horse Beta at 1–3 on (25 per cent chance), horse Gamma at 1–4 on (20 per cent chance), and horses Delta to Theta given the same odds of 1–19 on (5 per cent). It seems reasonable for Alfred, say, to believe Alpha will win. But what should Alfred think of Betty who believes Beta will win because she notices storm clouds in the morning and thinks Beta is better in the wet. Must Alfred believe Betty's views false and Betty mistaken? The correct response would seem to be that Alfred would hold his own belief to be better founded or to have a higher degree of confidence than Betty's

34

while not rejecting hers as necessarily false. In this situation then, Gardner's fallacy does not seem to get a hold.

Fundamental to the logic of belief structures is consistency; it is generally considered irrational to affirm an inconsistent set of beliefs. This means that while Alfred may not judge Betty's belief false (that Beta will win), he certainly would hold the conjunction of the two beliefs – that both Alpha and Beta will win – to be false (given that he knows only one horse will win). Or, to avoid using 'true' and 'false', he would consider (to use Forrest's expression) that the conjunction is inconsistent and self-refuting (Forrest, 1986, p. 55). This means we could reformulate Gardner's fallacy and scale it down to the *error* of tolerance which becomes: it is irrational to maintain an inconsistent set of beliefs.

So we still seem confronted with the problem – is it possible to avoid committing the error of tolerance? The answer is 'Yes'. The first step is to reject the first half of Gardner's error of tolerance, that it is *always* irrational to maintain an inconsistent set of beliefs. The second step is to adjust the degrees of belief in the sets of propositions so as to reduce what Forrest calls the epistemic 'stress' within the belief structure caused by this inconsistency (1986, p. 134). Epistemic stress is a measure of the logical disvalue which is introduced into the system by maintaining an inconsistent belief system. Although this stress could be relieved by jettisoning the inconsistent beliefs, this would be at the cost of losing important information, which may itself have a greater logical disvalue. The idea, then, is to find a way to reduce or minimise the stress within the system by adjusting the degrees of belief in the offending propositions. If this can be done Gardner's objections can be overcome.

Before we look more closely at this solution we might examine an example taken from a religious context. Let us consider two religious claims: 'Islam is the path to salvation' and 'Judaism is the path to salvation'. The question to confront us is: is the conjunction of these two claims inconsistent? We might recall that 'Both Alpha and Beta will win' was inconsistent only because Alfred knew there was one winner, otherwise it would not be inconsistent for it is possible for both horses to come equal first. Similarly, 'Both Islam and Judaism provide the path to salvation' will be inconsistent only if one is confronted with the additional claim, 'Only Islam (or Judaism) is the path to salvation'. This latter claim emerges if either Islam or Judaism asserts exclusive rights to salvation, or the claim can be inferred from holding one or other belief. Whichever of the latter occurs, we are confronted with what Forrest refers to as an 'inconsistent polyad' (1986, p. 71).

The error of tolerance now hangs on the question: 'is it always irrational to maintain an inconsistent polyad?' We have already suggested that it is not. Clearly, new evidence, E, might be inconsistent with an existing scientific theory, T_1, and with previous observation statements O_1, O_2, ... O_n, which it would be irrational to reject as such evidence may lead to the development of a new and more comprehensive theory, T_2. Thus it would be rational to maintain the conflicting evidence, E, together with the earlier observations and theory. However, and this is the crucial point, it would be irrational in such a situation not to adjust the degree of belief in some or all of the propositions E, T_1, O_1 ... O_n. In the case of scientific theories it would seem best to do as Forrest recommends (1986, p. 43) and give all of E, T_1, O_1, ... O_n a lower degree of confidence. In the case of conflicting religious claims, we contend that it is more rational to maintain T_1, O_1 ... O_n at a higher confidence level than E, leaving E at a lower epistemic value until sufficient evidence or new insights emerge which cause us to adopt a new theory, T_2. The justification for this will emerge in the next section with a discussion of a form of sophisticated relativism. If, however, E was the proposition '*Only* Islam (or Judaism) leads to salvation' from our earlier example, it seems more plausible to give a lower degree of confidence to this exclusivist claim, while maintaining a higher degree of confidence in the claim, 'Both Islam and Judaism lead to salvation.' Thus the error (or fallacy) of tolerance can be overcome, for clearly it is not irrational in this case to maintain an inconsistent polyad under these circumstances.

In general then, the second problem raised for the teaching of religious studies can be met by pointing out that while in the past religious doctrines have been held in a typically exclusivist way, this is not a necessary feature of religion. Moreover, the notion of degrees of belief allows a richer and more coherent way of comprehending religious propositions than a simple true/false dichotomy.

THE PROBLEM OF RELATIVISM

If we thus accept that it is possible to maintain degrees of belief in a range of different and possibly conflicting religious propositions, does this mean we are now in danger of falling into a relativist position? This is the third objection that may be made to religious studies programmes which will be investigated in this chapter. Apart from the specific concerns arising from the degrees of belief position, there is also the more general worry that any programme that looks at a wide range of competing religious beliefs without coming down clearly in favour of one is likely to encourage a relativist attitude to religion on the part of pupils.

The problem of relativism, like that of scepticism, has a long history stretching back to the time of Plato and Aristotle. In his *Nicomachean Ethics*, Aristotle says, 'fire burns in Hellas and in Persia; but men's ideas of right and wrong vary from place to place' (1953, v, vii, p. 2). Here his reference is to ethical relativism but the more general problem is epistemological relativism.

We may begin by distinguishing two types of relativism which we will call naive and sophisticated. The former is the more extreme version and according to it each person's view is as good as another's and there is no way of judging between them other than by personal preference. So, in relation to religion, we could say that all views are true (for the respective believers) which is tantamount to saying all views are false because there is no way of determining that one is any better than another. Keith Ward supports this latter claim. He submits that if we cannot decide between so-called equally 'true' religions then the correct conclusion is to 'admit the fallibility and theoretical uncertainty of my view', which provides 'a reason for denying any right to believe any view in this area' (1990, p. 13). However, the naive relativist's argument, 'if there are no rational grounds for deciding between religions, then all religions must be equally true', will not do because it is invalid. The correct conclusion (if we accepted the antecedent, 'there are no rational grounds for deciding between religions') should be, 'then we cannot decide which religions are valid'. Yet, to assert this is equivalent to denying that any religion can be judged to be true, and rather than leading to relativism, it leads to scepticism (which is the philosophical problem dealt with in the first section of this chapter).

The antecedent of the relativist's argument should be rejected because it is not true that there are no rational grounds for deciding between religions. The criteria for doing this are those of critical realism – developed more fully in Chapter 4 – which are: agreement with the data, coherence (both internal and external) with the dominant paradigm, scope or generality, and fertility or the ability to generate further insights or discoveries. In the specific area of religion, these may be understood to include criteria such as profundity, fulfilment of social and psychological needs, ethical value, aesthetic satisfaction, compatibility, and openness to other interpretations of life in the world. Also, in developing our notion of sophisticated relativism below we accept a level of mutual corroboration between different religions in respect of a core set of beliefs. These factors, then, do provide rational grounds for making decisions between religions.

In general, naive relativism makes the error of inferring from the empirical facts of cultural variations in religious beliefs the philosophical conclusion that all such variations necessarily represent equally true (or equally false) beliefs. This is to confuse sociological relativism with philosophical relativism. It also completely glosses over the distinction between strong and weak evidence for a proposition, regarding all evidence as equally good or bad.

At this point we should distinguish our position from Ward's soft relativism which asserts that a core set of shared beliefs between different religions can be factually established. The flaw in Ward's position is that he insists on focusing on particular truth claims, and on particular interpretations of them to see if they are warranted by the facts (1990, p. 4). However, separating facts from theory is a notoriously difficult thing to do. Hence there is a problem with Ward's overall piecemeal approach. His insistence on judging individual propositions as 'true' or 'false' would be better replaced by judging the rational justification for propositions within an overall religious belief structure – as in this chapter – and then comparing between belief structures.

If we now try to develop a sophisticated version of relativism, we still need to be able to explain why there are so many conflicting views in an area such as religion, most with a strong and committed band of adherents who believe their views have a rational foundation. One way of responding to this is to invoke two different levels of explanation. The first is to say that up to a point these apparently conflicting views are different (largely culturally and socially determined) ways of expressing a common set of core beliefs.

Because most religious traditions originally began in isolation from others, or at least in geographically separate communities, their interpretations of the nature of the divine were strongly influenced by social and cultural factors which determined to a large extent how they viewed the world. Over time these different interpretations of the divine developed a life of their own and generated a set of doctrines and codes which helped communities define their religious identities in contrast to other groups. This has often led to an accentuation of what distinguishes them rather than to a shared affirmation of what they hold in common.

A useful analogy is that of acquiring a language. We all need some form of language to make sense of our experience and communicate with others and naturally we are initiated into the language of our parents and the community in which we are raised. Yet we do not say that only one language is correct and that all the others are false; they are all valid ways of enabling thought and communication to take place. Of course there will be variations between languages in the range of concepts they distinguish and the richness and subtlety of the distinctions they make. However, the fact that we can translate from one language into another shows general agreement about a common set of basic concepts and experiences.

In the case of religion the same pattern holds true in many respects. As with language, we have to interpret our experience through some paradigm and we have little choice in the one we begin with. If we recognise this in our own case and see that it also applies for others, we will be more ready to accept that their way of expressing their experience of the transcendent may be just as valid as ours. This may in turn lead us to discover that we have more in common than at first appears, once allowance is made for the accidental and contingent facts of different cultural histories. However, unless and until new paradigms become clearly superior to our existing one it is quite rational to operate within that as the one that presently makes the most sense for us.

This notion of a primary paradigm that all children need to begin with is supported by various writers. Michael Polanyi (1962, 1967) calls it our 'fiduciary framework' which is the framework of beliefs and presuppositions we have come to hold as a result of our upbringing. These give us the basis or starting point from which to explore the world and develop our own particular interpretation of it. As long as we continue to check such inherited beliefs against our ongoing experiences of reality in a dialectical fashion, our religious belief structures can be said to be rational. As Polanyi says:

> Any tradition fostering the progress of thought must have this intention: to teach its current ideas as stages leading on to unknown truths which, when discovered, might dissent from the very ideas which engendered them. (1967, p. 82)

McLaughlin (1984) also discusses a similar idea when he refers to the notion of a 'primary culture', which was originally developed by Bruce Ackerman in *Social Justice in the Liberal State* (1980). McLaughlin argues that it is possible to combine initiation into such a primary culture with a liberal approach to child rearing which preserves the child's autonomy. This involves aiming at 'autonomy via faith' (1984, p. 79), which distinguishes the short-term aim of bringing about faith in a certain religion with the long-term aim of encouraging autonomous choice as to whether to accept or reject that faith. As McLaughlin points out, such a goal can be achieved if the methods of upbringing are not such as to permanently fixate the child in a certain way of thinking or render later questioning of one's beliefs impossible (1984, p. 81). (We will be exploring issues to do with parents', the State's and children's rights in relation to religious upbringing in more detail in Chapter 6.)

In answering the question, 'Do all religious traditions worship the same God?', Vroom says that in respect of some predicates 'like good, bliss (beatitude), omniscience, omnipotence, immutability, omnipresence, creator, ground of being, and maker' he is 'convinced they refer to the same divine reality'. But in respect of other incompatible predicates such as 'merciful, self-sacrificing, personal and distinguished from creation' on the one hand and 'non-personal, the all, and non-dual' on the other he thinks they do not (1990, pp. 87–8). So, while we can say that there is a shared interest in the supernatural or divine and that our different cultural interpretations may mask a common set of core beliefs in some instances, in others we have to accept that various beliefs may in fact be incompatible.

This leads us to acknowledge a second level of explanation of religious differences. What we have to do here is recognise that where there really are conflicting views these represent different judgements about a highly complex area where we cannot say with certainty just what is the correct answer. This lack of certainty should be reflected in the degree of belief accorded to such conflicting propositions, which should remain open for ongoing appraisal and critical analysis. This may lead to ultimate rejection of some beliefs but, as our earlier discussion of epistemic primitives showed, the foundational propositions of all belief systems raise complex epistemological issues. We should thus consider carefully the merits of alternative belief structures before too hastily jettisoning existing ones – as pointed out by Rescher in our earlier discussion of scepticism.

These arguments are supported by MacIntyre, whose solution to the problem of relativism requires transcending it, by going beyond the limitations of the standards of truth and rationality inherent in each belief system to a form of rationality which 'requires a readiness on our part to accept, and indeed to welcome, a possible future defeat of the forms of theory and practice in which it has up till now been taken to be embodied within [the] tradition...' (MacIntyre, 1994, p. 481). This solution requires the possible adoption of a new set of flexible standards for rationality and truth as, for example, those set out above in Forrest's logic of degrees of belief.

We may conclude that sophisticated relativism coupled with a logic of degrees of belief provides a rationally defensible means for acknowledging both agreements and conflicts between religions.

THE PROBLEM OF REDUCTIONISM

While the threat to studies of religion from scepticism, exclusivism, and relativism can thus be countered, a further threat arises from reductionism. Reductionism is not as much influenced by the problem of pluralism as the other three. Reductionism denies religious propositions their cognitive and ontological content – both of which are important properties for meeting the challenges of scepticism and relativism. Rather, it interprets religious propositions as merely human projections explainable in terms of psychology, sociology, morality, or some other epistemological domain. In western philosophy, Ludwig Feuerbach (1804–72) was one of the first to espouse such a reductionist philosophy, defining religion as 'the dream of the human mind' (Flew, 1979, p. 111). Feuerbach's legacy, as Hick observes, is that his 'projection theory ... has now established itself as a serious and indeed unavoidable possibility for the understanding of religion' (1989, p. 191).

The principal tenet of the reductionist thesis is that God is made in our human likeness. It suggests religious propositions say nothing about the nature of the Divine, or Real, or Transcendent, or Other, but only about human purpose and intention. Two other well-known reductionist accounts are found in the sociology of Karl Marx and the psychology of Sigmund Freud. Within modern philosophical circles, R.B. Braithwaite uses the logical positivists' thesis, which holds that only empirical or analytic propositions are valid, to argue that religious propositions can be reduced to moral assertions. In a more positive vein, Don Cupitt recognises both a moral and spiritual dimension in religious propositions but, as Hick points out, argues that 'like ethics, religion must be allowed to come of age, as the practice of a spirituality which is not dependent for its validity upon any outside authority and whose claim upon us is grounded in our own nature' (Hick, 1989, p. 200). He contends that, just as ethics represents a valid and autonomous moral discourse, so too religious propositions constitute a valid, autonomous, but non-realist, religious epistemology.

However, what must be asked about the reductionist arguments is whether they are valid and whether they adequately represent religious discourse. In Braithwaite's case, his argument is invalid as the underlying verificationist principle on which his argument rests is self-defeating – the verificationist principle is itself neither empirical nor analytic and so by its own definition is invalid. As a consequence of this, any argument based upon it is also invalid.

In Cupitt's case, metaphysical economy is achieved by reducing religious propositions to non-realist moral and spiritual ones, but if the decision to adopt such a position leads to a belief system which fails to adequately represent what religious adherents themselves believe then it may well represent a self-defeating position. As such the outcome of Cupitt's arguments could be seen as a *reductio ad absurdum* against the reductionist position. Hick's criticisms of Cupitt suggest that this is in fact the case, for he comments, '(t)here is, however, a fundamental anomaly in this non-realist position: namely that whereas the central core of religious discourse interpreted in a realist way constitutes, if true, good news to all humankind, on a non-realist interpretation it constitutes bad news for all except a fortunate minority' (1989, p. 205), because the promise of eternal salvation is taken away.

It seems, then, there is considerable epistemological disvalue in rejecting the ontological claims of religious propositions. Given this cost, one needs to question seriously whether the reductionist route is the maximally rational one to take. Similarly, one might question the rational justification for reducing to a single perspective, or only non-realist perspectives, such a logically and epistemologically complex domain as religion which can be analysed through multiple perspectives, such as psychology, sociology, history, and philosophy.

It is our belief that the strong appeal of the reductionist arguments must not only be recognised but also countered by critical discussion and debate. As is frequently the case, the most attractive option is not always the best founded. Similarly, reductions of religious propositions to psychological, sociological, or moral propositions might have a popular and perhaps even plausible ring to them, but when the underlying arguments are closely examined their validity seems much in doubt.

Moreover the common emphasis on phenomenological and sociological methodologies in studies of religion could lead to a de facto reductionism in the mind of students that religious propositions are somehow fully explained through sociological, psychological, and other concepts. Accepting this ignores the crucial ontological claims that all religions make. We therefore contend that it is better to view religious statements as making ontological claims and to hold these up for assessment, and if they do not stand up to examination to *then* reject them rather than dismiss them from the beginning with a reductionist interpretation.

This concludes our discussion of Part 1 of this book on the legitimacy and place of religious education in schools. In Chapter 1 we argued for a contemporary version of liberal education as its basic justification and examined the appropriate approaches and methodologies for the teaching of such a subject. In Chapter 2 we have examined four challenges to the place of religious education in the curriculum: scepticism, exclusivism, relativism, and reductionism, and found that none of these raises insurmountable problems for the teaching of the subject.

REFERENCES

Ackerman, B. (1980). *Social Justice in the Liberal State*, New Haven, CT, Yale University Press.

Aristotle (1953). *Nicomachean Ethics*, trans. J.A.K. Thompson, Harmondsworth, Penguin.

Ellis, B. (1979). *Rational Belief Systems*, Oxford, Blackwell.

Flew, A. (1979). *A Dictionary of Philosophy,* London, Pan Books.

Forrest, P. (1986). *The Dynamics of Belief,* Oxford, Blackwell.

Gardner, P. (1988). 'Religious Upbringing and the Liberal Ideal of Religious Autonomy', *Journal of Philosophy of Education*, 22, 1, 89–105.

Hick, J. (1989). *An Interpretation of Religion*, London, Macmillan.

Hirst, P.H. (1985). 'Education and Diversity of Belief', in M.C. Felderhof (ed.), *Religious Education in a Pluralist Society*, London, Hodder & Stoughton.

Laura, R.S. and Leahy, M. (1989). 'Religious Upbringing and Rational Autonomy', *Journal of Philosophy of Education*, 23, 2, 253–65.

MacIntyre, A. (1994). 'Relativism, Power and Philosophy', in J. Astley and L.J. Francis (eds), *Perspectives on Christian Education,* Leominster, Gracewing.

McLaughlin, T.H. (1984). 'Parental Rights and the Upbringing of Children', *Journal of Philosophy of Education*, 18, 1, 75–83.

McLaughlin, T.H. (1990). 'Peter Gardner on Religious Upbringing and the Liberal Ideal of Religious Autonomy', *Journal of Philosophy of Education*, 24, 1, 107–25.

Mill, J.S. (1962 [1859]). *On Liberty,* in M. Warnock (ed.), *Utilitarianism, On Liberty, Essay on Bentham*, London, Collins.

Polanyi, M. (1962). *Personal Knowledge*, London, Routledge & Kegan Paul.

Polanyi, M. (1967). *The Tacit Dimension*, London, Routledge & Kegan Paul.

Quinton, A. (1985). 'On the Ethics of Belief', in G. Haydon (ed.), *Education and Values: The Richard Peters Lectures*, London, Institute of Education, University of London.

Rescher, N. (1993). *Pluralism: Against the Demand for Consensus*, Oxford, Clarendon Press.

Vroom, H.M. (1990). 'Do all Religious Traditions Worship the Same God?', *Religious Studies*, 26, 2, 73–90.

Ward, K. (1990). 'Truth and the Diversity of Religions', *Religious Studies,* 26, 1, 1–18.

PART II

Responses to Pluralism in the Teaching of Religious Education

3

The Implications of Religious Diversity for Religious Education:
The Case for Extended Pluralism

When religious education is understood in the open-ended way advocated in Chapter 1 (where it is commonly known as religious studies), it generally takes a multi-faith approach in which a range of different religions are examined. This raises an interesting and important epistemological question. What is being assumed and taught (either implicitly or explicitly) about the truth status of the different religions covered? For instance, is one religion true and the others false, are they all true in some sense or perhaps are none of them true? These options are similar to the positions of exclusivism, relativism, and scepticism discussed in relation to the viability of religious studies programmes in general in the previous chapter. Here they will be looked at from the point of view of their significance in how studies of religion programmes should be organised and taught. In assessing how well such courses achieve the aims of liberal education discussed in Chapter 1, it would be very helpful to know what epistemological assumptions about the diversity of religions should underlie them and whether certain of these assumptions are more appropriate than others in allowing the courses to achieve their educational goals.

There are three different positions that can be taken on the question of religious diversity – exclusivism, inclusivism, and pluralism – which represent three broad ways of conceiving and representing the truth status of the various religious (or non-religious) viewpoints making up the programme. Although each of these positions raise important epistemological issues in their own right, here they are being examined essentially as alternative methodologies for determining how issues of the validity of one religion *vis-à-vis* another are to be dealt with in the teaching of religious studies.

These three methodological positions will now be examined in the order of their development away from the traditional model of focusing on just one's own religious tradition as being uniquely true. It will be seen that in regard to each position there is a range of approaches varying from to stricter to more open interpretations. What, then, are the distinctive features of exclusivism, inclusivism, and pluralism with regard to the fact of religious diversity and how appropriate are they as a basis for teaching religious studies?

EXCLUSIVISM

As the name implies this view maintains that one religion is exclusively true and thus all others are largely or completely false. At its most extreme the claim would be that one religion is absolute and unique and that no other religious beliefs are worth examining and (as is the case in some countries) their expression should be prohibited. This was perhaps the dominant view held by most religious believers in most traditions up until modern times.

A somewhat less extreme exclusivist view would be that while other religious views are held to be false their adherents should have the right to practise and teach their religion to their own members. This approach also has a long history and has been prevalent in various countries at various times, becoming more widely accepted in the last few centuries.

The most open version of exclusivism is one that has only attracted much following in the twentieth century with the widespread growth of pluralist societies. Largely as a result of mixing with people from a range of different traditions, some people, while remaining committed to their own religion as normative, have come to accept that they may not have the total and absolute truth and may have something to learn from others. While they are not open to changing their own basic beliefs they may develop a new perspective on them and while not accepting the views of others they may develop some respect for the people who hold them.

In each of these versions of exclusivism the movement from stronger to more open forms has taken place *within* religious traditions (for example, between Protestants and Catholics in the case of Christianity), as well as *between* religious traditions such as Christianity, Judaism, Islam, Hinduism, and Buddhism. In the case of Christianity, the growth of less rigid forms of exclusivist thinking has paralleled the end of European world dominance and the fall of the great European empires along with the migration of large numbers of former colonial subjects (representing a wide range of religions) into western countries. Clearly, exclusivist views are more at home in mono-faith societies, but the experience of pluralism has been a major factor leading to the questioning of such approaches in multi-faith societies. Of course purely philosophical or theological considerations also play a part in the development of pluralist views.

Some of the epistemological problems of exclusivism have been indicated in Chapter 2. Generally, it makes the questionable assumption that only one out of a possible range of versions of religious truth is valid, without an adequate exploration of the alternatives. It also eliminates one important way of assessing the validity of one's own beliefs, namely that of comparing them to the opposed beliefs of others. However firmly convinced the exclusivist is of his or her own religion, it is highly implausible, without detailed supporting argument, for any one religion to claim that it is uniquely true when one takes into account the great variety and richness of religious belief. It is one of the themes of this book, conveyed in the twin notions of epistemic liberalism (dealt with later in this chapter) and an ethics of belief (dealt with in Chapter 5), that we have a strong obligation not simply to eliminate but to consider conflicting yet relevant evidence which helps to test and perhaps leads us to modify our own beliefs. These criticisms apply most strongly to the first two versions of exclusivism discussed but also raise serious epistemological questions about the third.

In relation to religious education, the exclusivist model of religion has a clear and natural link with confessional or faith-oriented approaches. In historical terms the two have gone hand in hand in most countries. People who sincerely believe that their own religion is uniquely true would generally wish to teach their children this important truth and not confuse them with the false beliefs of other religions. When, however, religious education takes the form of religious studies, where educational rather than confessional criteria are paramount and where a range of religious traditions are examined, an exclusivist methodology is clearly problematic as we have seen in the previous chapter. Certainly it is hard to see how the aims of such a programme could be achieved if the two more extreme versions of exclusivism were to underlie it.

The third and more open version of exclusivism mentioned, whereby we accept that one religion does not necessarily possess the total and absolute truth, would perhaps allow some multi-faith study to proceed but even here there would be serious limitations. Such an approach assumes that other traditions can at best provide some new ways of better understanding the one true faith. This would preclude a fully open and genuinely educational engagement with them. It would in practice also preclude covering in the course anything which may be seen as seriously questioning the preferred religious faith, such as moral critiques of its practices or sceptical questions raised by non-religious world views.

INCLUSIVISM

In an attempt to move away from the one-sidedness and unsubstantiated claims of exclusivism, some theologians have developed inclusivist versions of religious belief. As most such attempts of which we are aware are from the Christian perspective, we will focus on these while noting that the principles could be applied across other religions as well. Perhaps the main stimulus to inclusivism is the belief that a good God would not refuse salvation to those who lead morally good lives but through no fault of their own are unacquainted with the Christian message. In order to accommodate such people, their religious beliefs are seen as implicit or partial versions of Christianity so that they can thus be included in God's saving grace. One of the most influential exponents of inclusivism, Karl Rahner (a theologian in the Catholic Church), invokes the notion of other believers as being 'anonymous' Christians:

> Christianity does not simply confront the members of an extra-Christian religion as a mere non-Christian but as someone who can and must already be regarded in this or that respect as an anonymous Christian. (1969, p. 131)

This modifies the traditional exclusivist Catholic doctrine of *extra ecclesiam nulla salus* (outside the Church there is no salvation), promulgated by the Council of Florence (1438–45). There is now in this inclusivist view the possibility of salvation outside the official Church provided these other believers can be seen as in some sense pursuing the Christian goal.

The problem with such versions of inclusivism is that they still prejudge the issue in favour of Christianity. Most adherents of other religions would not see themselves as anonymous or implicit Christians. Such an approach, while well-intentioned, seems to take a paternalistic and self-referential view of religion. The basic difficulty lies in the attempt to reconcile two incompatible beliefs: namely the belief that Christianity is the one true religion with the belief that there may also be truth in other religions. Moreover, for Christian inclusivism to be properly established it would have to be shown that there are good grounds for regarding Christianity as uniquely valid among the world religions, something that has yet to be satisfactorily done.

There is another possible way of interpreting inclusivism of which only hints have so far been made in the literature. This would be to say that other religious traditions may be valid in their own right but that one can only understand them from one's own perspective such as that of Christianity and where they seem to have compatibilities or parallels to Christian notions, their believers may achieve salvation within their own faith. In other words, believers of other faiths are not to be seen as anonymous Christians but as achieving through their own faith what the observer interprets as equivalent to Christianity. This view remains in the inclusivist rather than pluralist camp (with which it has affinities) because the judgement on the salvific potential of other religions is made from the Christian perspective and is still interpreted in Christian terms.

Because of their recognition that believers of other faiths may achieve salvation, both versions of inclusivism are more appropriate epistemological bases for religious studies programmes than are exclusivist views. However, they are in reality still more suited to faith-oriented programmes, albeit of a more liberal kind, because they still prejudge the issue of religious truth. If Christianity (or whatever religion is seen as definitive) is the norm by which all other faiths are to be evaluated, how can these other religions be given a full and fair hearing? Because their place in the programme is made dependent on their links to Christianity, their exposition will be from an external rather than an internal focus (that is, from how they are seen by their own representatives).

PLURALISM

The pluralist in religion rejects the claim that any one religion is superior to all others. This represents a major move away from traditional approaches to religion, a crossing of the 'theological Rubicon' one might say.

Religious pluralism as a theological or philosophical position needs to be distinguished from religious pluralism as a sociological fact. As a matter of fact most western societies are pluralist in religion (they have a wide range of practising religious groups), but the religious pluralist in the sense we are considering here goes beyond this sociological fact to argue that all (or at least most) of these different religions are in some sense potentially valid. No doubt the experience of living in a religiously plural society is one factor that has influenced many pluralists to take the position that they do but by itself it does not make such a position necessary. One could still remain an exclusivist or inclusivist and argue that one of these competing religions is superior to the remainder.

As with the previous two positions, a number of different versions of pluralism may be noted, ranging from restricted to more open forms. The first form to be distinguished may be called 'revisionist pluralism', following Keith Ward's discussion (1990, p. 17). This involves the radical revision of existing religious traditions to prune out any beliefs not compatible with post-Enlightenment critical thinking. As a result, religion 'can move to a more universal phase, in which insights are selected from many traditions, while most of their differences are relegated to the museum of dead beliefs' (1990, p. 17). As Ward says:

> If a Buddhist is prepared to regard belief in re-incarnation as a myth, a Christian thinks of the Incarnation as a mistaken fourth-century doctrine, and a Muslim agrees that the Koran is a fallible and morally imperfect document, they might well be able to agree on much more than they used to. (1990, p. 17)

What this would eventually lead to is a new world religion which encompasses the best and most commonly shared doctrines of all the major religions. However, such an approach is unlikely to appeal to orthodox religious adherents of the various faiths because it rejects the distinctiveness of their individual religious beliefs and more generally it lacks any clear criteria as to which beliefs should be rejected and which accepted. Consequently, it has not been put forward as a realistic option by many writers. It is rather akin to the attempt to popularise Esperanto as a universal language; it involves too radical a reconstruction of existing practices and ends up by imposing an artificial model that corresponds with very few persons' actual reality.

JOHN HICK'S INTERPRETATION OF PLURALISM

Another and far more influential form of pluralism claims that all the major religions are equally valid and equally salvific. The best known exponent of this position is John Hick (1989) who argues that all religions are culturally conditioned ways of responding to similar basic questions confronting all humans. To make his point he invokes the Kantian distinction between noumena and phenomena and says that we can never directly experience the noumenal realm, which he calls 'the Real' in itself but only the phenomenal realm made up of human religious responses to this Real. Religious growth is a process of transformation from self-centredness to Reality-centredness which takes place in all the major religions. Religion is thus interpreted by Hick primarily in a 'soteriological' sense, that is, as a means of achieving salvation by moving towards a higher and more profound state of awareness and being. Some religions interpret reality or the absolute in theistic terms (for example, Christianity, Judaism, and Islam), others in non-theistic terms (for example, Buddhism and some forms of Hinduism), and all these interpretations are equally authentic.

In order to maintain his position Hick has to argue that the claims to uniqueness of the various world religions can no longer be accepted as literally true because if they were they would rule out the incompatible claims of the other religions. Doctrines such as the resurrection of Christ have therefore to be interpreted mythically, expressing in a metaphoric way a great religious principle. Christ's life is understood as representing an extraordinary openness to the divine presence rather than him being seen as the second person of the divine Trinity.

Hick calls his theory a hypothesis, which indicates the non-dogmatic character of his approach. He likewise maintains that God presents him or herself (or itself) at a certain epistemic distance in a universe that is ultimately religiously ambiguous. This always leaves room for cognitive freedom or faith which, while it does not involve any direct sensation of the divine presence, is still based on human experience. Hick extends Wittgenstein's (1953, Part II, Section xi) notion of 'seeing-as' to all experience which he says is always essentially interpretive or 'experiencing-as'. Religious believers choose to interpret reality religiously on the basis of their experience and this, Hick maintains, is just as valid a response to the ambiguity of the universe as a naturalistic one. Because of various geographic, historical, and cultural factors, different groups 'perceive the transcendent through the lens of a particular religious culture with its distinctive set of concepts, myths, historical exemplars and devotional or meditational techniques' (1989, p. 8). All religions promote in their own distinctive way the soteriological goal of transformation from self-centredness to Reality-centredness.

The criticisms that have been made of Hick's account may be grouped under two headings: (a) the distinction he makes between the Real in itself and our different human responses to this in the various religions; and (b) the treating of all religions as having a common essence and as all being compatible in their goals.

With regard to the first of these, the question is raised that if we can never directly experience ultimate reality, how can we be sure it exists and how can we know that our human response to it is valid or not? Has Hick perhaps reduced religious experience to essentially a moral process? That is, is Hick guilty of reductionism as discussed in Chapter 2? He implies this when he says 'the transformation of human existence which is called salvation or liberation shows itself in its spiritual and moral fruits' (1989, p. 301). He also implies that non-religious movements can partake of the Real:

> [f]rom a religious point of view the basic intent of the Marxist-Leninist, Trotskyist, Maoist, and broader socialist movements, as also of 'liberation theology' and the contemporary drive for racial

and gender equality, has to be interpreted as a dispositional response of the modern sociologically conditioned consciousness to the Real. (1989, p. 306)

If such a wide range of responses are legitimate manifestations of the Real, does the notion have any real explanatory power? Is there any real difference between denying and affirming its existence? Hick is aware of this criticism and his response is that even if his concept of the noumenal realm is unclear and difficult to verify it must be posited if our religious experience of the world is to have any meaning, which he thinks it does. (Hick is here positing an epistemic primitive as discussed in Chapter 2.) He says of the noumenal realm, 'it is the concept of the inexperienceable and indescribable ground of the range of human religious experiences in so far as this is more than a purely human projection' (1991, p. 26). However, this still leaves us with some major unanswered questions concerning his notion of the Real and its place in religious understanding

The second major line of criticism of Hick is that his theory fails to account for the particularity and uniqueness of the individual religions by treating them all as having a common essence. As has been noted, Hick seeks to reinterpret those aspects of the various religions which directly conflict with one another in mythological terms. The danger here is that what is distinctive to a particular religion will be lost and such a reinterpreted description of the various faiths will be unacceptable to most followers. Most believers do hold that their beliefs are literally and not just mythologically true and that they are pursuing a distinctive religious path not shared by those outside their faith.

Some writers have broadened this critique of Hick to claim that what he is in fact doing is imposing a western liberal quasi-secularist view of religion onto all believers, many of whom would reject such an approach. According to Kenneth Surin, 'the dominant ideology of this new world reality declares that nations, cultures, religions and so forth, are simply obsolete if they are maintained in their old forms as fixed and intractable' (1990, p. 79).

Jürgen Moltmann makes a similar critique when he notes that, in the modern western world, religion has moved into an area reserved for subjective belief and private choice:

> Different religious traditions lose their capacity to be the binding element of societies and become instead mere objects for religious consumers to select for their own private reasons, reasons which are not to be argued about. Thus democratised, religions enter the

market place as objects of subjective choices in much the same way as brands of toothpaste and laundry soap. (1990, p. 152)

Moltmann likens this to Marcuse's notion of 'repressive tolerance', 'tolerant in allowing everything as subjective possibility, repressive in respect to scepticism about any objective reality being adequately mediated by religious symbols' (1990, p. 52). Surin likewise invokes the analogy of the McDonald's hamburger as a 'universal' food with the 'world ecumenism' advocated by the exponents of religious pluralism, both of which are western capitalist impositions (1990, p. 79).

Peter Donovan, in an interesting article entitled 'The Intolerance of Religious Pluralism' (1993), responds to such criticisms of Hick by pointing to an inconsistency in the arguments of people like Surin and Moltmann and conservative exclusivists in general. He shows how they use postmodernist arguments, such as the rejection of all world views as having any objective foundation, to buttress their attacks on liberal pluralists such as Hick. Liberalism itself is held to be an ideology which takes a secular, empiricist view of truth which liberals impose on all others in the guise of tolerance and openness. In the process other peoples' distinctive traditional convictions about the world including their religious beliefs are dismantled. Exclusivists can then claim that unlike such liberals they are not interfering with how other religious believers hold their beliefs and not expecting them to reconsider their basic traditional convictions (even though they believe them to be mistaken), and are in fact showing them more respect than the religious pluralist such as Hick does. In other words, people can agree to disagree and each maintain their own religious faith in the way they always have done.

However, there is something problematic about this strategy. Donovan captures this rather cleverly when he notes that 'a cynic might well be intrigued to see the descendants of Calvin and of the inquisition joining forces with the disciples of Nietzsche to give lessons on tolerance to the children of the Enlightenment!' (1993, p. 219). The conservative theologians' alliance with postmodernism can never really work out because they, 'even more than liberals and modernists, are in need of a realist, absolutist view of truth, if they are to hold their traditions and revelation to be the final word, rendering all others false or incomplete' (Donovan, 1993, p. 225). A postmodern epistemology is quite incompatible with an absolutist view of religious truth.

Nevertheless, the second line of criticism of Hick's thesis which we have been examining, namely its inconsistency with how religious believers actually hold their beliefs and its blurring of the distinctiveness of individual religions, remains relevant. Hick's response to this criticism is similar to that which he gave to the first: his position cannot be conclusively proved but it is a legitimate attempt to find meaning and value in all religions, not just one. If this leads to some sacrifice in the certainty and literalness with which religious beliefs have traditionally been held, this may be a price that has to be paid. It is perhaps a step that has become necessary now that the world has become essentially pluralist and global in perspective. We are now forced to confront the immediate reality of viewpoints fundamentally different to our own and make some considered response to this situation. As Huston Smith says, 'when people lived in tribes and cloistered civilisations, they were not aware of having views of reality; there was, for them, simply the way the world was' (1990, p. 661). We no longer live in such a world (at least most of us do not) and we are required to consider our view of reality, and Hick's approach is one that is worthy of our consideration.

An alternative response to this situation would be one of agnosticism which would maintain that it is at present impossible to decide whether all religions are equally valid or whether one is uniquely true or whether all are false, while not ruling out any of these as possible options. Such an approach would reflect what Hick calls the religious ambiguity of the universe which, as he points out, can be interpreted either religiously or naturalistically (1989, Part II). He lists a series of arguments in favour of a religious interpretation (for example, the widespread human experience of religion, the apparently designed character of the world) and a series in favour of an atheistic interpretation (for example, the problem of evil, the utterly insignificant place of human life within the universe, the ability of science on its own to explain the workings of nature). He argues that if we set all the reasons out in two opposed columns we have no way of concluding that one outweighs the other (1989, p. 123). Hick however does not himself draw an agnostic conclusion. He comes down on the side of religion but as we have seen presents this as a hypothesis which we may either accept or reject. It is quite reasonable to make such a commitment as Hick's as long as it is accepted that it is equally reasonable for someone else to make an alternative commitment (say, to a naturalistic interpretation, or to an agnostic one where the evidence is deemed to be inconclusive either way). Because of the genuine ambiguity of the universe, we have to remain open to the possibility of the correctness of any of the three positions while at the same time acknowledging that ultimately they cannot all be true.

A similar point was made by Rescher, as detailed in the previous chapter, in response to the global sceptic. As individuals we need to make a choice between competing positions in order to have a consistent and meaningful set of philosophical principles in life. This brings out the difference between the type of commitment appropriate for religious studies as a subject and that appropriate for an individual studying such a subject. Religious studies as a subject needs to remain open-ended to all major possibilities to allow freedom of choice for each individual between the different positions presented. The individual student will generally want to make a more definitive choice in favour of one specific position, be it religious, naturalistic, agnostic, or some variant on one of these.

EXTENDED PLURALISM AND ITS IMPLICATIONS FOR RELIGIOUS EDUCATION

What the above argument leads to is a third version of pluralism, the most open of the three, which may be termed 'extended pluralism'. On this approach no judgement is made in advance that any one religion is uniquely valid or that all the major religions are equally valid, nor that non-religious views are any less valid; but that all significant attempts to answer issues of ultimate concern deserve careful and open consideration. The only criterion for acceptance or rejection would be how well the relevant beliefs can be explicated and supported.

If we now apply these considerations to religious education, the appropriate methodological basis for organising a course in the studies of religion is that no one position is to be favoured over another but that all are deemed potentially valid until shown otherwise. The notion of the potential epistemological validity of both religious and non-religious interpretations of the universe was presented in Chapter 2 in response to the local sceptic and is of course linked to Hick's notion of the ambiguity of the universe discussed above. The decision which one ultimately makes will be made on the basis of appropriate criteria incorporated in the course. These would centre upon the three key conditions for liberal education presented in Chapter 1 – critical rationality, personal transcendence, and epistemological coherence. Students would thus come to decide that some beliefs are better based or more rationally defensible than others, are more consistent both within themselves and with other branches of knowledge, and lead to a more personally meaningful world view. While exploring such issues it would be quite rational for students to work from their existing primary paradigm or home religion (or non-religion) unless or until they feel there is sufficient reason to change to a new belief system as was argued in our discussion of sophisticated relativism in Chapter 2.

Such a version of pluralism as a methodology for treating the various belief systems in a religious studies course is preferable to that of Hick's because it has all the advantages of his approach with none of the disadvantages. Hick's version of pluralism is nevertheless a big step forward from exclusivism and inclusivism because it allows an impartial engagement with a range of different religions. It is also superior to revisionist pluralism as it allows each religion to be presented in its own distinctive terms and as worthwhile in itself. As a methodological basis for teaching religious studies it does therefore have considerable advantages. As Hick himself says:

> Academically, to acknowledge the unavoidable cultural element within the forms of religion frees us to observe and to be fascinated by the differences between the different traditions, without any pressure to homogenise them or to depict the objects of religious experience – Yahweh, Brahman, Shiva, the Holy Trinity, *sunyata,* the Dharma, and so on – as phenomenologically alike. (1985, p. 107)

The historical and phenomenological study of religion can thus flourish freely, as can the philosophical, whereby we can judge and criticise, where appropriate, distorted or morally suspect forms of religious experience and practice.

However, Hick's approach does require that people come ultimately to see their religious beliefs as not literally true but as culturally conditioned responses to the Real in itself, valid in so far as they promote movement towards Reality-centredness. While this is an interesting view it does provide a special account of how religion should be understood and thus could restrict the presentation of other ways of understanding religion in a religious studies programme. Another problem is that it would seem not to encourage adequate coverage of non-religious world views. Although Hick occasionally mentions that humanists, Marxists, existentialists, and so on, may somehow share in an understanding of the Real, his overwhelming emphasis is on religious (either theistic or non-theistic) means of personal fulfilment.

Extended pluralism, on the other hand, would allow all views to be presented impartially. It would also encourage a wider range of teaching strategies than Hick's approach and provide more scope for cross-religion and thematic approaches where certain topics such as ethical beliefs, social practices, and the role of women could be looked at across a whole range of religions. Similarly, the links between religious belief in general and other aspects of human experience (for example, religion and art, music, architecture, the media) would be very relevant topics. One aspect of religious study that would be especially stressed would be encouraging children to relate what is taught to their own personal search for meaning in life, what we have called personal transcendence.

Because no one position or no particular interpretation of religion is given favoured status a programme along these lines would encourage the students to develop, through careful consideration of all the appropriate issues, their own final stance on the range of positions explored. As has been indicated, a religious studies course based on extended pluralism would allow all relevant positions on ultimate issues to be presented including those supporting a non-religious interpretation of the universe. This is quite appropriate as it will provide a complete range of responses to the sort of questions to which religions are one type of answer. Children will at any rate be exposed to such positions in their wider life in the community (at least in western, secular societies) and by including them in the course it will allow students to weigh up in an informed and impartial way the pros and cons of all sides of the debate. Moreover, in a programme such as the one advocated here, non-religious believers are also likely to find value in studying various religious texts and perhaps discover insights there that help shape their beliefs. In other words, it is more likely to make religion accessible to all people.

A major aim of a religious studies programme based on extended pluralism would be to get people to hold whatever beliefs they reach in a non-dogmatic and flexible way. It may be argued by some that such an approach precludes a genuine religious commitment because such a commitment is a total and absolute one and would lose its force if held in this more open-ended way. While this may be true of how most religious believers have held their religious beliefs in the past (particularly in mono-faith societies), it is not, we would hold, a *necessary* feature of religious beliefs. Logically, people can hold a firm commitment to their religion while at the same time acknowledging the fact that they *may* be mistaken and could conceivably change their minds in the future. At present this is their considered position and they will act accordingly, but they refuse to be dogmatic or close-minded to alternative possibilities. This could be linked to the notion of degrees of belief, as discussed in Chapter 2, where there is a preparedness to adjust the degree of confidence with which people hold their beliefs when confronted with new evidence. It can also be understood in terms of the principle of fallibilism, which is discussed in Chapter 5. An approach such as this has been supported by Andrew Wright (1993, p. 64), who argues that the main aim of religious education should be 'allowing pupils to become religiously literate, to be able to think, act and communicate intelligently about the ultimate questions that religion asks' and to be able to do so whether the pupils are believers, agnostics, or atheists.

This is, of course, a different conception of what it means to be committed to religion (at least for most people), but one that would seem eminently appropriate for those living in modern, pluralist societies including those living in separate mono-faith communities in such societies. One thinks of examples such as Bosnia, Israel, and Northern Ireland. If, as a result of religious education of the type being recommended, a larger number of people did come to hold their beliefs in this more provisional, flexible way it would be an enormous step forward in helping to reduce the conflicts based on religious differences besetting so many parts of the world today. In this light we may consider Cardinal Newman's famous statement, 'Oh, how we hate one another for the love of God', or the contemporary popular physicist Paul Davies' assertion, 'Few would deny that religion remains, for all its pretensions, one of the most divisive forces in society' (1983, p. 4). Such negative characteristics of religion could be drastically lessened by the new approach to holding religious beliefs advocated here.

It may be objected that the approach to religious studies being recommended, which presents all viewpoints as open to critical examination, takes too rationalistic or cognitive an approach to the study of religion and neglects the essential affective elements present in all religions. Associated with this criticism is the view that it is too intellectually demanding an approach for young children. There is, however, nothing in this approach that prohibits treatment of the experiential side of religion; indeed this would be an important part of any phenomenological study of religion. The feeling of what it is like to be a believer in the different religions is an important part of such a study and one does not have to actually believe in the truth of the religion to appreciate the nature of these feelings. One can temporarily put oneself in another's shoes and use one's imagination in understanding the perspectives from which they view the world. Perhaps one could never fully share the feelings of what it is like to be on the inside of a particular religion unless one actually belongs to that religion, but understanding is not an all-or-nothing affair and there are many cases in education where less than total understanding is still meaningful and helpful.

In relation to the question of children's ability to handle religious studies of the form advocated here, naturally the programme would need to be adapted to their developmental level and the more intellectually demanding aspects reserved for the senior years and tertiary level. In the early years a more descriptive, phenomenological approach would be appropriate and children would not be expected to make critical evaluations or personal choice of life stances until later. In many cases children will be brought up in a particular 'home tradition' and this will provide them with the experience of seeing a religion from the inside which will aid them when they come to tackle the more searching task of reflecting on the validity of their own beliefs and developing their own, considered life stance.

EPISTEMIC LIBERALISM

The extended pluralist approach to the study of religion is of course much in tune with contemporary, secular liberalism as discussed below. As we have seen it has been attacked by writers such as Surin and Moltmann as imposing a particular western ideology with overtones of the market economy and consumerism when it comes into contact with other generally more traditionalist cultures. It would take us too far afield to undertake a detailed defence of liberalism against its critics but the following recent works on the topic may be consulted by those interested: Horton (1993), Kymlicka (1995), Mendus (1989), Rawls (1993), and Raz (1986).

For the present we would like to refer to an important distinction made by Donovan (1993) between *epistemic* and *ideological* liberalism, the former referring to respect for intellectual freedom and a commitment to rational procedures in deciding differences of opinion, the latter to commitment to liberalism as a total belief system and political policy which should be promoted as widely as possible. The critics of liberalism are focusing on ideological liberalism but as Donovan points out:

> Not all liberal thinkers by any means, we might argue, have been ideologically committed to a 'modernist' project whereby the beliefs and practices of others are to be progressively brought into line with a secular, scientific, and humanistic world-view, to form a uniform global culture. The intentions of most liberals involved in the study of religion have been far more modest: the conscientious application of the best scholarship they know to the questions before them. (1993, p. 220)

We may also turn to the classic exponent of epistemic liberalism, John Stuart Mill, to find how his account provides the principles which can guard against its becoming a totalitarian ideology. His stress on principles such as acceptance of fallibility, openness to refutation, and invitation to radical critical scrutiny are exactly the sort of epistemological values that should underlie a fully pluralist-based approach to the study of religion. They are also intimately connected to the liberal education criterion of critical rationality discussed in Chapter 1. Such principles would protect the programme from ideological bias from any particular quarter.

We may further note that the approach of epistemic liberalism is particularly appropriate for a pluralist society. It is the approach most likely to facilitate harmonious interaction between the different religious groups because it provides a common framework for meaningful and open-ended dialogue in which all can share and in which none are uniquely privileged. Contrast this with the traditional, exclusivist model where one group's perspective is imposed on all others, or (in its milder form) where there is a set of competing, inward-looking, religious perspectives disinclined to engage in dialogue with others because each thinks it has the whole truth. What are the likely implications of these models for long-term community harmony?

Michael Grimmitt (1994) makes a similar point when he argues that religious education can make a strong contribution to social harmony by helping to break down divisions and stressing the complementarity rather than the oppositions between religions. The subject is uniquely well-placed to do this because it reflects at a micro-level the issues which a pluralist society faces at the macro-level (1994, p. 144). The problem, in practice, is reconciling the distinctiveness of each religious tradition with the universal core values that underlie most of them. Grimmitt maintains:

> that there is something unreasonable about faith communities seeking to benefit from the promotion of these so-called educational values while resisting the application of other educational values to the process of studying religion – such as critical evaluation which is vital to promoting tolerance and appreciation. (1994, p. 141)

Epistemic liberalism is also very relevant in another way. Particularly for those involved in education, we do want to have some means of resolving questions of truth – this would seem to be almost a logically necessary requirement of any genuine educational process. As Donovan says, when it comes to religion we cannot avoid the question, 'who's right?' (1993, p. 226). Epistemic liberalism provides us with a means of grappling with that question. Even if asking this question may make many uncomfortable and risk stirring up deep-seated prejudices, a policy of 'agreeing to disagree' seems ultimately self-defeating and a block to intellectual and social progress. If, in the process of exploring such a question, people are led to make major modifications to their belief systems it will not be for the first time. And, as in the past, as Donovan points out, 'the experience of adjustment may prove to be for the overall enhancement, rather than the destruction, of the faith of those involved. "Great is truth", after all, and surely "it shall prevail"' (1993, p. 228). He then goes on to make the link between this goal and the role of religious studies: 'Liberal thinkers will take it for granted that academic religious studies should stand with them in this enterprise, providing them with a forum and many of the resources with which it can best be furthered' (1993, p. 228).

The principles of epistemic liberalism also provide a model for the teacher's role in presenting the conflicting ideas that make up the content of religious studies. Such teachers will have their own commitments to one of the religious (or non-religious) positions being presented but should not, of course, openly propagandise for such a commitment to be shared by the pupils. This is not to say that teachers cannot indicate their own position and in many ways it is better for this to be out in the open. What they should do is treat this as just another viewpoint to be critically considered by the pupils, not having any special status because it happens to be the belief of the teacher. The only commitment that should be actively pursued is that to the principles of epistemic liberalism as described above, which is another way of saying that it should be to a genuinely *educational* treatment of religion. This may be termed a 'meta-commitment' in that it is a commitment to following certain types of procedures in the study of religion rather than to any one specific position in the course. It follows from this that teachers from a wide variety of backgrounds and varying personal belief systems should, if they behave professionally, be able to teach religion in a genuinely educational way. The problem is not so much finding teachers who hold the 'right' sort of beliefs to teach studies of religion, but finding those who have the breadth of knowledge and extensive range of skills needed to teach such a subject effectively.

CONCLUSION

We have now covered the three major viewpoints that can be taken in response to the diversity of religious beliefs and seen how well they function as initial frameworks for the teaching of religious studies. It has been argued that the more open versions of each of these three positions are educationally superior models but that, in the cases of exclusivism and inclusivism, even these less restricted forms are unsatisfactory. The most appropriate foundations were found in pluralism – in John Hick's version and in the extended form of pluralism – with the latter being the preferred one because it had all the advantages of the former but allows a more unrestricted or open study of the subject.

It could even be argued that once you treat religion in an *educational* way (as religious studies programmes attempt to do) extended pluralism is already implied. Education, as opposed to indoctrination, involves such values as critical awareness, openness to differing perspectives, broad range and depth of understanding. This requires that questions of truth are not prejudged and no one perspective is given privileged status, and these are notions central to epistemic liberalism which, when applied to the study of religion, is most appropriately represented by the extended pluralist approach.

It was also pointed out that the three different viewpoints were being examined not as personal belief systems but in terms of their adequacy as a methodological basis for organising studies of religion. In other words, the concern was with how they structured the way in which the different religious and other world views would be presented in terms of their validity and how issues to do with their truth status were to be handled. The question of the teacher's own personal beliefs was seen to raise somewhat different issues and no judgement was made as to which are the most appropriate as long as such beliefs did not interfere with the educational goals of the programme.

REFERENCES

Davies, P. (1983). *God and the New Physics,* New York, Simon & Schuster.

Donovan, P. (1993). 'The Intolerance of Religious Pluralism', *Religious Studies,* 29, 217–29.

Grimmitt, M. (1994). 'Religious Education and the Ideology of Pluralism', *British Journal of Religious Education* 16, 3, 133–47.

Hick, J. (1985). *Problems of Religious Pluralism,* London, Macmillan.

Hick, J. (1989). *An Interpretation of Religion,* London, Macmillan.

Hick, J. (1991). 'Reply to Gavin D'Costa', in H. Hewitt Jr, *Problems in the Philosophy of Religion: Critical Studies of the Work of John Hick,* London, Macmillan.

Horton, J. (ed.) (1993). *Liberalism, Multiculturalism and Toleration,* London, Macmillan.

Kymlicka, W. (1995). *Multicultural Citizenship,* Oxford, Clarendon Press.

Mendus, S. (1989). *Toleration and the Limits of Liberalism,* London, Macmillan.

Moltmann, J. (1990). 'Is "Pluralistic Theology" Useful for the Dialogue of

World Religions?', in G. D'Costa (ed.), *Christian Uniqueness Recon-sidered: The Myth of a Pluralist Theology of Religions,* Maryknoll, NY, Orbis Books.

Rahner, K. (1969). *Theological Investigations,* Vol. 5, London, Darton, Longman & Todd.

Rawls, J. (1993) *Political Liberalism,* New York, Columbia University Press.

Raz, J. (1986). *The Morality of Freedom,* Oxford, Clarendon Press.

Smith, H. (1990). 'Postmodernism's Impact on the Study of Religion', *Journal of the American Academy of Religion,* LVIII, 4, 653–70.

Surin, K. (1990). 'A Certain "Politics of Speech": "Religious Pluralism" in the Age of the McDonald's Hamburger', *Modern Theology,* 7, 1, 67–100.

Ward, K. (1990). 'Truth and the Diversity of Religions', *Religious Studies,* 26, 1–18.

Wittgenstein, L. (1953). *Philosophical Investigations,* trans. G.E.M. Anscombe, Oxford, Basil Blackwell.

Wright, A. (1993). *Religious Education in the Secondary School,* London, David Fulton.

4

Critical Realism and the Role of Models in Religion

INTRODUCTION: THE PLURALIST PREDICAMENT

Anyone approaching the study of religion is faced with a bewildering array of conflicting religious paradigms in terms of the different religious traditions existing in the world and now increasingly present in western societies such as the UK, the USA, and Australia. Even within the main religious traditions there is a wide range of variations, and there is also a range of non-religious viewpoints available. This has given rise to what may be termed the 'pluralist predicament'. This predicament could lead students to draw one of the following inferences as a result of such competing claims: (i) a sceptical conclusion that it is not possible to decide between competing claims; (ii) an exclusivist conclusion that one must be right and all the others wrong – a conclusion a fundamentalist or dogmatist might happily live with; and (iii) a relativist or postmodernist conclusion that there is no objective knowledge independent of the knower. We regard each of these three conclusions as unduly negative with adverse implications for studies of religion. We have dealt with their weaknesses in Chapter 2 and so will not repeat them here. There is, however, a fourth possible response, the one this chapter will argue for, which is a critical realist position. This can only be drawn after some investigation of the growth of knowledge in both religion and science by examining the role of models and paradigms within each. This will be offered as a positive response to the pluralist predicament and will be examined in the next section.

A further reason for developing the critical realist response arises because of Hick's failure to establish a fully satisfactory realist epistemology for religion, as argued in the previous chapter. His appeal to a noumenal realm does not convey what most religious believers understand by the notion of a transcendent realm. While his use of the Kantian noumenal/phenomenal distinction is a useful response to pluralism, it does not give an adequate account of critical realism. Moreover, unless a satisfactory theory of critical realism can be established, the path is left open for the reductionist to argue that the ontological claims of religion are spurious.

THE CRITICAL REALIST RESPONSE

Critical realism accepts the pluralist predicament without adopting a sceptical, relativist, or exclusivist conclusion. One clear expression of critical realism is found in the epistemic logic of Forrest (1995). Another is found in recent work in the epistemology of science and religion by Barbour (1974, 1990), McFague (1982, 1987), Murphy (1990), and Peacocke (1984, 1990), which examines among other things the implications for religious epistemology of Kuhn's and Lakatos' study of scientific method . Two key concepts central to this latter debate are those of model and paradigm. By looking at the roles of models and paradigms in the growth of knowledge, it is possible to see similarities in the use of models in both science and religion which allows for a degree of freedom to explore interpretations of our experience of the world, within the context of a public external reality.

Forrest's (1995, p. 44) solution to the pluralist predicament is firstly to use Nozick's (1981) notion of 'tracking' to argue that while belief systems track reality, and that small differences in reality are reflected in small changes to the belief systems, nevertheless different belief systems do not track reality in identical ways because of different cultural or other background factors surrounding the formation of the belief systems. This part of his argument reflects a commitment to a correspondence theory of truth which maintains that the truth of propositions can be established by their reference to things in the world. Nozick's notion of tracking is an attempt to show how beliefs correspond with reality while at the same time acknowledging that reality is also dependent on our beliefs. (By 'reality' here we mean the amalgam of beliefs and experiences which constitute our understanding of the world.) For example, the proposition, 'It is raining', has a simple relationship or correspondence to the events around us, but the proposition, 'The forest ecosystem is in a degenerative phase', has no comparable simple correspondence to events at hand. It can only be understood by bringing to bear previous knowledge of ecosystems and their various phases. That knowledge is now corroborated by what one sees.

The second part of Forrest's solution deals with the strong internal coherence of the individual religious belief systems. This acknowledges that while a subset of propositions of belief system A may well conflict with propositions from a subset of belief system B, each subset nevertheless coheres well within its own belief system. More importantly, the effect of removing either of the conflicting subsets from their respective belief systems merely on the grounds of their mutual incompatibility is to reduce the overall coherence and consistency of each belief system. That is to say, the relative equilibrium of each belief system is maximised by keeping the offending propositions, and reduced by removing them. An example of this is given in Chapter 2 in our discussion on degrees of belief in the section on exclusivism.

This strong argument for resolving the pluralist predicament, which Forrest refers to as 'holistic correspondence' (1995, p. 43), is underpinned by a principle appealing to the rationality of maintaining maximally consistent sets of beliefs at the cost of accepting a degree of inconsistency between some propositions across different belief systems.

While Forrest's solution is philosophically elegant, the level and complexity of its arguments are not easily accessible to students of studies of religion where the counter-case to the possible negative conclusions deriving from pluralism needs to be put. On the other hand, the role of models and paradigms within scientific and religious epistemologies is more concrete and gives rise to more pertinent and colourful possibilities relevant to the student. For example, a consideration of conflicting models of God (for example, the Christian concept of Jesus as both God and man), or of the problem of incompatible models of the atom in science because of its wave/particle duality, can substantially parallel the discussion in the epistemic logic of pluralism but at a less abstract level. Hence, a critical appraisal of the solution of the pluralist predicament will be given in the first place from this standpoint, focusing on the role of models in the scientific realm and Barbour's four epistemological criteria of agreement with the data, coherence, scope or generality, and fertility.

Ian Barbour's most recent work, *Religion in an Age of Science* (1990), is a detailed analysis of the methodological parallels between science and theology and examines the roles of models and paradigms in each. Barbour does this in three steps: firstly, he looks at the relationship between data and theory in science and religion; secondly, he discusses the notion of paradigms; and, finally, he outlines the role of models in both domains.

In examining the relationship between scientific theory and data, Barbour notes a problem central to the pluralist crisis – the fundamental difficulty in linking observations and experimental data to scientific theories and concepts. The work of Thomas Kuhn (1970), investigating the growth of scientific knowledge, reveals further significant problems.

Rather than scientific knowledge growing architectonically out of the work of previous scientific theories, it is instead characterised by paradigm shifts and scientific revolutions. Disturbingly, subsequent theories are, in significant respects, incommensurable with previous ones. Thus, for example, Copernican cosmology does not grow out of and build upon Ptolemy's cosmology but replaces it with a new theory, engendering a cycle of paradigm crisis, scientific revolution, and paradigm shift. Kuhn argues that alternative theories are incompatible with each other. Accompanying a paradigm shift is a corresponding shift in meaning, wherein core concepts of the original theory are transformed into new meanings under the later paradigm. The implications of this for science are profound, ushering into science a pluralism not just of competing paradigms but of incommensurable paradigms – a problem very similar to the pluralist predicament in studies of religion.

Kuhn's philosophy of science has been roundly criticised by Imre Lakatos (Lakatos and Musgrave, 1970). The major stumbling block is Kuhn's incommensurability thesis and the theory of meaning underpinning it. Banner (1990) also mounts a series of arguments against Kuhn's position and argues that he fails to provide an adequate theory of meaning.

Lakatos rejects Kuhn's theory of paradigm shifts, built upon the incommensurability thesis, and replaces it with a theory of scientific research programmes. Under this regimen, scientific hypotheses are constructed within a broader scientific tradition in which scientific inferences are made and tested and theories modified in the light of them. When the research programme is no longer fruitful or cannot handle anomalies, it is replaced by an alternative research programme. While Lakatos' view is more in keeping with standard science it nevertheless ushers in a pluralism of its own. Under this scheme, science is characterised by various research programmes which continue, often in competition with each other, until one or the other proves to be the more fruitful line of enquiry.

Kuhn's and Lakatos' work highlights the important role of paradigms in the formulation of scientific theories. A useful definition of paradigm is given by Barbour:

> a cluster of conceptual and methodological presuppositions embodied in an exemplary body of scientific work, such as Newtonian mechanics in the eighteenth century or relativity and quantum physics in the twentieth century. A paradigm implicitly defines for a given scientific community the kinds of questions that

may fruitfully be asked and the type of explanations to be sought. (1990, p. 33)

The important aspect to note is the relationship between theories and paradigms. Scientific theories are set against a backdrop of conceptual and methodological assumptions, or a paradigm, which is resistant to change, whereas theories are flexible and adapt to new data or the discovery of significant implications implicit within them. Barbour suggests that scientific theories must satisfy four criteria: agreement with the data, coherence (both internal and external) with the dominant paradigm, scope or generality, and, finally, fertility or the ability to generate further discoveries or experiments.

While these four criteria accord well with scientific practice, they nevertheless give rise to considerable epistemological problems. If scientific theories are as flexible, adaptable, and revisable as the history of science suggests, then their correspondence with reality is seriously in doubt. The clear implication of this set of criteria is towards an epistemological instrumentalism or relativism – notwithstanding the solidly realist claims of scientists themselves. The question mark over the status of scientific theories is brought about by the fact that three out of the four criteria listed above are merely logical or rationality conditions on theories consistent with a coherence theory of truth which sets no conditions linking the theories to reality through a correspondence theory. Only one of the four criteria – agreement with data – seeks to do this.

It might be contended that the fourth criterion – fertility and the ability to generate further discoveries or experiments – is not simply a rationality or logical condition, but rather a strong condition linking theory to reality. That this is not so can be seen from the fact that the fertility condition can be stated more formally using the logical schema, 'If p then q'. The important point to note is that q, whether it is a discovery or a further experiment, is logically entailed by theory p. Its verification however is dependent on the further application of the four criteria.

The fact that three of the four criteria are rationality or coherence criteria gives rise to the problem that if multiple theories are consistent with the same data, then the question is no longer which theory is true or false but which theory is to be preferred – leaving open the further question of how this is to be decided. Kuhn suggests that the scientific community decides this point, principally by reference to the other three criteria. Lakatos, on the other hand, suggests that the four criteria define a research programme, and that at any one time multiple programmes are in progress.

Revisability of scientific theories presents a problem for the critical realist who has to steer a mid-course between the two extremes of instrumentalism with its anti-realist overtones and naive realism. Instrumentalism holds that scientific theories are merely convenient constructs to give the desired answer – if a theory is deemed lacking in scope or fertility another theory can be chosen in its place as long as it coheres with the dominant paradigm. The naive realist, on the other hand, resolves the problem by proclaiming that only one theory agrees with the data and makes correspondence with reality not only a necessary condition for a scientific theory but also holds revisability to be causally determined by the nature of reality.

A critical realist accepts the revisability of scientific theories for reasons other than just their correspondence with reality. The solution is to articulate a correspondence theory of truth which is consistent with not only a revisability thesis of scientific theories but also with the possibility of multiple, competing research programmes. On this point, Barbour proclaims himself a critical realist, stating:

> [m]y own conclusion is that the meaning of truth is correspondence with reality. But because reality is inaccessible to us, the *criteria* of truth must include all four of the criteria mentioned above. The criteria taken together include the valid insights in all these views of truth. (1990, p. 35)

The major problem with this argument is that the conclusion does not follow from the premises. For if truth is correspondence with reality and reality is inaccessible to us, then the correct conclusion to draw is that the truth about reality is inaccessible to us. This leads to scepticism. Barbour would have strengthened his argument here had he elaborated his brief suggestions made later in the same chapter where he states that, '[t]he basic assumption of realism is that *existence* is prior to *theorising*. Constraints on our theorising arise from structures and relationships already existing in nature' (1990, p. 44). Such an elaboration could have led to a more satisfactory explanation of how the critical realist understands correspondence and could perhaps have brought out some similarities between the idea of nature placing constraints on our theorising and Nozick's notion of beliefs 'tracking' reality referred to earlier. Then Barbour's conclusion that all four criteria (agreement with the data, coherence, scope, and fertility) are necessary would be more clearly established.

This highlights the point made earlier about Forrest's solution to the problem of truth and correspondence with reality in his holistic correspondence theory of truth. He suggests 'we should analyse truth in terms of knowledge, which we can then characterise using a reliabilist theory' (1995, p. 43), that is, one that measures the evidence in terms of a reasonable degree of confidence. Thus, for example, the truth of the claim, 'The forest ecosystem is in a degenerative phase', is best analysed by reference to our knowledge of forest ecosystems and not simply by looking at the forest as the naive realist would. So, if our beliefs track reality, and our systems of belief satisfy the criteria of coherence, scope, and fertility, then we can claim with a reasonable degree of confidence that our beliefs are true. It should be pointed out here that beliefs are true as a consequence of the conditions we impose upon knowledge, and not because of any direct or one-to-one correspondence with reality. That is to say, we gauge the truth-claim about the degenerative forest ecosystem by deduction from our extensive knowledge of ecosystems and their regenerative or degenerative phases along with the evidence we see before us.

It needs to be noted that Forrest's holistic correspondence theory of truth is a general theory which is just as applicable in an epistemology of paradigms and models as it is in the logic of belief systems. Forrest's theory thus enables us to make sense of a pluralist notion of truth.

Barbour is not alone in failing to produce an adequate correspondence theory. McFague (1982, 1987), Murphy (1990), and Peacocke (1984, 1990), who also argue for critical realist positions (and like him stress the role of models and bring out many useful links between understanding in science and in religion), similarly fail to put forward an adequate correspondence theory. Without such a theory the distinction between critical realism and anti-realism or instrumentalism is difficult to maintain.

We have now established a critical realist position for scientific knowledge satisfying the four criteria of agreement with data, coherence, scope, and fertility. What also needs to be realised is that models and paradigms are not only subject to these four criteria but that, in examining more closely how models work, we are examining how these four criteria operate and interrelate. We are now free to explore more fully the epistemologically fruitful implications inherent in the notion of models, namely, their scope and fertility.

Barbour (1990, pp. 41–2) points out that models have three very useful and fruitful characteristics: they are analogical; they contribute to extensions of theories; and they are intelligible as units. Firstly, they are analogical in that they permit new and unfamiliar processes to be understood in terms of already understood processes. Thus, for example, the theory of gases can be usefully understood in terms of the mechanics of billiard balls. Secondly, they permit extensions of theories to new phenomena such as the billiard-ball model which suggests how the kinetic theory of gases might be applied to gas diffusion, viscosity, and heat conduction. Finally, a model can be grasped as a whole, giving a vivid summary of complex relationships. While these three features of models are largely responsible for their success and fruitfulness in the scientific enterprise, they also give rise to problems (as they likewise do in the religious realm which is discussed below). For example, scientific theories can conflict. The theory of light is partly based on a particle model which successfully explains some of the properties of light, while other properties are best explained in terms of a wave theory. Clearly the two theories are not compatible, yet together they best explain the properties of light. This is an example of complementary but incompatible models: to drop one or the other impoverishes our understanding of the behaviour of light. This is another example of a situation where the notion of the degrees of belief discussed in Chapter 2 is quite appropriate.

Models permit the exploration and testing of various relationships and implications within them, but do so against a backdrop of concepts and methodologies taken from the particular paradigm in which they are situated. Critical realism, then, by stressing the role of paradigms and models, offers a way of combining elements of both correspondence and coherence theories of truth, and enables us to interpret reality in a creative and fruitful, but at the same time, valid way. This creativity and fruitfulness gives rise to multiple models for interpreting reality but, as has been shown above, these can be adequately tested by the application of the four criteria of critical realism. This provides a way of resolving the pluralist predicament mentioned at the beginning of the chapter.

To this point, we have concentrated mainly on models and paradigms in science. It is now time to look in more detail at the role they play in religion.

CRITICAL REALISM AND RELIGION

As has been indicated, critical realism stresses the fact that while there may be multiple interpretations of the world, it is nevertheless possible to decide between less or more adequate understandings of it. As Janet Soskice points out, we can refer to the world without claiming unrevisable or exhaustive descriptions of it (1985, p. 141). Critical realists do not deny that one can achieve objective knowledge, but do claim that all of our knowledge of the world must pass through the filter of human interpretation of our experience. In both science and religion we are obliged to use models, metaphors, and other forms of analogical thinking to help us make sense of our experience. This is brought out well by Wentzel van Huyssteen when he says:

> The necessity of metaphoric language – owing to a transcendent God who is at the same time invisible – also offers fascinating possibilities of comparisons with other sciences working with invisible entities such as atoms, values, and intelligence, for whom metaphor is therefore also indispensable. (1989, p. 136)

All religions rely heavily on the use of metaphors and models as well as myths, parables, and allegories, to convey their essential message. The different religions can themselves be seen as paradigms representing different historical and cultural communities' interpretations of their religious experience. Models in religion show many of the characteristics of models in science but differ in a number of important ways. Whereas scientific models are primarily based on observations and explanations of the physical world, religious models are more concerned with finding meaning and purpose in our existence. They involve a subjective, personal dimension not present to the same extent in science. This is not to say that religious models lack a cognitive basis, only that they are more heavily overlaid with affective meaning.

Science and religion have usually been seen as alternative approaches to understanding reality but now, increasingly, are perceived as interacting and even complementary approaches. This is seen in the work of many of those involved in the 'new physics', such as Paul Davies (1992, 1995), who find that the more deeply they examine the ultimate nature of the universe, the more it raises for them similar questions to those raised by philosophers of religion and theologians. For example, scientists are now finding new evidence of the presence of design or mind in the way the universe is structured and are raising fascinating questions as to the source of this.

Science and religion, through their reliance on the use of models to explain our experience, are now seen by many to share a stress on knowledge as involving interdependence and interaction between the knower and the known. As a result, we now see the world more in terms of structures and relationships expressed through models, rather than in terms of isolated, objective entities. This was, of course, part of the paradigm shift from Newtonian mechanics to Einstein's theory of relativity and quantum mechanics in which the relation of the observer to the observed is stressed. It is paralleled in religion by a growing conviction among many religious believers that our talk of God can only be in terms of a complex interdependence and interaction between the religious believer and God and that we can never directly know God's nature. It is precisely in this context that the power of models comes to the fore with their ability to illuminate different aspects of our human experience and understanding of the divine. It is through an examination of such multiple perspectives or diversity of interpretations that we are able to move towards a more comprehensive and coherent position of our own. Critical realism thus requires dialogue between religions as van Huyssteen points out: 'A critical theology that has thus learned to see its reflective processes as a creative conceptual construction will never be able to proceed from established confessional contrasts between churches, but should be essentially ecumenical' (1989, p. 145).

Seeing religion in terms of models can also help counteract the apparent irrelevance of traditional theology to many young people today. It can help bring forth new, contemporary, and relevant models of God for the twenty-first century. This is a good example of the fourth criterion of critical realism mentioned earlier, namely fertility.

If we consider, for example, Christianity, the traditional models stressed God's transcendence, his separation from the world, his infinite power, and have used the metaphors of God as father, monarch, and ruler to express this notion in personal terms. However, a number of contemporary theologians, especially feminist writers (for example, McFague, 1982, 1987), have questioned the appropriateness of such models for us today, particularly because of their patriarchal overtones. They fail to convey the richness and complexity of the divine–human relationship and a broader model of parent–child or, alternatively, of God as guide/companion/inspirer has been suggested. This would allow us to imagine God in terms of models such as mother, lover, friend, liberator – all of which raise interesting and fruitful ideas.

These approaches suggest a model of God which stresses human liberation, including the liberation of women as well as men, the oppressed as well as the successful. As McFague says, the divine–human relationship 'as modelled in the parables and in Jesus as parable of God is intrinsically destructive of conventional power arrangements and hence liberating to those who are oppressed, whether by their sex, race, economic situation, or other factors' (1982, p. 165). Hick (1989) also sees religion in terms of human liberation but in his case the stress is more on personal liberation which he describes as moving from a state of self-centredness to Reality-centredness.

It should be stressed that these new images of God are not meant to describe God's nature so much as to suggest different ways of understanding our *relationship* to God and seeing this in a very broad and flexible way. They signal a shift from a model of God as in total control of the world and humans as completely dependent on his will to one where we share with God responsibility for the world. God's power is seen as exercised through love rather than domination. Such a re-emphasis in the Christian tradition is made all the more relevant by the fact that we humans now have, for the first time, the capability to destroy the world (through nuclear power) and, therefore, have to accept at least partial responsibility with God for its future. If we can also replace the old static, deterministic models of nature with more dynamic ones, we are then likely to see humanity and nature as interdependent (rather than humanity seeing itself as having some sort of licence from God to dominate and destroy the natural environment). This will, in turn, have very positive implications for attitudes towards care and concern for our planet earth.

In attempting to decide between alternative models of God we can use similar criteria to those suggested above for evaluating scientific models, namely, agreement with data, consistency (coherence), comprehensiveness (scope), and fertility. Within the religious domain, these criteria can be interpreted to include factors such as profundity, fulfilment of social and psychological needs, ethical value, aesthetic satisfaction, compatibility, and openness to other interpretations of life in the world. In line with the principles of critical realism it is difficult to prove that any one model is necessarily superior, but we can ask if it is better substantiated than the alternatives or if it offers adequate solutions to meaningful problems.

Applying some of the above criteria to the evaluation of religious models, some of the key factors to look for in each case are now described. In regard to agreement with the data (sometimes called 'empirical fit'), the key question is whether the model adequately illuminates and explains our experience. In doing this it may also serve to fulfil various social, psychological, and spiritual needs. With reference to the criteria of consistency and comprehensiveness, it is obviously important that the models used within a paradigm fit together and complement each other, but they should also be open to new perspectives and not narrow the acceptable models down to one limited set. As we have seen, Christianity has tended to stress the patriarchal, hierarchical, monarchical models – God as father, lord, or king, rather than models of God as mother, lover, liberator, and friend. Many would now argue that these new metaphors can complement in a valuable way the traditional models because they reflect more accurately the pattern of relationships which constitute our experience of God and are also consistent with the Christian tradition.

Another question raised by a model's consistency and comprehensiveness is its ability to deal with anomalies, which is also, as we have seen, a key element in Lakatos' successful 'research programmes'. In the case of Christianity a major anomaly that has always caused serious problems is the existence of evil and unmerited suffering in a world supposedly created by a benevolent, omnipotent being. How could such a God allow, for example, the Jewish holocaust to occur, or a young child to be stricken with leukemia? This issue cannot be discussed here but it is one that continues to raise major difficulties for traditional Christian models of God. Another anomaly is that already mentioned, namely the fact that traditional Christian models tend to exclude the experience of women and also images of women.

Finally, the criterion of fertility is an interesting one for models in religion. Metaphorical theology (that is, a theology which stresses the role of models and metaphors in interpreting religious experience) is a great advance here as it does encourage openness to alternative interpretations and it does try to seek models that are compatible with contemporary scientific, political, and spiritual views of the world.

The models we use, therefore, both discover and create reality; they are not arbitrary in that they do refer to the world, but not in the sense of picturing it exactly, rather in the sense of making meaningful a particular network of structures or relationships. These networks are paradigm dependent – whether the model is a valid one or not depends on whether it corresponds with the assumptions or ground rules of a given paradigm. For example, that which is a valid model in Christianity may not be in Buddhism and vice versa.

A number of critical realist writers argue that there exists in the shared historical experience of a particular religious community, certain recurring central metaphors which point to the fact that there is some common reality to which they refer. For instance, in relation to Christianity, van Huyssteen maintains that:

> it is in the history of our theological reflection, too, that the success of certain theories over a long period not only guarantees continuity with the basic biblical metaphors but also provides adequate grounds to believe that certain models or theories do indeed refer to something, and that something of the Reality theologians speak of is constructively and progressively realised in that reference. (1989, p. 196)

Similarly, Peacocke (1990) argues that 'critical theological realism takes as central the past and present religious experience of one's own and others, so that there is also a continuous community and interpretative tradition, in comparison and in contrast with which one's own experience can be both enriched and checked' (1990, p. 15–16). This spells out the notion of a 'home tradition' (discussed in Chapter 2) as the initial frame of reference from which to begin our evaluation of our own and other religions.

We have to date focused particularly on the use of metaphors and models in our discussion of metaphorical theology. Other forms of analogical thinking that have an important place in religion are allegories, parables, and myths. These are more narrative forms each of which has its own distinctive characteristics. Myths in particular play a central role in nearly all religions. They involve stories which try to capture important elements of human experience in terms of key symbols and images. They often provide people with a way of finding meaning and significance in their daily lives by seeing the latter in terms of some broader perspective. All myths contain models: as Barbour says, models 'are the enduring structural components which myths dramatise in narrative form' (1974, p. 27).

We may conclude our discussion of critical realism and the importance of models and other analogical forms of thinking in religion by reiterating that such an approach provides a very helpful response to the epistemological predicament posed by the wide range of competing paradigms in religion. It does this by allowing rational deliberation to proceed in the area of religion while fully responding to the issues raised by pluralism. It steers a mid-course between two extremes: on the one hand, naive realism or positivism, which in the religious sphere is often expressed as literalism or fundamentalism, and, on the other hand, instrumentalism or relativism which denies any possibility of objective knowledge. Moreover, the approach to religion through a focus on models and metaphors, provided it remains aware of what Barbour calls the 'constraints on our theorising [which] arise from structures and relationships already existing in nature' (1990, p. 44), is a very fruitful and intellectually exciting one. Furthermore, because of its openness to new possibilities, it is particularly relevant for the study of religion today. The next step is to explore the implications of such an approach for the teaching of religion in schools and universities focusing particularly on studies of religion programmes.

IMPLICATIONS FOR STUDIES OF RELIGION PROGRAMMES

Studies of religion courses are now offered up to matriculation level in schools in many English-speaking countries as well as in universities. These courses do not aim to bring about commitment to any one particular religion and their focus is *educational* rather than *confessional*. They explore a range of religions and religious issues and use a diversity of methodologies by which to study them. We regard these programmes (which may also be taken to include the multi-faith compulsory religious education courses in the UK) as a major step forward in the teaching of religion at school level and have written earlier in this book about the philosophical and educational issues they raise.

The critical realist position fits in very well with the approach to religious education taken in these courses. As we have noted, it is particularly appropriate for a pluralist, multi-faith society in encouraging openness to a range of religious perspectives represented through different metaphors and models. This has benefits both in terms of acquiring valuable insights from other religions as well as learning to become more tolerant of people with different beliefs to ourselves. Critical realism discourages any notion of there being a final and absolute truth which is the same for all. It would reject fundamentalist and exclusivist approaches to religion. It raises imaginative new ways of conceiving the divine–human relationship, some of which are more appropriate to the contemporary life experience of the students than many of the traditional models.

Because of its tentative and inquiring approach to knowledge, critical realism encourages intellectual virtues such as open-mindedness, flexibility of outlook, and critical awareness, which are crucial elements of genuine education in any sphere as pointed out in our discussion of the liberal education model in Chapter 1. At the same time, it would strongly support the use of a diversity of methodologies for the study of religion as Barbour has argued. He mentions in particular the phenomenological, sociological, psychological, historical, philosophical, and theological approaches (1974, pp. 173–6), all of which are commonly used in studies of religion syllabuses (although as will be indicated in Chapter 7, the philosophical approach is often underemphasised).

However, the critical realist approach, by virtue of its commitment to realism and the correspondence theory of truth, would seek to try eventually to resolve conflicts between different religious models. It would do this at two levels. Firstly, it would critically examine the various models and metaphors within a religious community to see which most adequately reflect the religious experiences or traditions of that community. Secondly, it would examine the models put forward by different religious communities to seek to maximise areas of agreement between these models and thus seek some convergence on how the data of religion in its broadest sense should be interpreted. This is where Barbour's notion of nature placing 'constraints' on our theorising (1990, p. 44) is very apposite: for not every model will be equally valid – there should be a cumulative process of seeking to arrive at ever more adequate understandings of the pre-existent structures and relationships that give rise to religious experience.

None the less, we are unlikely ever to reach total consensus on the proper understanding of religious experience. This is because of radically different starting points or underlying assumptions on how the data should be interpreted. For example, is the ultimate reality personal or impersonal? Is there one God or many? Did the universe have a beginning or is it eternal? The different answers given here will have significant implications for which models are deemed acceptable, but as John Hick (1989, p. 369) has argued, it is not possible to decide definitively which of these starting points is superior to the others. Therefore, the critical realist must work within these parameters and aim to maximise agreement where possible, but where it is not, to at least be clear where we differ, and why and how our different models reflect such a difference. This point is captured in our notion of sophisticated relativism in Chapter 2. Hick argues that such disagreements do not imply that one religion is right and the others wrong, but that:

> each of the great traditions constitutes a context and, so far as human judgement can at present discern, a more or less equally effective context, for the transformation of human existence from self-centredness to Reality-centredness. (1989, p. 369)

For Hick, the various religious traditions are just different 'religio-cultural "lenses" through which the Real is humanly perceived' (1989, p. 369). While this is not a conclusion that all critical realists would necessarily accept, it is one that is quite consistent with critical realist thinking, as it highlights a common core reality that all religious models seek to realise. Hick himself advocates critical realism as a desirable mid-point between naive realism and instrumentalism. As he says, 'Critical differed from naive realism mainly in taking account of the conceptual and interpretive element within sense perception' (1989, p. 174). On the other hand, he acknowledges:

> critical realism holds that the realm of religious experience and belief is not *in toto* human projection and illusion but constitutes a

range of cognitive responses, varying from culture to culture, to the presence of a transcendental reality or realities. (1989, p. 175)

The critical realist approach to religion has another educational advantage in that it brings out how the essential ideas and concepts of any religion have both cognitive and affective meaning and thus provides a link with the holistic approach discussed in Chapter 1. It avoids stressing the one type of meaning at the expense of the other and, in presenting models of different ways of conceiving our relationship to God, it captures what is at the heart of all religions with a vividness and immediacy that is lacking in purely conceptual approaches. In deciding which model is most meaningful for them, students also have a clear set of criteria to judge by, as outlined above. They may, for instance, find one model more fruitful or illuminating than others, or more comprehensive, or more compatible with other models to which they are committed.

One helpful way of bringing out the relevance of critical realism for religion would be to include a unit dealing with the place of models in religion in a religious studies programme. This could serve to show their central role in all religions, as well as highlighting the place of other analogical forms such as metaphors, symbols, images, allegories, parables, and myths. It could examine central models arising in the various religions, look at alternative ones that have been suggested, compare and contrast models across the different religions, and so forth. It could use the criteria suggested in this chapter to critically evaluate the various models and thus serve to contribute to the students' quest for a rationally informed and personally satisfying position of their own. Ideally, a course in science would also bring out the central role that models play in that subject.

Many studies of religion syllabuses raise issues to do with religion and social justice. Here the Christian models of God as friend and liberator, reflected both in our contemporary religious experience and dialogue as well as in the Christian tradition, are particularly apposite and there is a whole series of models, parables, and allegories where Jesus is portrayed as on the side of the outcast and the oppressed that could be explored. Here, also, the affective components of such models which involve emotions of care and compassion for those who are suffering are an especially relevant part of such a study. It should be noted that although the religious examples cited in this chapter all come from Christianity, similar points could be made about alternative models in various contexts in other religions, and these are, of course, equally relevant in studies of religion programmes which are multi-faith in orientation.

We may conclude this chapter by reiterating that the pluralist predicament in studies of religion need not be seen as unresolvable. In fact, by drawing on the rich epistemological potential of the critical realist position and its associated stress on models and paradigms, there is both a solution available to this predicament and the basis for a very fruitful way of approaching the study of religion in our contemporary, pluralist society.

This concludes Part II of this book which presents the two major responses to pluralism in the teaching of religious education and we turn in Part III to a new range of problems of both a topical and contentious nature relating to the ethical, political, and social dimensions of religious education.

REFERENCES

Banner, M.C. (1990). *The Justification of Science and the Rationality of Religious Belief*, Oxford, Clarendon Press.

Barbour, I.G. (1974). *Myths, Models and Paradigms*, London, SCM Press.

Barbour, I.G. (1990). *Religion in an Age of Science*, London, SCM Press.

Davies, P. (1992). *The Mind of God*, London, Simon & Schuster.

Davies, P. (1995). *The Cosmic Blueprint*, London, Penguin Books.

Forrest, B. (1995). 'Maya and the Pluralist Predicament', *Australasian Journal of Philosophy*, 73, 1, 31–48.

Hick, J. (1989). *An Interpretation of Religion*, London, Macmillan.

Kuhn, T. (1970). *The Structure of Scientific Revolutions*, 2nd edn, Chicago, Chicago University Press.

Lakatos, I. and Musgrave, A. (1970). *Criticism and the Growth of Knowledge*, Cambridge, Cambridge University Press.

McFague, S. (1982). *Metaphorical Theology*, Philadelphia, PA, Fortress Press.

McFague, S. (1987). *Models of God*, London, SCM Press.

Murphy, N. (1990). *Theology in the Age of Scientific Reasoning*, Ithaca, NY, Cornell University Press.

Nozick, R. (1981). *Philosophical Explanation*, Cambridge, MA, Harvard University Press.

Peacocke, A. (1984). *Intimations of Reality*, Notre Dame, IN, University of Notre Dame Press.

Peacocke, A. (1990). *Theology for a Scientific Age*, Oxford, Blackwell.

Soskice, J. (1985). *Metaphor and Religious Language*, Oxford, Clarendon Press.

van Huyssteen, W. (1989). *Theology and the Justification of Faith*, Grand Rapids, MI, W.B. Eerdmans.

PART III

Ethical, Political, and Social Dimensions of Religious Education

5

The Ethics of Belief Debate and its Implications for Religious Education in a Liberal Democratic Society

The teaching of the studies of religion is complicated by the fact that religious statements involve a broad range of logical types including cosmological, ontological, theological, moral, historical, and sociological propositions. Accordingly, studies of religion syllabuses tend to focus on those types of statements thought to be most meaningful for students. This leads to the widespread use of methodologies such as the phenomenological, historical, and sociological. This chapter will argue that independently of the particular logical types into which religious statements fall, there are ethical principles deriving from membership of epistemic and democratic communities which dictate that an axiological approach should be part of the study of the subject. An epistemic community is one committed to the principles of rational inquiry (or critical rationality, as is the term used in Chapter 1). An axiological approach is one concerned with the teaching of values which, within the context of this chapter, are those values concerned with an ethics of belief.

The ethics of belief debate is made up of two separate but logically connected levels of concern. The first involves our moral responsibility in how we acquire the beliefs we hold and the extent to which certain ways of acquiring beliefs may diminish our personal autonomy; the second stems from the fact that beliefs guide actions and false or insufficiently understood or justified beliefs may give rise to actions which cause harm or injury to others in the community. A simple way of distinguishing the two levels is to say that the first is concerned with our epistemic duties in acquiring beliefs, while the second is concerned with the moral consequences of holding those beliefs.

Principles and values from an ethics of belief complement democratic values to provide ethical and epistemological norms which should inform the teaching of religion and act as a guide to how religious differences should be handled in the curriculum. However, we believe that such an approach is deserving of more prominence than it presently has in studies of religion syllabuses in the UK, the USA, and Australia.

THE ETHICS OF BELIEF DEBATE AND THE EPISTEMIC COMMUNITY

The concerns of an ethics of belief are not new, their origins can be traced back to Plato's doctrine that knowledge is goodness which maintains that a person cannot knowingly choose evil; they are also evident in Aristotle's notion of the intellectual virtues which would include such things as honesty, respect for evidence, clarity, non-arbitrariness, impartiality, and consistency. However, it was not until the nineteenth century that William Clifford coined the actual phrase 'ethics of belief' and in a seminal article of that title set forth his central dictum: 'it is wrong always, everywhere, and for any one, to believe anything upon insufficient evidence' (1986, p. 24). In justifying this principle he provides the example of a shipowner of an emigrant-ship which is about to put to sea who fails to resolve his doubts about the seaworthiness of the vessel and simply convinces himself all is well. When the ship sinks with all hands on board he has no moral compunction about collecting the insurance. Clifford's example has given rise to a wealth of discussion. Two recent works, one by McCarthy (1986) which examines nineteenth- and twentieth-century reactions to Clifford, and the other by Pojman (1986) which explores the implications of this debate for religious belief, help inform the critique adopted in this chapter.

Pojman examines arguments both for and against Clifford's dictum. On the positive side he quotes Richard Gale's deontological argument (Pojman, 1986, pp. 106–7) that it is morally wrong to believe against sufficient evidence, as doing so gives rise to false beliefs which impair a person's free will and autonomy. Maintaining a person's free will and autonomy is held to be a moral absolute and so believing against sufficient evidence is wrong. Some may reject Gale's Kantian absolutism that it is always wrong to reduce a person's freedom of choice. There may well be some justified cases for doing so as, for example, with children whose reduced capacity for moral judgement may necessitate reducing their scope for choosing certain actions. While criticism of such an absolutist claim seems well-founded, this in no way diminishes the importance of our overall moral duty not to impair our personal autonomy. Such a principle is generally accepted in liberal democratic societies as a primary moral obligation.

A second argument in favour of Clifford's principle is put by J.T. Stevenson, who argues for the utilitarian principle that a community's survival and welfare depends upon a stock of highly justified beliefs (cited in Pojman, 1986, pp. 108–9). Because of this, one has a 'doxastic responsibility' (p. 107) to the community to hold only highly justified beliefs. While this argument has strong intuitive appeal it suffers from the problem as to what constitutes the set of criteria for well-justified beliefs. In addition, it seems to run counter to the fundamental right to freedom of thought, for it begs the question of who decides what is well justified and what one may or may not believe, especially in political and religious thought. While these criticisms provide important restrictions on Stevenson's principle of doxastic responsibility, nevertheless we believe Stevenson correctly identifies a duty we have in the community by virtue of the fact that our beliefs guide our actions. If these beliefs are false or spurious then the actions derivative from them will have significant adverse effects at the community level.

The major objection that has been made to Clifford's principle and his ethics of belief questions the voluntariness of beliefs. This objection derives from the principle that 'ought implies can' and so we can only be held responsible for beliefs if their adoption is in some way voluntary or constitutes an intentional act. Central to this objection is the contention that beliefs are not simple voluntary acts. Bernard Williams, for example, argues that we cannot simply will beliefs to be true (cited in Pojman, 1986, p. 110). Williams takes the case of a father who refuses to believe his son is dead. To support this belief the father must systematically alter other beliefs which strongly imply his son's death as, for instance, the son's vacant room, giving rise to an unstable belief system ultimately leading to the destruction of the world of reality. Williams' objection seems plausible and has given rise to a position known as 'indirect voluntarism' which holds that, although we cannot directly will our beliefs as true, we can control to some extent the manner in which we arrive at our beliefs. In other words, we do have the ability to weigh up evidence and can be held accountable if we do not carry out adequate enquiry before passing judgement, or are not sufficiently concerned to determine rationally the issue one way or the other. Indirect voluntarism, in our view, correctly reflects the fact that we do hold people responsible for their biases or prejudices arising simply from ignorance. Similarly, we condemn the political or religious fanatic's narrowness in not considering all the available evidence or for not considering alternative viewpoints.

Transferring this debate to the educational context, Dearden (1984) and Degenhardt (1986) adopt an indirect volitionalist position and strongly support an ethics of belief. Dearden speaks of the 'normative requirements' (1984, p. 108) of specific subject areas and the need for close attention to the standards of evidence within a discipline. Such an approach is necessary for developing personal autonomy and its correlative of independent thought. Dearden also refers to Aristotle's intellectual virtues (mentioned above) and their crucial role in the overall development of character which requires both intellectual and moral virtues (1984, pp. 108–9). Degenhardt adopts a similar position and argues that it offends against an ethics of belief to 'formulate beliefs by passively acquiescing to authority and social pressures' (1986, p. 110).

However, others such as Harvey (1986, p. 193) reject indirect voluntarism as still too strong. Harvey contends that philosophers as diverse as Quine, Polanyi, and Wittgenstein have argued that it is impossible to justify all of our beliefs as a large part of our thinking has to be based on a network of acritical beliefs which form a 'picture of the world, that is, a loosely connected network of propositions in which the consequences and premises are mutually supporting'. We acquire many of our beliefs not by 'testing or investigation but simply by belonging to a community bound together by science and education' (1986, p. 193). This would seem to shift the responsibility for the testing of beliefs onto the specialists in the various domains of knowledge and in the educational context onto the teachers as a necessary part of their role. This ties in with Harvey's second point that the ship-owner is not guilty because of his unsubstantiated beliefs in general but because of his specific failure to fulfil his role as a ship-owner with a direct responsibility to know about and guarantee the vessel's seaworthiness. Rather than simply 'believe' it is seaworthy, he has a duty to take steps to 'know' that it is so. Thus, Harvey asserts that if we claim to 'know' something this implies we can produce the proof or evidence, and that this is not the case with mere belief.

In the case of teachers, there is a special duty to produce the evidence for what they teach and to aim to instil this respect for truth in their students. This would then serve to counteract G.M. Young's scathing indictment that:

> our schools have for years been discharging into the world young people without the slightest capacity for, or the remotest interest in what, for brevity, one might call scientific thinking. And the proof is this, that whether they believe or disbelieve, the grounds of their faith or scepticism are purely emotional, traditional, or it might seem accidental. What the schools have failed to teach is that a man has no more right to an opinion for which he cannot account than to a pint of beer for which he cannot pay. (cited in Harvey, 1986, p. 199)

However, speaking more generally, we would argue against Harvey that, regardless of our role, whenever our beliefs may have an impact on other people we have a duty to seek to base such beliefs on sound evidence. This arises even more strongly when our beliefs (for example our views on birth control or euthanasia) may directly affect others' freedom to act in a certain way. Thus, what emerges from the discussion of epistemic responsibility up to this point is that we all have a duty to attend to the evidence where this can reasonably be expected and to obtain beliefs having some guarantee of truth.

Another way to put this debate into an educational context is through D'Agostino's (1989) concept of an 'epistemic community'. Such a hypothetical community is one which acknowledges not only the fact of disagreement between competing viewpoints but also the need for a method of adjudicating between them, in much the same way as the legal system has institutionalised procedures for resolving disagreements between litigants. Taking epistemological disagreement as his starting point, D'Agostino seeks to determine the set of conditions or principles which must be present in the community if the process of resolving differences is to succeed. At the very outset, D'Agostino considers four underlying principles as necessary if the adjudicative process is to be possible at all. These are commitments to: (i) realism, (ii) fallibilism, (iii) rationalism, and (iv) respect for others. D'Agostino believes that unless there is this minimal commitment, it is not possible to reason with others at all. He contends that these principles have a 'transcendental' justification, since 'rational argument presupposes a commitment to these principles' (1989, p. 244). These four principles constitute what D'Agostino refers to as the epistemic ethos (1989, p. 241), which he describes as a commitment 'to try to discover and to test and comparatively to weigh the p-relevant reasons of the other' (1989, p. 235) in situations where disputants disagree about the truth of some proposition p.

D'Agostino argues that adhering to realism entails that one cannot at the same time both affirm and deny a proposition p, unless of course one is an epistemological relativist in which case the issue of disagreement over the truth of p would not arise (but of course the general problems arising from a relativist position discussed in Chapter 1 then occur). It should be noted that the sense of realism discussed by D'Agostino is equivalent simply to a rejection of relativism and does not convey the broader connotations of 'critical realism' as discussed in the previous chapter.

Hand in hand with realism goes a commitment to fallibilism. This emerges from the fact that disagreement about the truth of a proposition implies the possibility that one of the beliefs about p is false. Entertaining the possibility that one's beliefs are false, or that your opponent's are true,

D'Agostino refers to as fallibilism. The alternative to this position is dogmatism which holds that one's own beliefs are not open to criticism and that 'any refusal to acknowledge [their] truth is tantamount to an admission of imbecility or of "bad faith"' (1989, p. 232). An important proviso here is that neither disputant is an authority on the matter at hand, but that both are seeking to decide about it responsibly and rationally. (However, even in an educational context where the teacher is an authority, dogmatism and indoctrination – its conceptual correlative – are ethically untenable.) We have argued in Chapter 3 that programmes in religious education should encourage students to hold their religious beliefs in a fallibilist way.

If fallibilism implies the possibility of error about p, then it also implies a commitment to the third principle, that of rationalism. This provides a means of deciding the truth or falsity of p by determining the best reasons for or against p. It might be noted that while the fact of disagreement implies the need for some adjudicative process, given the assumption of the disputants' desire to resolve the disagreement, it does not necessarily entail rationalism – for one could just as well toss a coin to decide the issue. Rationalism emerges only where there is a commitment to deciding the truth of a proposition on the basis of the best available reasons.

Finally, the epistemic ethos involves a commitment to respect. This requires our assuming, whether rightly or wrongly, that those who disagree with us have good reasons for doing so and that we therefore need to consider seriously their point of view.

If we accept these four commitments of realism, fallibilism, rationalism, and respect as constituting the epistemic ethos then three important rules of adjudication can be derived. D'Agostino refers to these as the rules of non-interference, responsibility, and publicity.

The rule of non-interference stems from the fact that disputing parties have good reason, if they are rational, not to interfere with the presentation of the other's reasons for affirming or denying p. Simply put, the affirmation of one's own beliefs should involve listening to and evaluating the other's reasons. Another way of stating this is as a rule of tolerance. The second rule, that of responsibility, requires not only that disputants not interfere with each other's presentation of reasons for affirming or denying p, but, more positively, that each disputant responds with counter-reasons against the reasons put by the other for or against p. It is not sufficient simply to reject the other's reasons out of hand or not give them adequate consideration, there is a duty to say why those reasons are inadequate or wrong. This latter aspect of assessing the reasons and counteracting them where possible, or affirming them as the case may be, requires that the supporting reasons be publicly accessible and can be independently confirmed by each of the parties. This is stated as the third rule, that of publicity.

In the commitments and rules enunciated by D'Agostino we substantially recognise J.S. Mill's principles, mentioned in Chapter 3, which are encapsulated in the concept of epistemic liberalism.

In summary, we need to suggest the two major aspects of the ethics of belief debate which lead to a definition of an axiological approach and its relevance for teaching (particularly of studies of religion). In the first place, we need to reiterate the general concerns of the broader ethics of belief debate centred on Clifford's dictum. Within this broader ethics of belief debate two concerns emerge. Firstly, that we have a responsibility to ensure that the beliefs we acquire do not in any way impair our personal autonomy or transcendence. The second major concern is our responsibility to the community to ensure the beliefs we hold have a high measure of validity and justification. J.L. Stevenson (cited in Pojman, 1986, pp. 108–9) suggested the reason for this was the survival and continuity of the community itself. While this may seem slightly hyperbolic, nevertheless there is an important truth contained in it. That is this: the beliefs we hold guide our actions, both at a personal and communal level. What we believe on important issues within the community is going to determine how we decide, and so, in a very real way, will have a significant impact on the type of community which results. Where people make decisions based on ignorance or bias, or where an attitude of seriously weighing up the evidence both for and against an issue has not been instilled in citizens, then important public decisions will be put in jeopardy. As Harvey (1986, p. 189) notes in reporting Clifford: 'Credulity, the readiness to hold unjustified beliefs threatens the very foundations of society. Every belief, no matter how trivial, is significant because it prepares the mind to receive more like it.'

The second aspect of an axiological approach is that which gives effect to the rules and principles of an epistemic community. This requires a commitment to the principles of realism, rationalism, fallibilism, and respect for the other's reasons, and to the rules of non-interference, responsibility, and publicity. The notion of an epistemic community clearly has close links to the approach of epistemic liberalism discussed in Chapter 3 and provides a useful model of how the principles of epistemic liberalism can be put into practice in an educational context.

If both of the above approaches are included in teaching subjects such as studies of religion within the secondary school then many of the concerns of an ethics of belief will have been met. We may finally reiterate that an axiological approach puts a special responsibility on teachers to be able to provide the evidence for the statements they make and to nurture in their students a particular care for the intellectual virtues.

IMPLICATIONS OF AN ETHICS OF BELIEF FOR THE UNDERSTANDING OF RELIGIOUS BELIEFS

In this section we seek to examine the implications for the holding of religious beliefs deriving from an ethics of belief. There are four specific implications which need to be addressed. The first concerns the nature of the evidence for religious beliefs; the second concerns the exclusivist claims of religious beliefs and associated connections with an infallibilist position; the third involves the nature of religious beliefs as requiring a 'leap of faith' or as cultivating the 'will to believe'; finally, there is the question of how we should hold religious beliefs given the fact that the evidential requirement of an ethics of belief cannot be fully satisfied within the religious domain. Let us now look at each of these in more detail.

One of the most obvious problems with religious beliefs is the problem of what constitutes the evidence or proof for their truth. As Harvey notes:

> The morality of believing arises most obviously and acutely ... in situations dealing with matters of evidential belief ... [but is] an entirely different matter when dealing with beliefs that are not evidential or where there is no accepted repertoire of procedures for their assessment and adjudication. (1986, p. 203)

Harvey notes this difficulty with the evidence for religious beliefs but does not attempt to deal with the problem. He holds there is a serious moral conflict when the 'ethos of a role-specific mode of enquiry is violated' (1986, p. 203). What he seems to have in mind here is where there is a conflict between the rigorous evidential standards of, say, historical enquiry and religious claims such as the Israelites crossing the Red Sea dry-shod. In such a situation, Harvey would give priority to the historical mode of enquiry and would see it as a matter of ethical consequence not to do so (1986, p. 202). But this leaves the question of the strength of the evidence for religious beliefs untouched. There is, however, a moral responsibility on those teaching religious studies to both acknowledge and address the problem. In other words, we should draw students' attention to the difference in evidential support for religious beliefs as against, say, historical beliefs. Another difficulty which emerges here is in regard to the epistemic community's rule of publicity. This rule forbids members putting forward reasons for their beliefs which cannot be independently assessed by each of the parties. Therefore, religious adherents will need to give careful consideration to this requirement when making religious assertions.

The second major implication of an ethics of belief concerns the difficulty about the exclusivist claims of religious beliefs and the implications of an infallibilist position that this leads to. This stems from the fact that most religions claim to possess an exclusive path to knowing God or to represent the whole truth in religious matters. Logically, the exclusivist is committed to asserting that if proposition p is true then not-p is false and if one is an adherent to the truth of p then one is logically committed to holding that those not believing p are wrong. This errs against the epistemic community's commitment to fallibilism which requires my entertaining the possibility that my belief in p is false. We have dealt with this problem in Chapter 2 and believe the answer lies in rejecting a straightforward true/false logic in favour of a logic of degrees of belief with its commitment to the provisional nature of religious propositions. In a situation such as this, one's own beliefs are always open to revision in the light of further evidence, and where there is open conflict between my own beliefs and those of others then I am required to lower the degree of belief with which I entertain relevant propositions.

The third implication of an ethics of belief concerns the nature of religious beliefs as requiring a 'leap of faith' or as cultivating the 'will to believe'. Quite clearly notions such as these are open to all the major objections raised against voluntarism with its notion of willing beliefs to be true. We hold with Bernard Williams that once one starts willing propositions to be true against validation and justificatory reason, then one's grasp on the world of reality becomes seriously diminished. What is implied here is that unless religious educators can clearly establish the rational foundations for believing, then merely suggesting one should have faith or make the effort to believe seriously offends against an ethics of belief.

The final question is how we should hold religious beliefs, given the fact that the evidential requirements of an ethics of belief cannot be fully met. Harvey notes this problem but fails to address it. Pojman says of this problem:

> For many religious people there is a problem of doubting various credal statements contained in their religions. Often propositional beliefs are looked upon as a necessary, though not sufficient,

condition for salvation. This causes great anxiety in doubters and raises the question of the importance of belief in religion and in life in general. It is a question that has been neglected in philosophy of religion and Christian theology. (1986, p. 212)

However, while acknowledging the problem, Pojman endeavours to deal with credal statements not as truth-functional propositions but as statements of hope or optative statements (1986, pp. 217–30). He endeavours by this means to circumvent the problem. Our own view is that such a logic of hope statements is untenable. We contend that credal statements do seek to make an epistemic claim which, as such, must be adjudicated. Our own view is that a logic of degrees of belief, coupled with a sophisticated relativism, allows for the degree of belief in a religious statement to be reduced where there is genuine conflict. In cases where the logical complexity of the issue does not admit an easy adjudication, this permits the religious believer to give a higher degree of belief to his or her home religion as the primary religious paradigm, while holding the belief open for possible revision at a later date.

Furthermore, Pojman points out that if we have ethical duties to seek the best justified beliefs then we cannot be held unrighteous for not believing propositions not satisfying those standards of belief. He further contends:

> that a moral God would not judge us according to which beliefs we did or did not hold but according to how well we responded to criticism of our beliefs, including our religious beliefs, how faithful we have been to the truth as we have seen it. On this basis it might well be the case that in heaven (or purgatory) Calvin, Barth, Billy Graham and Jerry Falwell may have to be rehabilitated by taking catechism lessons in the ethics of belief from such archangels as David Hume and Bertrand Russell. (1986, p. 230)

THE SCHOOL AS PART OF A DEMOCRATIC COMMUNITY AND THE ROLE OF THE TEACHER

We have seen how the role of the school as an epistemic community gives rise to certain principles that have both an epistemological and moral dimension. If all parties respect such principles then the chances of resolving differences of opinion by discussion rather than conflict will be greatly enhanced. However, there will always be cases where such disagreement cannot be so easily resolved. The first and most prominent is where one or more of the parties refuse to fully accept and act on such principles. Secondly, even where there is general acceptance of the principles, there may still be different views about how we should act because of deep seated differences in substantive religious, moral, or political beliefs. An example of the first case would be a fundamentalist religious believer who is not prepared to accept the epistemic condition of fallibility and maintains that only one religious view is correct and that non-believers should be discriminated against. An example of the second case would be where two people who share the principles involved in an epistemic community have differing views about the sacredness of life (based on differing religious beliefs) and thus come to take opposing positions on questions such as abortion or euthanasia.

To respond to such situations we need to consider the social and political framework in which such differences occur and, in the context of the present book, this is that of the liberal democratic community. It is our contention that the democratic model provides a basis for resolving conflicts arising from such differing value positions, in that broader democratic values may justifiably take precedence over sectional religious values. Democracy may be seen as the social manifestation of the epistemic principles of reason, justification, fallibility, and respect. It is the form of government in which such principles can be most fully realised because by its very nature it is committed to resolving differences between people by discussion rather than by coercion.

Richard Peters (1981, pp. 37–41) distinguishes three groups of values implicit in the democratic way of life: (i) values such as concern for others, impartiality and respect for persons, that underpin procedural consensus; (ii) values associated with the pursuit of truth and the attempt to decide matters by reason (for example, consistency, precision, respect for evidence); and (iii) values associated with the pursuit of a personal good which would involve notions such as personal fulfilment and transcendence. It will be noted that these are all primarily procedural values rather than stating any particular substantive view of the good life and this is their particular strength and usefulness in providing a way of resolving disputes such as the ones mentioned at the beginning of this section. Thus, both religious believers and non-believers have every right to their own beliefs, but no right to discriminate against those who do not share them. Similarly, those with different views on issues such as abortion and euthanasia have the right to follow their own beliefs (within the confines of any relevant laws in their society) and to argue for their acceptance by others, but not to impose their views on them. Furthermore, where religious beliefs of an extreme kind lead to policies such as the refusal to allow blood transfusions or are used to justify practices such as female genital mutilation, which conflict with widely shared moral values within a democracy such as the protection of children's rights, then the broader democratic values should be given precedence. Thus, the laws regulating behaviour in a democratic society should themselves ultimately reflect a democratic consensus or at least the majority view in a particular society.

Of course, such a democratic consensus does not necessarily make the view morally right, but it does at least ensure that, where there is a conflict of values and a decision has to be made one way or the other, the wishes of most people will be taken into account. It could also be argued that the majority view in a democracy is likely to have some rational basis as it should (if it is a genuine democracy) be based on a wide-ranging and open discussion. Thirdly, although democratic values are primarily procedural ones, there may be some core values (for example respect for others, justice, tolerance) that have both procedural and substantive implications which would give significant moral credibility to democratically based decision making.

The values of democracy also provide a clear set of principles upon which to base the role of the school. In fact, we would argue that it is only in a democracy that education in its fullest sense can flourish. Without the openness to competing world views that characterises democracy, education very easily collapses into indoctrination. The promotion of moral and intellectual autonomy is the distinctive function of education democratically conceived and this means that teachers as agents of such a society have certain role specific obligations. One of these is to develop the values of critical enquiry, justification, tolerance of opposing viewpoints, search for truth, and similar goals, in their pupils and to resist any desire to impose their own specific religious or other personal commitments. It is here that the notion of an ethics of belief again has relevance. Because, as we have seen, beliefs guide actions and because teachers are in positions of authority over young children, they have a particular duty to make children aware of the ethical requirements of basing their beliefs on good reasons and noting how their behaviour towards others will reflect their own belief patterns.

Another way of making these points is to use Charles Bailey's (1984, p. 155) notion of 'caring for reason' as a central aim of education. As he argues, this is a necessary condition of acting morally, particularly in relation to its highlighting of the necessity to justify one's behaviour towards others. The notion of justification is central to both epistemology and morality; one can be neither reasonable nor ethical without it (that is, without being concerned to justify our beliefs or behaviour). Our treatment of other people must also take account of the fact pointed out by Bailey (see Chapter 1) that persons are by nature reasoners and justifiers. So not only should we aim to avoid causing them pain, we should also treat them as autonomous agents who are deserving of an explanation of why we treat them as we do. (This is another way of expressing D'Agostino's rule of responsibility.) Liberal education is the institutionalised expression of this notion.

Because caring for reason and justification involves affective as well as cognitive concerns, it will not be possible for teachers to engender them merely by pointing out their importance. Teachers must exemplify them clearly in their own behaviour. As Bailey says, they should 'provide an atmosphere in which concern for reason is patently at work and can be absorbed by those operating within it'. If children can thus be brought to really care about reason then the basic ideals of the school as an epistemic community and as a central part of a democratic community are likely to be realised. This will also manifestly assist the work of the teacher of studies of religion and make such programmes much more likely to achieve their aims.

IMPLICATIONS OF THE ETHICS OF BELIEF FOR THE TEACHING OF RELIGION IN A DEMOCRATIC COMMUNITY

Let us now examine the implications of the ethics of belief for the actual teaching of religion in school. We will focus on implications for studies of religion or multi-faith religious education courses rather than for education in faith programmes (that is, instruction in a specific religious set of beliefs). It is the former where most of the interesting new curriculum developments in schools are presently being made and, more significantly, it is these programmes which have the greatest potential to achieve the goals of an ethics of belief as outlined above. This is because their primary rationale is an educational rather than a faith-development one and so they are well placed to develop the broader epistemological and moral understandings implied by an ethics of belief. This is not to say that an ethics of belief is not also relevant to religious education of the more traditional type and that schools which aim to foster commitment to a particular faith should not also aim to respect the values of an epistemic community. Moreover, as such schools exist within the framework of the democratic community and are preparing future citizens of the State, the values they promote should not be openly inimical to broader democratic principles as was suggested earlier.

In terms of the present chapter, one aspect of most existing studies of religion courses in western countries which we would like to see strengthened is the axiological dimension of the study of religion, in particular encouraging students to appreciate the moral significance of grounding their religious beliefs on rational foundations rather than merely on authority, custom, prejudice, superstition, and so forth. Such a goal is implicit in many existing syllabuses but is not generally given the centrality we think it deserves. The dangers of dogmatism, intolerance, and credulity in relation to religious belief need to be more strongly emphasised and this may, on occasion, require the treatment of potentially contentious issues. At present most syllabuses generally tend to avoid anything that may be controversial or could be seen as critical of a particular religion or group of religious believers. However, children are likely to be already making their own judgements on some of these questions as a result of their experience of living in a multicultural and multi-faith society and would benefit from some help from the school in making their judgements as rational and informed as possible.

Children are also daily reminded through the media of the devastating effects of religious and ethnic conflict in countries such as the former Yugoslavia, Northern Ireland, Israel, and Rwanda. They see the results of fundamentalist versions of religion in countries like Iran and Saudi Arabia, including examples of religious intolerance, as in the death sentence placed on Salman Rushdie, and discrimination, as in the treatment of women. They observe how the activities of religious cults can bring about massive disasters as occurred with the Branch Davidians in 1993 in Waco, Texas, or the Heaven's Gate followers in 1997 in San Francisco. They are also constantly reminded of the close linkages between religious beliefs and attitudes to a range of moral issues such as the status of women, rights of children, tolerance of minority groups, sexual practices, issues of life and death (for example birth control, abortion, euthanasia, suicide). In fact, for many children these political and ethical dimensions of religion could be the dominant experience they have of the effects of religious belief on human behaviour. Apart, therefore, from the general moral duties to base one's beliefs on sound evidence and to be aware of the linkages between our beliefs and our actions that flow from an ethics of belief, there are pressing practical reasons why any course in the study of religion should provide some guidance for children in dealing with ethical issues such as the above as they arise in religion.

A typical statement found in a studies of religion syllabus is the following one from the NSW, Australia syllabus where it is stated that:

> Any religious tradition must be treated on its own terms, and the focus is not on comparison of religious traditions but on the understanding of the aspect being examined and its expression and place in religious traditions. (NSW Board of Studies, 1991, p. 47)

Such a phenomenological approach, common to many syllabuses, implies an inappropriate degree of neutrality and insufficient level of critical scrutiny at least for students at the senior secondary level. As Brian Hill says, 'All religions are not equal ... They are not equal in the power of their intellectualisations of the world, nor their moral standards, nor their ability to take root in cultures different from their origin' (1991, p. 68). This inequality needs to be recognised and confronted.

There are also a number of issues which deserve greater prominence than they are presently given. These involve cases where there may be a conflict between one group's moral and religious beliefs and those of other groups or of society in general. One such issue is that arising from the worldwide growth of fundamentalist versions of religion in most western countries. Fundamentalism, which generally involves strict adherence to certain dogmatic beliefs (as taken to be revealed unambiguously in relevant sacred texts) without impartial weighing up of the evidence for and against, almost by definition is a negation of the principles involved in an ethics of belief. A fundamentalist group could not be considered to be an epistemic community as we have defined it and provides a clear instance where the holding of beliefs in a certain way has definite ethical implications. If the search for truth is restricted to a very narrow range of possibilities, then alternative explanations are never really given proper consideration. This can readily result in a very one-sided view of the issues which can then easily lead to morally indefensible practices such as religious intolerance, indoctrination, and the placing of adherence to dogma over individual human rights.

The ethical implications of fundamentalism are rarely mentioned in any of the studies of religion syllabuses we have examined but given its prevalence today they should be, and children should be prepared to adequately understand its specific limitations. Similarly, highly questionable beliefs that often grow out of fundamentalism, such as creation science, should be discussed and the strong scientific evidence on the other side pointed out to children who will then be in a position to make an informed judgement on such questions.

That there is reason for concern here is evidenced by a consideration of the sort of curriculum material often taught in fundamentalist Christian schools. One of the standard curriculum packages used in a number of countries is the ACE (Accelerated Christian Education) programme originating in the USA. Some examples from this programme follow. In the *Science* text, when discussing chemical elements, it is stated that:

> nitrogen comprises about 78% of the atmosphere. This ratio of oxygen to nitrogen is no accident, even though evolutionists believe that it is. God used nitrogen to dilute the oxygen in the atmosphere because nitrogen is a very stable element that does not react easily with oxygen. (ACE *Science* [1114], 1992, p. 10)

In the *English* [1120] workbook there is a cartoon (1989, p. 17) of a ship called 'Public Education' sinking and next to it a ship called 'Christian Education' picking up survivors with the Captain saying, 'We'll rescue all we can'. In the *English* [1107] workbook all of the examples used to teach grammar and sentence construction are statements reflecting religious assertions, for example, 'I will give Christ control of my life', 'He made me a certain gender for a purpose' (1987, pp. 3–4).

In the text *Collectivism* [138], the theme of Fascism and its philosophical antecedents is explored. This text includes a wide range of material, some of it quite philosophically abstruse, for example the philosophical ideas of Schopenhauer and Nietzsche, which are sometimes distorted and oversimplified. The *bête noire* of fundamentalists, Charles Darwin and his theories, is described as follows:

> On November 24, 1859, a balding, middle-aged, self-styled naturalist and former divinity student published a 400 page dull, pedantic, and down-right boring tome ... The overall evolutionary hypothesis may be considered to be an integral part of pantheistic polytheism, which can be traced back to the Babylon of Nimrod, and ultimately to Satan himself. The Renaissance and the Enlightenment of modern Western civilisation were nothing more than resurgences of those same humanistic and pagan philosophies ... Charles Darwin's actual personal scientific accomplishments were meagre indeed. He had earned no degree in any science and was totally unqualified to fill the position of naturalist on the HMS *Beagle* Expedition, which enabled him to develop his theories ... The Omniscient God, speaking through the Apostle Peter, told us over 1700 years before that men like Lyell and Darwin would in the latter days assert such pseudo-scientific theories as uniformitarianism ... From the above types of view [for example natural selection] it is but a short step to out-and-out racism and the 'Master Race' syndrome

of the future Nazis. (ACE *Collectivism* [138], 1979, pp. 35–6)

These examples show some of the typical features of the ACE programme – the way that all subjects are imbued with religious connotations, the question-begging nature of many of the assertions, the rejection of non-fundamentalist scientific explanations, and the hostility to the public education system. To anyone committed to an ethics of belief as outlined in this paper all of this raises serious problems, including the fact that children exposed to this sort of education are likely to have serious intellectual and moral conflicts in accommodating their views with those of the wider, liberal, pluralist society once they leave school.

Another contentious issue arises in relation to the beliefs and practices of certain mainstream religions which, it may be claimed, offend against some of the ethical principles argued for in this chapter. Whether or not they do would be a matter for debate and one which could arouse strong feelings on both sides. If handled carefully and if the arguments on both sides are fully and fairly presented, such issues could provide a valuable component of a studies of religion programme, at least at the senior secondary level. Students are already likely to have opinions on these issues and their treatment of them in an open and frank way could have beneficial effects and perhaps pre-empt potential social conflicts. Some instances of such difficult issues are: the Roman Catholic Church's stand against birth control and its effects in countries seriously troubled by over-population; the treatment of women and restrictions on freedom of religious expression in certain Muslim countries; the strong control over the minds of young children and a narrowing of their educational experiences exerted by some (not all) Charismatic and Pentecostal Christian churches; and, finally, the hard-line religious believer from any faith who sees AIDS as a divine punishment for homosexuality and its victims as not deserving of any special care and attention. While such issues may be seen by some as 'too hot to handle' or too divisive at the school level, they are nevertheless raised here as showing the sorts of curriculum implications that result if an ethics of belief is taken to its logical conclusion in the area of religious education.

CONCLUSION

We may conclude by noting some of the educational and political difficulties involved in incorporating the suggestions made here into studies of religion programmes, and how these difficulties may be responded to. The two main objections that are likely to be made are: (i) that these suggestions require too high a level of intellectual sophistication in students especially in terms of philosophical reasoning skills; and (ii) that they are likely to stir up too much hostility and division between children of different religious backgrounds or between children and parents. We would respond to the above objections in the following ways:

1. Even if these suggestions are not formally taken up in the various syllabuses, it is important that those involved in the planning and teaching of religious studies are aware of the considerations arising from an ethics of belief so that this can at least inform their understanding of the subject and perhaps influence their approach to it.

2. If it is still felt that some of the material we are advocating is just not appropriate for school students it would seem to have a legitimate place at tertiary level where studies of religion is now a widely taught undergraduate and postgraduate subject. If it turns out that students in such courses are preparing to teach this subject in schools it would do no harm for them to be exposed to these ethical dimensions themselves.

3. Another option would be to restrict some of the more controversial issues we have raised to the elective part of the school programme, giving the unit a title such as 'Controversial Issues in Religion' or 'Religion and Contemporary Ethical Issues'. It could be made clear in advance what is to be covered and perhaps parental permission could be gained for children to undertake it to forestall any potential difficulties between school and parents.

4. If studies of religion is correctly seen as a subject of a totally different nature to traditional faith-oriented religious education then these suggestions would seem less controversial. There is no reason why religion should not form a legitimate topic of academic enquiry as with any other curriculum subject and, considered in this light, the sorts of critical enquiry approaches we have outlined have as much place here as they would in, say, history or literature. This would in fact give religion a higher status as a subject rather than trying to preserve some sort of 'privileged' or 'protected' position for it, not accorded to other subjects.

One implication of these points is that teachers of the subject need special training (which would include aspects such as comparative religion, history, and philosophy of religion) and that the traditional preparation of religious education teachers in terms of training to pass on a specific faith is clearly inadequate on its own. This is not to say that such persons are not appropriate individuals to teach the subject but that they would need some broader training or experience to do it properly.

5. While some of the issues suggested for exploration are difficult and controversial they are by no means beyond the experience of senior secondary students who would be exposed to them regularly through the media and peer-group interaction. What such students probably will lack is an informed and structured framework for grappling with them and this is something a good studies in religion programme could provide. As liberal democracy relies on an informed and open-minded citizenry, such a course could provide a very important service in reducing ignorance, superstition, prejudice, and unthinking acceptance of traditional dogmas in these areas.

6. The goal of intellectual autonomy has been progressively accepted in a range of curriculum subjects from history to literature to social studies and, most recently, in morality. Religion seems to be the last area of the curriculum where the goal of autonomy has yet to be fully accepted. By religious autonomy we mean the capacity to work out for oneself, based on a thorough and impartial examination of the evidence, one's own thought-out position on the place of the transcendent in human experience, and this we would see as the most appropriate aim of a studies of religion programme.

REFERENCES

Accelerated Christian Education Inc. Handbooks: *Collectivism* [138] (ed. J.R. Bennie III) (1979), *English* [1107] (1987), *English* [1120] (1989), *Science* [1114] (1992), Texas, Accelerated Christian Education Inc.

Bailey, C. (1984). *Beyond the Present and the Particular*, London, Routledge & Kegan Paul.

Clifford, W.K. (1986). 'The Ethics of Belief', in G.D. McCarthy (ed.), *The Ethics of Belief Debate*, Atlanta, GA, Scholars Press.

D'Agostino, F. (1989). 'Adjudication as an Epistemological Concept', *Synthese*, 79, 231–56.

Dearden, R.F. (1984). 'Education and the Ethics of Belief', in R.F. Dearden, *Theory and Practice in Education*, London, Routledge & Kegan Paul.

Degenhardt, M.A.B. (1986). 'The "Ethics of Belief" and Education in Science and Morals', *Journal of Moral Education*, 15, 2, 109–18.

Harvey, V.A. (1986). 'The Ethics of Belief Reconsidered', in G.D. McCarthy (ed.), *The Ethics of Belief Debate*, Atlanta, GA, Scholars Press.

Hill, B.V. (1991). *Values Education in Australian Schools,* Hawthorn, Victoria, Australian Council for Educational Research.

McCarthy, G.D. (ed.) (1986). *The Ethics of Belief Debate*, Atlanta, GA, Scholars Press.

NSW Board of Studies (1991). *Studies of Religion Syllabus Years 11–12,* Sydney, NSW Board of Studies.

Peters, R.S. (1981). 'Democratic Values and Educational Aims', in R.S. Peters, *Essays on Educators*, London, Allen & Unwin.

Pojman, L. (1986). *Religious Belief and the Will*, London, Routledge & Kegan Paul.

6

The Rights of Parents, Children, and the State in Religious Upbringing

This chapter will explore the relative rights of parents, children, and the State in regard to religious upbringing. This represents a vexed issue of competing rights and duties in liberal democratic and pluralist societies today. Parents have a fundamental responsibility for the religious and general education of their children and certain rights for passing on their own values. Children have a right to an education that equips them to flourish in a liberal, pluralist, democratic society, which is also a post-industrial, information-driven society. The State has a corresponding duty to oversee the form of education that will promote this. The balancing of these various rights and duties raises many complex issues about the very nature of a liberal society. This is particularly evident in the debate about the rights of religious minority groups who do not necessarily subscribe in their own communities to the liberal values of the broader society.

We will argue in this chapter that the criteria for resolving these issues can be found in some of the key concepts presented earlier in this book. We will maintain that the form of education that is necessary for the maintenance of a liberal pluralist society requires adherence to the values of comprehensive liberalism, as distinct from the more restricted political liberalism (discussed below), and that this form of education is best encapsulated in the notion of liberal education presented in this book which stresses the values of critical rationality, personal transcendence or autonomy, and epistemological coherence.

What rights then do parents have to pass on their religious beliefs to their children? We will consider this first at the level of individual parents and then at the level of parents as members of communities or minority religious groups. The original issue of the rights of parents as individuals was widely debated in the literature in the 1980s (Bridges, 1984; Callan, 1985, 1988; Crittenden, 1988; Gardner, 1988, 1991; Hobson, 1984; Laura and Leahy, 1989; and McLaughlin, 1984, 1990). The latter issue of the rights of parents as members of religious minority groups and the related issues of maintaining community identity and the place of separate religious schools has been widely debated in the 1990s (Burtonwood, 1996; Burwood, 1996; Gutmann, 1995; Halstead, 1995a, 1995b, 1996; Hobson and Cresswell, 1993; Horton, 1993; Kymlicka, 1995; Leicester, 1992; Macedo, 1993, 1995a, 1995b; Mclaughlin, 1992; Rawls, 1993; Walzer, 1995; and Wringe, 1995).

The main context in which these debates have taken place is western, liberal, pluralist democracies such as the UK, the USA, and Australia. In such societies post-war immigration has led to the growth of multiculturalism and various minority religious groups. The issue of how far the State should require adherence to traditional liberal values by parents and such minority groups is a contentious one.

A key liberal value is the right of each individual to freely pursue and appropriate their own conception of the good life without interference from the State. The role of the State is to act as umpire to ensure that one person's pursuit of the good life does not interfere with that of another. An implication of the individual's right to pursue their version of the good life is their right to seek to convey that view to others. One limitation to this right is that such views do not cause harm to the recipient or to others. Another limitation refers to the status of the recipient of such views – a necessary requirement is that they are able to make a free and informed choice about the beliefs being conveyed, or that they have the capacity for full consent. In the case of children, these conditions will not be met as their rational faculties have not been fully developed. Children are also vulnerable to harm where their upbringing is so restricted as not to prepare them fully for participation in contemporary society. These liberal considerations are also reinforced in a human rights ethic such as the UN Convention on the Rights of the Child (1989).

POLITICAL AND COMPREHENSIVE LIBERALISM

The question, then, is how far does the liberal State have the right to intervene to protect its own values? In order to answer this question we need to distinguish between two types of liberalism: political and comprehensive. This distinction was popularised by John Rawls (1993). 'Political liberalism' is the more restricted form confining itself to procedural values necessary for democratic citizenship such as tolerance, respect for others, freedom of opinion, freedom of religion, and the rule of law. 'Comprehensive liberalism' on the other hand would actively promote the more substantive liberal values of critical rationality, autonomy, holding beliefs in an open and flexible way, and being exposed to a wide range of points of view. We will argue in this chapter for the necessity for both political and comprehensive liberalism indicating the different contexts in which they should apply. Together these will provide clear guidelines for when the liberal State should intervene to protect its own values.

A problem has been raised in regard to comprehensive liberalism's requirement for individuals to stand aside from their beliefs and evaluate them in an open and flexible way. Rawls contends that, 'Citizens may have, and normally do have at any given time, affections, devotions, and loyalties that they believe they would, and indeed could and should not, stand apart from and objectively evaluate from the standpoint of their purely rational good' (1985, p. 241). Rawls' solution to this perceived problem is to require only political liberalism for the functioning of a liberal society. He considers the value of objectively evaluating one's beliefs is a substantive value, rather than a procedural one, which stands in direct competition with the more traditional ways a community may have for holding their beliefs. What is at issue here is what possible justification liberal society has for imposing its substantive values over the more traditional values of the minority community.

Mark Halstead follows Rawls in drawing the distinction between comprehensive and political liberalism, requiring only political liberalism as a condition for participation in a liberal state. Halstead uses the phrase 'cultural liberalism', which he maintains particularly favours autonomy and individuality, and which he says 'is inhospitable to other cultures, for example to those which emphasise group interests at the expense of individual freedom' (1995b, p. 268). He interprets this as equivalent to Rawls' comprehensive liberalism and argues that this should take its place as just one of a number of competing conceptions of the good life (1995b, p. 269).

While we agree with Rawls and Halstead that political liberalism with its associated values of tolerance, respect for others, freedom of opinion, freedom of religion, and respect for law is sufficient for the harmonious operation of a multicultural society, we would maintain that it is not sufficient for flourishing in the complex, technological societies in which we are living today.

To flourish in such societies, critical rationality and autonomy are essential, particularly with regard to children and their education. This is supported by Joseph Raz, who, as pointed out in Chapter 1, argues for the necessity of autonomy for all citizens:

> it is an ideal particularly suited to the conditions of the industrial age and its aftermath with their fast changing technologies and free

movement of labour. They call for an ability to cope with changing technological, economic and social conditions, for an ability to adjust, to acquire new skills, to move from one sub-culture to another, to come to terms with new scientific and moral views. (1986, pp. 369–70)

He goes on to argue that, 'for those of use who live in an autonomy supporting environment there is no choice but to be autonomous; there is no other way to prosper in such a society' (1986, p. 391).

Children in particular, if they are to be able to develop to make free and informed choices in contemporary society, need an education that develops their autonomy and critical rationality. This is brought out well by Mr Justice White, one of the judges in the Wisconsin *v.* Yoder case in the USA involving the rights of Amish parents to restrict their children's education. As he says:

the State is not concerned with the maintenance of an educational system as an end it itself; it is rather attempting to nurture and develop the human potential of its children, whether Amish or non-Amish: to expand their knowledge, broaden their sensibilities, kindle their imagination, foster a spirit of free enquiry, and increase their human understanding and tolerance. It is possible that most Amish children will wish to continue living the rural life of their parents, in which case their training at home will adequately equip them for their future role. Others, however, may wish to become nuclear physicists, ballet dancers, computer programmers, or historians. And for these occupations formal training will be necessary ... A State has a legitimate interest not only in seeking to develop the latent talents of its children but also in seeking to prepare them for the life style they may later choose, or at least to provide them with an option other than the life they have led in the past. (Wisconsin *v.* Yoder *et al.* 406 US 203 (1972), quoted in Feinberg, 1988, pp. 137–8).

In today's computer-driven technological age such an education becomes even more critical. We now live in a post-industrial, information-based society. Such a society is one where successful participation depends on the capacity to tap into communications networks and to access electronic forms of information that increasingly underpin all aspects of society's functioning. With the sheer volume of information obtainable today on virtually any and every topic, the capacity to critically evaluate information is essential. Not only is the volume of knowledge doubling every three to five years, but knowledge in many areas becomes obsolescent over the same time-scale. A consequence of this is that individuals are required to constantly re-evaluate their life choices in the light of this new information. This has massive implications for children's education which need to be taken into account in the whole debate. This aspect of contemporary society has, however, been underemphasised in the contemporary debate about parents', children's and the State's rights. If children are to be able to succeed in such complex modern societies they will need to be self-directed, informed, flexible, and critically aware and thus receive an education that reflects the values of comprehensive liberalism.

It should be added here that while the above argument could be seen as primarily an instrumental one, the educational values involved are also intrinsically valuable as pointed out in our discussion of liberal education in Chapter 1. It will also be remembered that we made the point there that Bailey's account of liberal education has the virtue of bringing out that its key values, which include critical rationality and autonomy, have both intrinsic value in terms of promoting human understanding and personhood as well as instrumental value in regard to their enhancing and facilitating a greater range of choices a student can make in life.

As well as its role in preparing children to live in a technological, post-industrial society, comprehensive liberalism is also necessary to achieve the goal of personal transcendence, as discussed in Chapter 1. To be able to make a free and informed choice between alternative views of the good life, it is necessary to have achieved the goals of critical rationality and moral and intellectual autonomy. Coupled with this is the notion of positive tolerance in which children learn not merely to 'put up with' the ideas of others (what may be termed negative tolerance) but to actually welcome diversity and look on this as a valuable stimulus in their own search for meaning. Another way of expressing the values of positive tolerance is through Mill's (1962 [1859], p. 180) notion that truth is more likely to flourish in a free marketplace of ideas. This is also closely linked to our notions of extended pluralism and epistemic liberalism, developed in Chapter 3, that stress the importance of being open to a wide range of points of view and being flexible in how one holds one's beliefs.

Other writers, such as Halstead (1996, p. 311), distinguish celebration of diversity from tolerance, which they understand as necessarily linked to beliefs or conduct which are disapproved of. However, we believe the notion of positive tolerance as contrasted with negative tolerance is a more useful way of making the distinction because it maintains the historical links with one of the most fundamental values of liberalism. In fact, as Kymlicka points out, the development of religious tolerance is one of the historical roots of liberalism, 'Religious tolerance in the West emerged out of the interminable Wars of Religion, and the recognition by both Catholics and Protestants, that a stable constitutional order cannot rest on a shared religious faith' (1995, p. 155). Although this originally could be understood as negative tolerance, today with the ecumenical movement in Christianity there has developed a more positive notion of religious tolerance.

Education therefore has a vital role to play in pluralist societies in developing commitment to the values of positive tolerance as an essential aspect of comprehensive liberalism. This is particularly important in the current political context in the west where extremist conservative figures such as Jean-Marie Le Pen in France, David Duke (former leader of the Ku-Klux-Klan) in the USA, and Pauline Hanson in Australia are threatening the social cohesion of multicultural society.

Another response to the question raised earlier of how far the liberal State has a right to intervene to protect its own values is found in an ethics of belief, as discussed in Chapter 5. There are two arguments presented there which further strengthen the case for comprehensive liberal values. The first is Richard Gale's deontological argument (cited in Pojman, 1986, pp. 106–7) that it is morally wrong to believe against sufficient evidence, as doing so gives rise to false beliefs which impair a person's free will and autonomy. While one may not necessarily support Gale's Kantian absolutism that it is always wrong to reduce a person's freedom of choice, such a principle is generally accepted in liberal democratic society as a primary moral obligation. The second argument is the utilitarian one put forward by J.T. Stevenson who argues that a society's survival depends upon a stock of highly justified beliefs (cited in Pojman 1986, pp. 107–9). If our beliefs are false or spurious then the actions derivative from them will have significant adverse effects within society. These two arguments highlight our moral duty to pursue autonomy – they are additional to our earlier arguments for comprehensive liberalism in terms of the educational necessity of autonomy. Because they lead to a moral rather than a legal duty, they still would not on their own justify the State making comprehensive liberalism obligatory for all citizens but they do provide strong backing for the State to support and encourage such values.

It should be added that comprehensive liberalism need not be seen as an ideology imposed on all against their will. As we argued in Chapter 3, when distinguishing epistemic from ideological liberalism, liberalism does not have to involve the imposition of secular humanist, global values, as has been claimed by some of its conservative critics, but just the commitment to careful and continuing examination and elucidation of one's beliefs with an openness to change. Similarly, it was pointed out there that it was possible to hold one's beliefs in a revisable but committed way consistent with living out a fully religious way of life. It will be noted that this is a view different to that of Rawls in terms of how religious beliefs may be held, but is a quite legitimate one, particularly in the context of a pluralist society.

While comprehensive liberalism does involve commitment to particular substantive values such as autonomy and critical rationality, it still allows a degree of freedom to choose alternative world views as long as such a choice meets certain criteria. Thus, one could choose a religious or non-religious view or a wide range of moral and political views. Comprehensive liberalism therefore is not a totalistic belief system as described (in the religious context) by Stephen Macedo. People with such belief systems, he says, are:

> those who would be guided by religious imperatives in all spheres of their lives, those who refuse to honour the political supremacy of reasons that can be shared with those outside one's church, as often seems the case with religious fundamentalists ... (1995b, p. 227)

Similarly, totalistic belief systems could operate in moral and political contexts.

The great advantage of comprehensive liberalism as a belief system is that it allows reference to public criteria of evaluation that do not rule out in advance any position (unless it is blatantly irrational). It in fact protects the rights of people with totalistic belief systems to exist alongside others with conflicting belief systems. We may draw on a variation of Rawls' (1972) 'veil of ignorance' argument here – if persons holding totalistic belief systems were to choose the sort of society in which to live without knowing the form of totalism involved, they would have good reason to choose a liberal society rather than one organised according to a totalistic belief system (for example a theocracy). They could happily exist in the former but not in the latter if it happened not to be the one they subscribed to (for example a fundamentalist Muslim in a fundamentalist Christian society or vice versa). In other words, liberalism allows a variety of world views, whereas a totalistic system imposes a unitary view.

One way in which comprehensive liberalism differs from ideological liberalism in the religious sphere was mentioned in Chapter 3 when describing epistemic liberalism, which is a very similar concept to comprehensive liberalism. (It is one that focuses more on the epistemological and educational context of liberalism whereas comprehensive liberalism focuses more on the political context.) We agued in that chapter for extended pluralism (in which all opinions, religious or otherwise, are open for critical examination) as a methodology for religious education, in preference to Hick's form of pluralism which held that all religions are equally valid. Hick's version of pluralism could be seen as ideological in that it requires acceptance of a certain view of the nature of religious truth, whereas extended pluralism involves no such requirement.

We may conclude that the values of comprehensive liberalism provide essential criteria for educating children for successful membership of contemporary technological, multicultural societies such as the UK, the USA, and Australia. They provide necessary conditions for the flourishing of such societies at all levels but, nevertheless, the State does not have the right to impose the values of comprehensive liberalism on adults, although it does have the right to encourage and promote such values in non-coercive ways. On the other hand, it does have the right to expect the values of *political* liberalism to be generally adhered to as these are the minimum necessary for the harmonious functioning of a multicultural society. Two examples where such adherence may need to be enforced are where the activities of a group interfere with the right of others to pursue their concept of the good life or where the activities of a group cause actual harm or injury to others or to those within its own group.

Two questions may be asked at this juncture. The first is to do with the distinction between children and adults with regard to the place of comprehensive liberal values. The second is to do with the distinction between political and comprehensive liberalism.

Why exactly should comprehensive liberalism be required for children but not adults? We have argued that such values are necessary to flourishing in contemporary society on two grounds, one related to the requirements of living in a post-industrial, technological society; the other to living in a multicultural pluralist society. It is in both the individual's and the wider society's interest that the attitudes, skills, and understandings involved in comprehensive liberalism are developed as fully as possible.

However, if adult citizens make a free choice not to subscribe to comprehensive liberalism, maybe preferring to follow a custom-bound, unreflective way of life, the State, we would argue, should not force them do otherwise. To do so would be to move towards ideological liberalism which we have suggested here and in Chapter 3 is an unwarranted forced extension of liberalism to the adult community. Children, on the other hand, are in a different situation and in their case we argue that the State does have the right to expect comprehensive liberal values to be promoted in their upbringing where possible or when other important values are not seriously infringed. This is because children, by nature of their immaturity and limited experience, are not able to make a rational decision for themselves about what is in their long-term best interest and the only way of ensuring that they can make such a choice is by developing their autonomy and critical rationality. If they ultimately choose to reject such values and lead an unreflective, tradition-bound life, at least they have been able to make an informed choice to so do. It will be remembered that Mill excepted children from his general renunciation of paternalism in *On Liberty* on similar grounds.

A second reason why the State may require children to be brought up according to comprehensive liberal values is in terms of its own interests. The State has a right to protect its own future as a technological, multicultural society by ensuring that future generations will be equipped with the necessary skills and attitudes for such a society to flourish. It may also be argued in this context that the liberal State has a right to promote those values which make up its philosophical rationale and which have been developed historically through its particular political experiences.

The second question we need to consider at this stage is that of the precise relation between political and comprehensive liberalism. It has been argued (for example Gutmann, 1995; Kymlicka, 1995; and Macedo, 1995a) that political liberalism either collapses into comprehensive liberalism or is sufficient on its own to achieve the values desired by comprehensive liberals. Without going into the fine details of this debate, we would argue that the distinction is worth maintaining and the separate case be made for comprehensive liberalism on the grounds that the two are distinct conceptually and that comprehensive liberalism provides a clear and explicit ideal for the flourishing of modern democratic, pluralist, multicultural societies. In particular it provides a rationale for the upbringing and education of children in such societies that sets clear goals for parents and schools to follow.

RIGHTS OF PARENTS AS INDIVIDUALS

Let us now more closely analyse the rights and responsibilities of parents, children, and the State in regard to religious upbringing, using the values of comprehensive liberalism as well as key concepts developed in earlier chapters as central criteria by which to assess them. We will focus ont he differing rights of parents as individuals and as community members as a way of bringing out the central issues in regard to the various rights and responsibilities of three groups. The right of parents as individuals to pass on their religious beliefs to their children is one that has been widely accepted in liberal societies in terms of freedom from interference from the State in regard to their private lives. However, when such transmission of beliefs involves indoctrination of their own children, this conflicts with another prized liberal value, namely the right of each individual to be self-determining. Also, if the beliefs or the values transmitted cause harm to others, this would be ruled out by the principle of respects for persons.

Some (for example, Callan 1985, 1988; and Gardner, 1988) would question the rights of parents in a liberal society to pass on any religious beliefs at all to their children on the grounds that this always involves indoctrination. However, this seems to us too extreme a view for the following reasons: (i) children require in the early years a stable set of beliefs consonant with those of the family (what we called a 'primary culture' in Chapter 2) from which to begin to interpret their experience; (ii) it is unavoidable that the way parents interact with their children will be influenced by their values and religious beliefs and therefore children have a right to know what these are; (iii) to be able to critically evaluate alternative religious beliefs children need an initial framework from which to interpret others' religious belief systems; and (iv) parents have certain rights to pass on to their children those beliefs and values they hold to be fundamental and necessary for their children's own good.

Parents thus have a right to pass on their own religious beliefs, but comprehensive liberalism provides restrictions and safeguards on how such a primary culture should be conveyed to a child. These restrictions are designed to ensure the possibility of the child's making an autonomous choice about religion at a later stage when she or he has the capacity to do so. Any methods that involve permanently fixating a child in a certain way of thinking would be ruled out, as would any methods that involve excessive physical and emotional pressure. Furthermore, the child should be made aware that other people hold different beliefs and while parents may disagree with these, they should convey to the child a sense of tolerance and respect for those holding different views. Also, children should be encouraged to hold their beliefs in an open and flexible way, thus avoiding the problems of dogmatism.

As the child matures, the parents' role (according to the comprehensive liberal position argued for here) changes from that of 'determiners' to that of 'trustees' for their child's beliefs, to use McLaughlin's phrases (1994, p. 94). Once a primary culture has been absorbed by the child and she or he is ready to think independently, the parents should gradually step back and allow their child to make an autonomous choice whether to stay with their primary culture or strike out in some new direction. This also involves the parent as playing the role of an intermediary between their child and the school or other outside influences. They should continue to act as a guide to their child in helping to make sense of experience, but now see themselves as only one agent of influence and encourage their child to learn in fruitful ways from other sources and institutions in society. In this way they will promote their child's growth to eventual full autonomy and independence.

However, what if parents do not subscribe to liberal values and wish to either indoctrinate their children or continue an unquestioning acceptance of a primary culture well past the age at which children are ready to think for themselves? Does the liberal State have the right to intervene to protect the child's right to an open future?

Because of the invasion of parental rights involved in intervention by the State in private family matters, coupled with the practical difficulties involved in doing this with any degree of success, it would seem that the most the State can do in this area is through its monitoring of educational provisions in society. It can do this through compulsory education requirements and through legislation concerning curriculum provisions and educational standards that have to be met by schools, or by parents who wish to educate their children at home. With regard to religious education in particular it can regulate the place of both education in faith and studies in religion in state schools and oversee what takes place in separate religiously-based schools. Historical and cultural factors will influence the precise balance that occurs in these areas in different countries. As a result, provisions differ markedly in the different western nations that are the focus of this book, ranging, for example, from compulsory religious education (albeit interpreted very broadly) in the UK, to legal prohibition of religious education (interpreted as education in faith) in the USA, with Australia and other countries somewhere in between. We shall explore these different educational contexts for religious education in the next chapter and see how far they meet the criteria for the subject developed in the earlier chapters.

For the present, the main points to be made concern the role of the state school in this domain. In the light of our earlier arguments regarding the values of comprehensive liberalism, we would maintain that the public school in a liberal, pluralist, democratic society has a right to implement such values and thus seek to develop each child as an autonomous individual. This would involve encouraging the critical evaluation of a range of world views, religious and non-religious, as exemplified in the liberal education approach in general and that of studies of religion in particular as discussed earlier in this book. Whether studies of religion should be made a required subject for all pupils (at least in the senior years) is a moot point, but this would appear to be a logical implication of implementing the values of comprehensive liberalism in an educational setting in a multi-faith democratic society.

Whatever conclusion is reached here, it would seem desirable that at some stage in their school career all pupils undertake some examination of the alternative world views competing for a place in their society. Such an examination should include not merely understanding but (at least in the senior years) also critically evaluating them, as we have argued throughout this book (as for example in our presentation of extended pluralism as a methodology for the teaching of studies of religion in Chapter 3). In other words, questions of truth should not be put on hold but actively explored and debated. Mill himself advocated such an approach when he spoke of the need to confront opinions opposed to our own in the search for truth (1962 [1859], p. 180). Those forms of liberalism that argue for putting the truth status of all world views on hold or maintaining a scrupulous neutrality between them seem to us to hold too limited an understanding of the concept, which is perhaps sufficient for political liberalism but not for comprehensive liberalism. For those parents who desire a more specifically religious upbringing there is the option of separate, private religious schools. Exactly what role these should play in a liberal pluralist state will be discussed later in the chapter when we look at the rights of communities to pass on their beliefs to their children.

Overall then the main way the State can and does act to protect the child against indoctrination or a severely limited upbringing by individual parents is through regulations regarding education. It can also support the role of the schools in this area by providing resources and encouraging activities in the wider society that help to promote positive tolerance and the celebration of our cultural and religious diversity. It would only be in extreme cases of parental behaviour leading to physical or measurable psychological harm that it would directly intervene in family affairs. (For a discussion of some of the issues involved in such cases, see Hobson and Cresswell, 1993).

RIGHTS OF PARENTS AS COMMUNITY MEMBERS

We now need to consider the rights of parents as members of communities to pass on religious beliefs through the family, schooling, or other means. We have already touched on some of the central issues here in our defence of comprehensive liberalism. As we said earlier, a central issue in this context is the right of minority groups to maintain their own separate cultural identity. This is a particularly pressing issue for ethnic or religious minority groups in western multicultural societies such as the UK, the USA, and Australia.

This issue becomes even more contentious because many of these subgroups do not subscribe to the liberal values of the broader community but uphold more traditional and communitarian beliefs. This is less of a problem with regard to how adults hold their beliefs, and even those committed to comprehensive liberalism would not intervene to ensure these are held in a liberal open-ended way. However, when it comes to transmitting these beliefs to their children and to the educational process in general, it does raise the question of children's rights to an open future or to an education that promotes free or autonomous choice. Moreover, the State has a legitimate interest in ensuring that future citizens are equipped to play a full role in contemporary society. This was expressed quite clearly in the judgement by Judge White in the Amish case referred to earlier.

On the other hand, these factors need to be balanced against the rights of minority and religious ethnic communities to maintain their cultural identity by ensuring that their children inherit their particular belief system and values. The question now is whether they have the right to set up separate religious schools to achieve this. This has become a heated issue in a number of western countries, particularly with regard to Muslim and Christian fundamentalist groups who are claiming state funding for schools on the basis that other more mainstream religious groups receive funding for their schools, as for example in the case of Catholic and Anglican schools. As commented earlier, this strand of the debate about the rights of minority groups to preserve their cultural identity has emerged as an important and significant variation in the 1990s. The debate is couched not simply in terms of the right of a minority group to pursue its version of the good life as one group among many within a liberal democracy, but rather in regard to the more serious claim that the values taught in public schools are inimical to those of the minority group. This is seen to undermine their children's appropriation of those values and threaten the very survival of the culture as a whole. Such groups, as with the Amish in America and fundamentalist Muslim groups in Britain, demand the right to opt out of the public school system either by leaving early, or by setting up their own schools. Not to allow them to do so, they argue, threatens the survival of their culture and represents a direct interference by the state in their pursuit of the good life. They further claim that the principle of tolerance provides for cultural diversity rather than its restriction, and requires, as Iris Young claims, a politics that 'attends to rather than represses difference' (1990, p. 7). Implicit in such arguments is the notion that all cultures are of equal worth.

This situation is a particularly difficult one for liberals as the arguments used against them are based on liberal principles, in this case the principle of tolerance and the principle of non-interference. The problem is how liberals can resolve this predicament without either repudiating their own principles or vitiating them by invoking numerous qualifications. There are two ways to resolve this dilemma. The first is to show that the appeal by the minority groups to the principle of tolerance involves committing a logical inconsistency. The second is to show that any attempt to accommodate diversity, and so ameliorate the charge of State interference, by reducing liberalism from comprehensive to political liberalism still involves an inconsistency, but this time on the part of the liberals.

Kymlicka exposes the error in the appeal to tolerance by examining the origins of the general concept of tolerance. As mentioned above, religious tolerance is a key concept in the historical development of liberalism and grows out of Europe's dissatisfaction with the endless feuding between religions and the recognition that universal agreement on religion was not necessary for a stable society. Kymlicka agrees with Rawls that while the principle of tolerance emerges historically from the desire to achieve religious tolerance, nevertheless the concept of religious tolerance itself has subsequently evolved in the west into a highly specific form, 'namely, the idea of individual freedom of conscience' (Kymlicka 1995, p. 156). This latter concept has taken on the status of a fundamental human right. The important point to note here is that the principle of tolerance itself entails the right of individual freedom of conscience. Consequently, the appeal to the principle of tolerance by illiberal religious minority groups to opt out of public education involves them in the logical inconsistency of justifying actions that would deny individual freedom of religious choice to their members by employing a principle which upholds that very same freedom. Hence, the arguments based on liberal principles by non-liberal minority groups for separate schools teaching one religion in an unquestioning way do not really stand up to scrutiny.

The second response to the argument from diversity by minority groups elicits the concession from some liberals, such as Rawls, of expecting only political rather than comprehensive liberalism as discussed earlier in this chapter. Political liberalism requires commitment to the common political good, and common social values such as peace, prosperity, and equal liberty, but does not intrude into their community life.

In other words, Rawls' accommodation requires minority groups to be liberal in their public life but not so in their private life. Kymlicka suggests this is an incoherent position. He questions whether people who, according to Rawls (1985, p. 241), do not normally 'stand apart from and objectively evaluate from the standpoint of their purely rational good' their constitutive religious views, will nevertheless happily do this in their political personas. That is, why would they 'accept the ideal of autonomy in political contexts unless they also accepted it more generally?' (Kymlicka, 1995, p. 160). Clearly there is a problem with a solution that requires not only inconsistent responses to political and private ends but also a highly improbable one as regards such groups' basic religious goals.

Thus, the call by illiberal religious minority groups to opt out of an adequate public education as a threat to their way of life cannot be sustained in this case by an appeal to the principle of tolerance, nor can their call for non-interference be accommodated by the lesser claims of political liberalism. This means the State retains the duty to oversee the provision of an adequate education for children according to comprehensive liberal principles.

However, if arguments based on liberalism itself cannot be used to justify separate schools teaching non-liberal values, are there nevertheless other arguments more explicitly in terms of preserving cultural identity that may be mounted? Halstead is one writer who believes that there are and attempts to develop a model of education for cultural attachment that is appropriate for schools in a liberal pluralist society. He suggests three necessary aspects of the curriculum for such schools: (i) education for democratic citizenship, which is equivalent to Rawls' concept of political liberalism; (ii) education for specific cultural attachment, which is different in different schools; and (iii) education for cross-cultural understanding which involves learning about the beliefs and values of other groups in society (1995a, pp. 372–4). The first and third aspects of Halstead's curriculum have considerable appeal and are closely in line with what we have been arguing in this chapter. The second, however, raises quite different issues. Nevertheless, Halstead makes a strong case for it in terms of the rights of the child to have his or her cultural identity respected at school. As he says, certain kinds of cultural identity are especially vulnerable to negative stereotyping in schools, particularly those connected with ethnic and religious subgroups. He gives the following example: 'A Jehovah's Witness child may have a strong self-identity at home as a member of the true faith but may pick up very different messages about the peculiarity of her identity at school' (1995a, p. 365).

We would agree with Halstead that considerable harm can be caused to the child in situations of ongoing negative re-enforcement of his or her cultural identity as may occur at schools. However, unless children are to be permanently isolated from the rest of society, they will at some stage have to adapt to the needs and requirements of the broader community. Even if this may pose some difficulties for individual children, it is better for them in the long run to start to do this at school rather than be cocooned in an artificial environment during their formative years. Particularly by the time of their secondary schooling, as we have argued earlier in this chapter, they should be ready to consider questions about their identity and reflect on its beliefs and values in comparison to others.

Another major difficulty with Halstead's proposal emerges when he points out that, for the minority groups about which he is talking, 'their religious identity is something which they believe should permeate the whole of life' and what they are seeking is a form of 'voluntary apartheid' (1995a, p. 366). A clear example of what this might lead to in the educational context is given in the previous chapter in our examination of the curriculum in Christian fundamentalist schools using the ACE (Accelerated Christian Education) programme. It was found that in such schools all subjects are imbued with religious connotations, non-fundamentalist scientific explanations are rejected, and the public education system is generally denigrated. Similar problems may well arise in the case of separate Muslim schools which are the ones Halstead is particularly concerned with. Further problems arise in those communities whose cultural values are in direct conflict with those of liberalism on such issues as equal opportunities for women, or the right to mix with children of different religions, or to be exposed to differing moral or religious views.

To anyone committed to the values of comprehensive liberalism or an ethics of belief such examples raise serious problems, including the fact that children exposed to an education based on these beliefs and practices are likely to have serious intellectual and moral conflicts in accommodating their views with those of the wider, liberal, pluralist society once they leave school.

There is a paradox here which Halstead fails to see. In seeking to avoid one sort of harm by promoting the value of cultural attachment he is opening the door for another sort of harm in impairing the child's ability to participate in the broader, multicultural society. It also needs to be pointed out that Halstead does not spell out in sufficient detail what his education for cultural attachment involves, and in particular he does not rule out that the curriculum might be taught in a very narrow and indoctrinatory way.

There is a further problem for Halstead's curriculum in that there is a clear values conflict between the second strand on the one hand and the first and the third on the other. As Burtonwood says, '[t]hese latter two elements are properly concerned with the educational imperative to go beyond culture and this stands in marked contrast to the transmissionist concerns of a curriculum for cultural attachment' (1996, p. 298). Walzer brings this out very strongly when he argues that education for democratic citizenship includes the development of appropriate attitudes. As he says, 'A certain democratic consciousness – open, questioning, hostile to dogmatism – must be at work in every course' (1995, p. 186). These values are likely to be inconsistent with the values in an education for cultural attachment.

This discussion highlights the need to establish a clear set of criteria to use as a yardstick to gauge the adequacy of education in religious schools if students are to be adequately prepared for life in a complex technological and liberal democracy. There are two approaches to this task. The first is to set out what the principles of comprehensive liberalism (or at least of political liberalism) require as regards minority groups and the passing on of their religious beliefs. The second is to set out specific requirements regarding the values schools should promote through the curriculum and their general functioning. We will now examine and comment upon various recent attempts in both these directions. In regard to the first we will refer to the writings of Burtonwood (1996), Kymlicka (1995), Macedo (1995b), Popper (1994) and Wringe (1995).

Burtonwood argues that an 'appropriate model for multicultural education would start from a view of culture and identity which recognises individual agency, internal differences within all cultures and an orientation of openness to other cultures' (1996, p. 299). He goes on to quote Popper on this point who says that 'the effort is amply rewarded by what we learn in the process about our own views, as well as what we learn about those we are setting out to understand' (Popper, 1994, p. 34). Burtonwood and Popper are here presenting principles very similar to those involved in the model of liberal education we have argued for in Chapter 1 and the methodology of extended pluralism advocated in Chapter 3.

Kymlicka highlights how liberal tolerance stresses freedom of individual conscience:

> Liberal tolerance protects the rights of individuals to dissent from their group, as well as the right of groups not to be persecuted by the state. It limits the power of illiberal groups to restrict the liberty of their own members, as well as the power of illiberal states to restrict the liberty of collective worship. (1995, p. 158)

Kymlicka thus brings out the strong connection between liberal tolerance and autonomy which he describes as the freedom of individuals to assess and potentially revise their existing ends. Once again this is a key concept that has been argued for throughout this book in regard to its importance for religious education in a democratic pluralist society.

Macedo states the case strongly for limiting the educational rights of non-liberal communities. Speaking of religious fundamentalists in America, he argues that living in a diverse society sets clear requirements:

> Here, I think is where sensible defenders of liberal democracy must bite the bullet in a way that multiculturalists often refuse to do. A liberal order does not and should not guarantee a level playing field for all the religions and ways of life that people might adopt and sincerely espouse. That some people have a hard time passing on their convictions to their children in circumstances of peaceful, liberal diversity is not anything to apologise or (necessarily) to adjust for. We have no reason to be equally fair to those prepared to accept and those who refuse to accept, the political authority of public reasons that fellow citizens can share. (1995b, p. 227)

This is also consistent with the principles argued for throughout this book especially in regard to an ethics of belief in Chapter 5 and the remarks about totalistic belief systems in this chapter.

Finally, Wringe points out that group membership in a democratic society should not be seen as circumscribing too rigidly our choices and future possible courses of action:

> To the democrat ... there can be no moral justification for demanding that unwilling individuals should simply accept pre-existing hierarchies or value systems which presume to prescribe whom they shall serve, what knowledge they shall have access to and whom they may turn to in satisfying their needs. (1995, pp. 290–1)

This has clear implications for the rights of children belonging to traditionalist minority groups to an education which respects their right to an open future.

Let us now turn to two writers (Burwood, 1996; and Crittenden, 1988) who set out more specific requirements regarding the values which schools should promote in a liberal multicultural society. Burwood introduces his criteria by arguing against the commonly held cultural relativism according to which all cultural beliefs and practices should be respected regardless of their educational or social value. (We also criticise such a notion in our discussion of naive relativism in Chapter 2.) By way of example, a minority culture that believes in gangland thuggery, or the oppression of women, or the taking of addictive drugs should not, he argues, be valued by schools (1996, p. 424). He points out that schools can tolerate a wide range of religious and cultural views, but require a common framework of moral values according to which people can interact harmoniously in a multicultural society.

In regard to how the school should respond to the multiplicity of values in such a society he provides the following very useful checklist which is worth repeating in full:

1. those values that are educationally valuable should be promoted;
2. those that are socially valuable to the extent that they contribute to a core, common moral framework should be promoted;
3. those values that are neutral in as much as they are neither educationally valuable nor anti-educational should be tolerated;
4. those that are neutral in as much as they do not actively promote a common moral framework, but do not challenge it, should be tolerated;
5. those values that are positively anti-educational should not be tolerated, but should be condemned;
6. those that challenge the common moral framework of a liberal democratic society should not be tolerated, but should be condemned. (1996, p. 427)

He says that the school has to judge collectively which values are educationally valuable and which are socially valuable but points out that a liberal democratic society would apply the following broad criteria in determining such values:

> Those that are educationally valuable might promote discussion, argument, criticism and the weighing up of evidence, as opposed to promoting practices which reject these in favour of, say, the acceptance of unquestioned beliefs handed down in sacred texts, interpreted by religious leaders and learned by rote. Those that are socially valuable might, inter alia, promote tolerance, freedom of expression, the rule of law, and the willingness to settle differences by argument rather than violence and terrorism. (1996, p. 426)

Crittenden argues along similar lines but gives a more detailed account of the curriculum requirements of schools in a liberal democratic society. The essential elements are:

(a) The values of the basic social morality together with those connected with the fundamental liberal democratic belief in the equal freedom of each individual

(b) The essential knowledge and skills on which participation as a citizen in the process of political democracy depends. (1988, p. 201)

In addition, recognising the complexity of modern society, he requires the curriculum 'to include pre-vocational skills and knowledge of particular importance for taking an effective part in the economic life of the society' (1988, p. 202). While suggesting that liberal education might in fact be the best preparation for a society that is rapidly changing and offers such a diversity of roles, he nevertheless acknowledges there is considerable debate between those arguing for a liberal education and those arguing for a more instrumental and vocational education. However, regardless of the outcome of this debate he believes the above two features (including the economic factors mentioned above) should be a component of all schools.

For those schools seeking public funding Crittenden would impose five further restrictions (1988, p. 206). The first is that students must be progressively brought to see the underlying reasons for beliefs and practices, as well as the strengths and weaknesses of the methods of enquiry used in the relevant areas of knowledge. Secondly, the values underpinning the particular way of life of the school should be subject to scrutiny and counter-evidence. Thirdly, there should be a comparative study of the 'major kinds of interpretations within the society of what it is to be human and how human beings should live'. Fourthly, both primary and secondary students should have access to a wide range of subjects allowing them to choose from the sciences, the arts, and the humanities. Fifthly, the precise epistemic status of any subject should always be clearly manifest. Crittenden refers to an education based on these five principles as one that works towards the ideal of rational self-determination.

In many respects this parallels the requirements of the liberal education tradition argued for in this book although the second requirement, to examine critically the values underpinning the way of life of the school, and provide counter-evidence to them, seems to be asking more than many religious schools could be expected to include. It might be sufficient to examine alternative systems of values, to suggest to students that there are different positions adopted by others. This approach might then encourage students to enquire further. In fact, the third requirement of looking at different ideals of humanity and morality might very well achieve this in a more balanced way. Nevertheless, we believe

Crittenden's criteria are generally very useful in ensuring the comprehensive liberal values of society will be maintained and that students' autonomy will not be compromised. Furthermore, the stringency of these requirements is appropriate for schools seeking public funding.

In conclusion, we believe that all the above writers have provided useful guidelines for assessing the role of separate minority culture schools in contemporary, liberal, pluralist societies. Some of the key features of the more general criteria of comprehensive liberalism are well summarised by Burtonwood, Kymlicka, Macedo, Popper and Wringe. The more specific criteria for separate schools are set out by Burwood in terms of the broad educational and social values required and by Crittenden in terms of the curriculum necessary for our contemporary and rapidly changing society.

Schools which are unable to provide an appropriate context for education for citizenship in present-day society which is both multicultural and technologically advanced should not be subsidised by the State. In other words, comprehensive liberal values should be promoted in all schools seeking public funding. In extreme cases, where schools actively deny liberal values, for instance not even respecting the more minimal requirements of political liberalism, the question of their right even to exist must be raised.

We may now conclude this chapter dealing with the rights of parents, children, and the State in religious upbringing by stressing that the best interests of the child should be the paramount value. This may be interpreted in the educational context in terms of the child's need to develop autonomy and critical rationality in order to flourish in contemporary technological and multicultural society. The philosophy of comprehensive liberalism provides the underlying rationale for such an interpretation. Both the parents and the State have rights in this area but these always need to be balanced against the prior rights of the child.

This completes Part III of the book which has explored the ethical, political, and social dimensions of religious education. In Part IV we will look at some more practical issues to do with the teaching of religious education, beginning with an examination of the policies and programmes for religious education in the UK, the USA, and Australia and concluding with some recommendations for teaching the subject and the development of a charter for the teacher of religious education in a liberal, pluralist, democratic society.

REFERENCES

Bridges, D. (1984). 'Non-Paternalistic Arguments in Support of Parents' Rights', *Journal of Philosophy of Education*, 18, 1, 55–61.

Burtonwood, N. (1996). 'Beyond Culture: a Reply to Mark Halstead', *Journal of Philosophy of Education*, 30, 2, 295–9.

Burwood, L. (1996). 'How Should Schools Respond to the Plurality of Values in a Multi-Cultural Society?', *Journal of Philosophy of Education*, 30, 3, 415–27.

Callan, E. (1985). 'McLaughlin on Parental Rights', *Journal of Philosophy of Education*, 19, 1, 111–27.

Callan, E. (1988). 'Faith, Worship and Reason in Religious Upbringing', *Journal of Philosophy of Education*, 22, 2, 183–93.

Crittenden, B. (1988). *Parents, the State and the Right to Educate*, Melbourne, Melbourne University Press.

Feinberg, J. (1980). 'The Child's Right to an Open Future', in W. Aiken, and H. La Follette (eds), *Whose Child?: Children, Rights, Parental Authority and State Power*, New York, Littlefield Adams.

Gardner, P. (1988). 'Religious Upbringing and the Liberal Ideal of Religious Autonomy', *Journal of Philosophy of Education*, 22, 1, 89–105.

Gardner, P. (1991). 'Personal Autonomy and Religious Upbringing: The "Problem"', *Journal of Philosophy of Education*, 25, 1, 69–81.

Gutmann, A. (1995). 'Civic Education and Social Diversity', *Ethics*, 105, 557–79.

Halstead, M. (1995a). 'Should Schools Reinforce Children's Religious Identity?', *Religious Education*, 90, 3/4, 360–76.

Halstead, M. (1995b). 'Voluntary Apartheid? Problems of Schooling for Religious and Other Minorities in Democratic Societies', *Journal of Philosophy of Education*, 29, 2, 257–72.

Halstead, M. (1996). 'Liberalism, Multiculturalism and Toleration' (review article), *Journal of Philosophy of Education*, 30, 2, 307–13.

Hobson, P.R. (1984). 'Some Reflections on Parents' Rights in the Upbringing of Their Children', *Journal of Philosophy of Education*, 18, 1, 63–74.

Hobson, P.R. and Cresswell, R. (1993). 'Parental Rights, Education and Liberal Tolerance', *Discourse*, 14, 1, 44–51.

Horton, J. (ed.) (1993). *Liberalism, Multiculturalism and Toleration*, London, Macmillan.

Kymlicka, W. (1995). *Multicultural Citizenship*, Oxford, Clarendon Press.

Laura, R.S. and Leahy, M. (1989). 'Religious Upbringing and Rational Autonomy', *Journal of Philosophy of Education*, 23, 2, 253–65.

Leicester, M. (1992). 'Values, Cultural Conflict and Education', in M. Leicester and M. Taylor (eds), *Ethics, Ethnicity and Education*, London, Kogan Page.

Macedo, S. (1993). 'Toleration and Fundamentalism', in R.E. Goodwin and P. Pettit (eds), *A Companion to Contemporary Political Philosophy*, Oxford, Blackwell.

Macedo, S. (1995a). 'Liberal Civic Education and Religious Fundamentalism: the Case of God v. John Rawls?', *Ethics*, 105, 468–96.

Macedo, S. (1995b). 'Multiculturalism for the Religious Right? Defending Liberal Civic Education', *Journal of Philosophy of Education*, 29, 2, 223–38.

McLaughlin, T.H. (1984). 'Parental Rights and the Religious Upbringing of Children', *Journal of Philosophy of Education*, 18, 1, 75-83.

McLaughlin, T.H. (1990). 'Peter Gardner on Religious Upbringing and the Liberal Ideal of Rational Autonomy', *Journal of Philosophy of Education*, 24, 1, 107–25.

McLaughlin, T.H. (1992). 'The Ethics of Separate Schools', in M. Leicester and M. Taylor (eds), *Ethics, Ethnicity and Education*, London, Kogan Page.

McLaughlin, T.H. (1994). 'The Scope of Parents' Educational Rights', in M. Halstead (ed.), *Parental Choice and Education*, London, Kogan Page.

Mill, J.S. (1962 [1859]). *On Liberty*, in M. Warnock (ed.), *Utilitarianism, On Liberty, Essay on Bentham*, London, Collins.

Pojman, L. (1986). *Religious Belief and the Will*, London, Routledge & Kegan Paul.

Popper, K. (1994). *The Myth of the Framework*, London, Routledge.

Rawls, J. (1972). *A Theory of Justice*, London, Oxford University Press.

Rawls, J. (1985). 'Justice as Fairness: Political not Metaphysical', *Philosophy and Public Affairs*, 13, 3.

Rawls, J. (1993). *Political Liberalism*, New York, Columbia University Press.

Raz, J. (1986). *The Morality of Freedom*, Oxford, Clarendon Press.

United Nations Convention on the Rights of the Child (1989), United Nations General Assembly (adopted 20 November, 1989).

Walzer, M. (1995). 'Education, Democratic Citizenship and Multiculturalism', *Journal of Philosophy of Education*, 29, 2, 181–9.

Wringe, C. (1995). 'Educational Rights in Multicultural Democracies', *Journal of Philosophy of Education*, 29, 2, 285–92.

Young, I.M. (1990). *Justice and the Politics of Difference*, Princeton, NJ, Princeton University Press.

PART IV

The Teaching of Religious Education: Case Studies and Recommendations

7

Surveys of Religious Education Policies and Programmes in the UK, the USA, and Australia

Policies and programmes for religious education in western liberal societies vary markedly from country to country. At one extreme we have the situation in the UK where religious education is a compulsory subject for all pupils up to the sixth form; at the other extreme we have the situation in the USA where there is a complete separation of Church and State and denominational religious education is prohibited in state schools. Somewhere in between are countries like Australia where denominationally based religious education, while prohibited from the official curriculum in state schools, can be taught during school hours by visiting religious representatives. However, in nearly all western countries religious studies, as an educational rather than faith-oriented subject, may be taught as an elective study, and the number of pupils choosing it is steadily growing.

There is, similarly, a wide variety of ways of teaching this subject, ranging from traditional confessional approaches to very open-ended, multi-faith and pupil-centred courses, using a range of methodologies such as phenomenological, sociological, historical, and philosophical. We will examine the various programmes in religious education using criteria developed in the previous six chapters to assess their appropriateness for today's multi-faith, pluralist democracies.

The criteria are as follows: in Chapter 1 we develop a contemporary model of liberal education which draws on the three essential criteria of critical rationality, personal transcendence, and epistemological coherence which are important features of any religious education programme. Chapter 2 investigates four philosophical challenges which may be mounted against religious education programmes and discusses how they can be avoided. These are the problems of scepticism, exclusivism, relativism, and reductionism. We need to assess how well various programmes respond to such philosophical challenges, especially as these problems are implicit in any multi-faith study. In Chapter 3 we develop the model of extended pluralism as an appropriate epistemological methodology for the teaching of religious education. In this approach questions of the truth status of the various positions studied, religious or non-religious, are not prejudged and no one position is given privileged status. This model draws upon the concept of epistemic liberalism and provides a useful criterion for evaluating religious education programmes in pluralist, liberal democracies. Chapter 4 explores the pluralist predicament and develops the case for critical realism as an appropriate epistemological response to this dilemma. Associated with this approach is the use of models, myths, and metaphors as useful tools for exploring religious experience. These enable us to adapt traditional religious understandings to contemporary experience. It will be found that syllabuses vary to the extent to which they use and explore such models. Chapter 5 develops an argument for an ethics of belief which stresses the duty to pay careful attention to the evidence for our beliefs. This obligates us to attend to the truth status of religious beliefs and their moral implications – issues requiring a philosophical perspective in the study of religions. Finally, in Chapter 6 the values of comprehensive liberalism are developed as a criterion for resolving disputes between the competing rights and responsibilities of parents, children, and the State in religious upbringing.

We will now consider religious education policies and programmes in the UK, the USA, and Australia in the light of these considerations, beginning in each case with a brief introduction to government policies and provisions for religious education in general. We will apply the criteria in a flexible way, focusing particularly on those cases where they are either strongly present or noticeably absent. We will only examine government-endorsed programmes, not those specific to denominational schools, as it is the former where the public debate has been focused.

UNITED KINGDOM

Government Policies on Religious Education in England and Wales

In the United Kingdom there are three separate systems of education: (i) England and Wales, (ii) Scotland, and (iii) Northern Ireland. Owing to considerations of space we will focus in this chapter just on the situation in England and Wales.

The 1944 Education Act made religious education compulsory for all schools fully funded by the State and each day was to begin or end with an act of collective worship. The Act further required that religious education be taught in accordance with an Agreed Syllabus drafted by a conference representing each Local Education Authority of which there were over one hundred. The conference consisted of four committees comprising representatives of the Church of England, other local religious denominations, the teachers' unions and the local authorities. Each group had one vote and decisions needed to be unanimous. Religious education was not to be denominational but it was assumed it would be basically Christian in character. Parents had the right to withdraw their children from religious education classes but this right was rarely exercised.

Apart from schools fully funded by the government (known as county schools) there were, and still are, a range of voluntary schools (from 1998 to be called foundation schools) which are partly funded by religious bodies. Of these there are three types: Aided, Special Agreement and Controlled. The first two of these organise their own form of religious education while the Controlled schools follow the pattern of the county schools in teaching from an agreed syllabus. All of the schools mentioned thus far come under the broad banner of 'maintained schools'; the remaining category comprises the independent or privately funded schools, such as the great public schools, which cater for fewer than 10 per cent of the overall school population and also devise their own form of religious education which tends to be influenced by current trends in the subject.

During the period from 1944 to the present day, major social and cultural developments have led to significant changes to the form of religious education taking place. The first of these developments was the growth of the multi-faith and multicultural society resulting from widespread post-war immigration – particularly from the West Indies and the Indian subcontinent. Another development was a change in educational philosophy from a traditional to a more pupil-centred approach where children were encouraged to think for themselves. A third factor was the increasing decline in the influence of established religions and further secularisation, a process that had already begun before 1944. These changes together led to the development of agreed syllabuses such as those of Birmingham (1975) and Hampshire (1978) which reflected a move towards multi-faith and critical enquiry approaches to the study of religion. Such approaches became widespread by the 1980s.

This set the scene for the 1988 Education Reform Act which reinforced the existing dual system of schooling but established a National Curriculum to be followed by all publicly supported schools. Religious education, while remaining compulsory (although the only subject with an explicit 'opt-out' clause) and thus part of the basic curriculum, was not made part of the National Curriculum. The 1988 Reform Act extended both religious education and the act of collective worship to all pupils up to the sixth form and went further in stating that the act of worship 'shall be wholly or mainly of a broadly Christian character'(Great Britain, 1988, Section 7.1). It was made mandatory for each Local Education Authority to set up a Standing Advisory Council on Religious Education (SACRE). (This had previously been optional.) It was to have the same four membership groups as the Agreed Syllabuses Conferences and have a broad supervisory role regarding religious education in its own area. The Act requires that any new or revised agreed syllabuses must now 'reflect the fact that the religious traditions in Great Britain are in the main Christian while taking account of the teaching and practices of other principal religions represented in Great Britain' (Great Britain, 1988, Section 8.3). This represents a compromise position between the conservative Christian groups and those from a more liberal perspective in that while entrenching the place of Christianity as predominant it explicitly acknowledges the reality of a multi-faith society and thus is a move towards recognising the values of comprehensive liberalism as set out in the previous chapter. It also explicitly rules out any notions of indoctrination in religious education, stressing the educational role of the subject.

Alongside the compulsory requirements for religious education which are understood as requiring only one period per week to be devoted to the subject, there has been since the 1950s an elective course at GCSE and A level. This allows more in-depth study of religion and is an examined subject which can be taken as part of an advanced humanities course and is chosen by a growing number of pupils. The GCSE replaced the old GCE (O level) and CSE exams. There is now a 'half GCSE' (short course) in religious education which is quite widely taken.

Programmes in Religious Education

As indicated above, each Local Education Authority works from an Agreed Syllabus for religious education which needs to meet broad government guidelines. The Government's School Curriculum and Assessment Authority (SCAA) published in 1994 two model syllabuses which reflect the authority's understanding of how religious education should be interpreted under the Act. While not being mandatory or designed as actual teaching syllabuses they are meant to act as a guide to the construction of agreed syllabuses. Model 1 is 'structured around the knowledge and understanding of what it means to be a member of a faith community'. Model 2 is 'structured around the knowledge and understanding of the teachings of religions and how these relate to shared human experience' (SCAA, 1994a, Model 1, p. 3). However, both models are very similar and consist primarily of a summary of the teachings of the six major religions represented in Great Britain today. These are Christianity, Buddhism, Hinduism, Islam, Judaism, and Sikhism.

These model syllabuses represent the main official guide to syllabus development in religious education since the 1988 Act and will thus form the focus of our discussion on the British scene.[1] Because they set the guidelines for religious education that will be experienced by all pupils in maintained schools they deserve detailed consideration. The syllabuses have been welcomed in most quarters as representing a significant step forward in acknowledging the multi-faith nature of modern British society. Also they attempt to bring out the educational dimension of religion in stressing how pupils can learn *from* religion as well as learning *about* religion. However, they have at the same time generated considerable controversy with most supporters generally coming from politicians and religious leaders on the one side and most detractors coming from academic religious educators and teachers on the other. The controversy predominantly revolves around the methodology adopted by the model syllabuses for teaching religious education. The model syllabuses analyse religion through studying each religion separately rather than adopting a more thematic or generic approach. Although the possibility of cross-religion studies is acknowledged in the introduction to some of the key stages, this is not developed to any extent in the detailed outlines for each key stage.

One of the main critics of the new syllabuses, John Hull, describes the theology underlying the syllabuses as one of 'religionism', which he defines as 'the form taken by religion when tribalistic or exclusive forms of personal or collective identity are maintained' (Hull, 1996a, p. 161). He sees this as perpetuating divisions between religions and religious groups rather than encouraging interaction and learning from each other. He says, '[w]hen we consider the responsibility of religious education towards the world-wide problems of peace and reconciliation, we are bound to have reservations about an approach which begins not with the assumption of mutuality and dialogue, but with the assumption of separation' (1995, p. 15). Hull and others like him would prefer to see religion studied in a generic way which stresses the common religious experience of humankind. In such an approach, thematic or cross-religion studies would be given far greater prominence.

Another related criticism is the fact that the model syllabuses promote primarily a descriptive approach rather than a critical, questioning, issues-based methodology. This is due to the fact that the content is very largely a summary of the teachings of the different religions. While such information is important, it is felt by many that the pupil's own personal quest for meaning and the philosophical issues of the validity and truth status of the beliefs presented need to be given more prominence.

There is also the danger of assuming that any one interpretation of a religion accurately captures its 'essence'. The accounts of the various religions in the model syllabuses are based on the views of small groups of selected spokespersons as presented in the *Faith Communities' Working Group Reports* (SCAA, 1994b). As Jackson (1997, p. 69) argues, such descriptions should be balanced against 'more personal accounts which link individual experience to social experience' and 'which give more recognition to the internal diversity of religious traditions, and, incidentally, [give] attention to religious phenomena that do not fit neatly into taxonomies based on six world religions'.

A further limitation of the syllabuses is the fact that despite the recognition in the introduction to Key Stage One that some of the pupils will have no religious beliefs, a non-religious or humanist perspective is not included at any stage.[2] This represents a serious limitation for a programme dealing with matters of personal belief in the closing years of the twentieth century. As the Religious Education Council working party report states, 'if RE is "open" it is necessary for pupils to learn that there are many who do not believe or practise a theistic or religious world-view. Indeed if pupils did not learn this, it could be said they were victims of indoctrination' (Religious Education Council of England and Wales, 1991, p. 42). Similarly, in terms of the arguments presented in this book, the absence of such a perspective fails to meet our criteria of extended pluralism as the appropriate methodology for teaching religious education.

Some of those who have felt this way have developed an alternative syllabus called the 'Third Perspective', which employs a wider definition of religion and is relevant to all pupils whether they are believers, atheists, or non-committed. The authors of the 'Third Perspective' divide the syllabus into seven major areas of enquiry: Who Are We? (The Human Condition); The Natural World (Cosmology); Looking Further (Metaphysics); Morality (Ethics); Religious Practices (Ritual); People and Communities (Social); and Communication and Expression (Language and Symbol) (Bowness, 1995, p. 39). The ideas of the various religious and non-religious world views would be explored in relation to these seven topics. They see this as preferable to treating each religion in isolation. While the syllabus has no official status, it represents a suggested approach which is felt to be a valid alternative and more in line with current liberal thinking about religious education in representing a

136

stress on personal development rather than religious understanding as the key goal of religious education.

A further criticism which can be made of the model syllabuses is their lack of any overarching analytical schema for cross-religion or thematic studies, as for instance given by Smart's (1968) six dimensions of religion which provide children with some means of making sense of the bewildering array of world religions. A second major shortcoming is an absence of any significant discussion and use of different methodologies which are available for analysing and evaluating religions, such as the phenomenological, sociological, theological, historical, or philosophical. The methodology used seems to be primarily theological in which the major doctrines of each religion are presented separately. As we will see when we come to discuss the Australian studies of religion syllabuses, one way of implementing such an approach is in the NSW syllabus which explicitly acknowledges its use of a multi-methodological approach to study religion and draws upon the phenomenological, historical, sociological, and theological dimensions.

Regarding the question of how the syllabuses respond to the philosophical challenges of scepticism, exclusivity, relativism, and reductionism there is some cause for concern. In treating the six religions as largely self-contained and independent belief systems, one generates significant problems in how to deal with conflicting truth claims and the related questions of exclusivity and relativism. Very little attention is given to these important epistemological issues in the syllabuses.

In spite of the above criticisms there are some strong points in the model syllabuses which tend to have been neglected by some of the critics. In the introduction to each key stage there is a useful distinction between what the pupils can learn *about* religion and what they can learn *from* religion. The learning from religion is particularly valuable in relating the material they study to the pupil's own search for meaning. This is further developed in the outlines for the different religions under the heading of Different Learning Experiences. For example, from Key Stage Three, under Christianity 3a, we have, 'Share experiences of making important decisions in their lives, and what influenced their choices' (SCAA, 1994a, Model 1, p. 43). Key Stage Four, Christianity 4a and 4b, lists the following: 'Reflect on things which have an emotional or spiritual relevance in their own lives, and the reason for their importance' (SCAA, 1994a, Model 1, p. 61). Another strong point is the listing of the skills and processes in religious education including such things as investigation, interpretation, reflection, evaluation, analysis, synthesis, and application which provide a useful elucidation of significant goals in religious education. As well, key attitudes that the syllabuses state should be developed, such as commitment to a set of values, fairness, respect, self-understanding, and enquiry, are all relevant to any modern religious education course.

Another positive aspect of the syllabuses is the provision of generally clear and accurate information on each of the six religions, which provides a useful resource. However, as argued above, such information should not be seen as capturing the 'essence' of any religion and needs to be supplemented by other sources of data on the various religions (such as that provided by ethnographic studies as in the Warwick RE project – see Jackson, 1997, Chapter 5). At least the model syllabuses do acknowledge that the information given does not have to be used exactly as it is presented there. In the introduction to the syllabuses it is stated that an agreed syllabus conference wishing to use the models could: 'use various sections unchanged; select materials from different sections to draw up their own models; adapt the sections for their own purposes; use parts of the sections and add others of their own devising' (SCAA, 1994a, Model 1, p. 61).

Furthermore, if we take the criteria developed in this book, we find a number of examples where these are given strong mention. With reference to critical rationality, the introduction to Key Stage Three suggests that pupils 'follow or take part in debates on religious or moral issues clearly identifying contrasting views and giving well-argued reasons for taking one view rather than another'. In regard to personal transcendence, in the introduction to Key Stage Four it is suggested that pupils should learn from religion by 'beginning to formulate their own responses to life's issues, and recognising that life poses questions which remain puzzling'. The importance of epistemological coherence is promoted in the introduction to Key Stage Three where pupils are encouraged to learn from religion by 'relating their knowledge of religions to other curricula areas and their general knowledge of the world'. In the same place, the values of an ethics of beliefs are strongly promoted in the expectation of students 'developing a sense of responsibility in relation to the community, and relationships in the community'. Once again in the same place, the values of comprehensive liberalism are highlighted in the requirement of pupils 'developing positive attitudes towards other people and their right to hold different beliefs by developing an understanding of how beliefs and values contribute to personal identity'. In Key Stage Four it is stated that pupils could 'explore the values of metaphor, allegory and symbolism as a means of expressing deeply held feelings and convictions' which reflects our discussion of both the importance and fruitfulness of models in analysing religions and its role in adapting religion to their own lives. The philosophical dimension of religious education studies is recognised in the introduction to Key Stage Three where pupils are to learn from religion by 'considering questions of meaning, e.g., the existence of God and the problem of suffering, what characterises these questions and why they are difficult to answer'. Further, in Key Stage Four there is the expectation that 'pupils should also be comparing the teachings of religions on key moral and metaphysical questions'.

If interpreted carefully and flexibly, these model syllabuses do provide some useful guidelines to the construction of appropriate agreed syllabuses for modern-day British pupils. However, their key weakness is their lack of a generic approach to the study of religion and their primary stress on a descriptive rather than issues-based methodology. Such approaches are essential for helping students make sense of the complexities of a multi-faith society and so be able to work out for themselves a suitable response to the issues of meaning and purpose in life. These shortcomings may require some additional modifications in the future building on the positive aspects that are already there.

UNITED STATES OF AMERICA

Government Policies on Religious Education

The situation regarding religious education in the public schools in the USA is the opposite to that in the UK. In America there is a complete separation of Church and State and no denominationally-based religious education is allowed in public schools. The First Amendment to the Constitution states: 'Congress shall make no law respecting an establishment of religion or prohibiting the free exercise thereof.' Those prohibitions were extended to the states by the Fourteenth Amendment. They are often referred to as the Establishment Clause and the Free Exercise Clause.

There has therefore been a long-standing secular tradition in American education which arose historically out of a desire to avoid the religious feuding that took place in Europe. There has always been a private, church school presence in American education but it has not had the strong influence that it has had in England and other European countries. The idea of the 'common' or public school which was to serve as a non-sectarian unifying force for all the different groups in America was strongly promoted by educational thinkers such as Horace Mann (1796–1859) and John Dewey (1859–1952). The following quotation from Horace Mann, writing in 1837, is indicative of this powerful tradition in American education:

> ... the tendency of the private school system is to assimilate our modes of education to those of England, where churchmen and dissenters – each sect according to its own creed – maintain separate schools, in which children are taught, from their tenderest years to wield the sword of polemics with fatal dexterity; and where the gospel, instead of being a temple of peace, is converted into an armory of deadly weapons, for social, interminable warfare. Of such disastrous consequences, there is but one remedy and one preventive. It is the elevation of the common schools. (1957 [1837], p. 33)

The trend towards secularisation has intensified in the twentieth century. In 1925 the Supreme Court explicitly required all states to apply the First Amendment (through the due process requirements of the Fourteenth Amendment) to their schools. This made the legal prohibition of religion clear to all and various court decisions over the ensuing years have confirmed and extended this prohibition. In 1948 visiting ministers were no longer allowed in state schools. In 1962 the saying of prayers and in 1963 Bible readings were ruled illegal. Similarly, restrictions on State aid to private schools were extended throughout the 1970s, the only significant form of support now allowed is through tax concessions for educational expenses incurred in sending children to such schools. The only way in which any religious education of a sectarian variety is allowed for public school pupils is through the use of 'released time' provisions whereby classes may be held by the churches during the last part of agreed school days where children who wish to attend are released early.

Overall, the proportion of children attending state schools in the US is higher than in England or Australia. Only about 12 per cent of pupils in America attend private schools. These have traditionally been mainly Roman Catholic but in recent years the number of Catholic school students has declined at the same time as a massive growth in the number of fundamentalist Protestant school pupils has occurred. There are now well over one million children in this latter category. This represents a somewhat worrying trend in the light of concerns expressed in other parts of this book (Chapters 5 and 6) about religious fundamentalism. This concern is exacerbated by the fact that many of these schools have substandard facilities (for example they are often located in church basements) and under-qualified teachers. They also often refuse to obtain State accreditation. That such schools are popular is due in large part to what some parents see as the prevailing 'secular humanistic' ethos of the State system.

Fundamentalist Christian attempts to influence government policy on education have a long history. Various subjects have been criticised on religious grounds such as physical education because of the dress required; dancing, as conflicting with religious beliefs; English because of the use of unsuitable literary texts; history due to what is seen as unfavourable representation of religious events; and moral education and sex education because these are not specifically taught in terms of Biblical requirements. One area that has created particular controversy is biology, in regard to the teaching of evolution. Certain states were even pressured to enact laws forbidding the teaching of evolution. A famous legal case took place in Tennessee in 1923 when John Scopes was found guilty of infringing that state's so-called 'monkey law'. The conviction was later overturned on a technicality.

In more recent years and particularly in the period from the 1960s to the present day, there has been a continuing skirmish between fundamentalists and liberals on the issue of what should be taught about the origins of life in biology courses. Some states (for example, Arkansas and Mississippi) attempted to ban the teaching of evolution but this was ruled unconstitutional in 1966. Following their loss in this case the fundamentalists pushed for the notion of a 'balanced curriculum' whereby both evolution and creation science were to be given equal coverage and legislation requiring this was passed in over 20 states. This was eventually also ruled unconstitutional by the Supreme Court in 1987 on the grounds that the teaching of creationism represented a promotion of religion and was, therefore, an infringement of the First Amendment. This is where the matter stands legally at the present time but the issue is by no means dead and there is continuing pressure from fundamentalists in regard to school curricula in this area.

We may conclude this section on American policies regarding religious education[3] by noting that the First Amendment restriction on the teaching of religion in schools allows two important exceptions: (i) in the case of private schools denominational religious education is allowed; and (ii) in the case of state schools, education *about* religion or religious studies is also allowed. We will now turn to examine what programmes are available in relation to the latter.

Programmes in Religious Education

The complexities of the constitutional debate surrounding the teaching of religion in public schools has given rise to considerable confusion on the part of teachers as to what they can teach about religion; to considerable caution on the part of textbook publishers against including any materials on religion at all; to a very careful and cautious drafting by district Boards of Education on policies about teaching about religion in public schools; and to a dearth of courses at the tertiary level in public institutions for preparing teachers to teach religion in schools. A further level of difficulty is the controversy and debate surrounding the interpretation of 'teaching about religion', as is constitutionally permissible, and whether this entails teaching about religion only within the context of other courses currently in the curriculum such as history, art, music, and literature or whether it permits teaching courses about religion, such as studies of religion courses in the UK and Australia, which exist as areas of study in their own right. The cumulative result of this is the virtual absence of studies of religion courses across the USA in public schools. A positive outcome, nevertheless, from this caution about studies of religion has been to focus attention on what the educational outcomes of such courses should be and the appropriate methodology for teaching them.

In discussing the state of religious studies in public schools, Warren Nord comments that several states (California, North Carolina, and Utah) require the study of religion in schools and there is interest in many others, but in the vast majority of cases religion is taught by inclusion in other subjects, not as a subject in its own right (1995, p. 316). A 1989 survey showed that only three states (Idaho, Tennessee, and Wisconsin) actually licensed religion teachers, and only four others (California, Idaho, Wisconsin, and Michigan) had laws or regulations dealing with the preparation of teachers to teach about religion (Nord, 1995, p. 316).

Consideration of a few specific examples will show the caution with which this whole issue is approached. In formulating its policy, the Committee on Religion in the Curriculum in the Des Moines County, Iowa, documents the general state of confusion on studies of religion while endeavouring to provide teachers, parents, and administrators with a clear set of guidelines on how to include religion in the curriculum. It notes that:

> teachers have transferred the aversion to teaching about religion to other topics and many times will ignore teaching about and/or discussing decisions of conscience because of a mistaken belief that to teach about social and moral responsibility is to teach religion. (Haynes, 1994, Chapter 6)

Similar results can be found in other states. Research by Pamela Sisemore in California and Hawaii about teachers' knowledge of what the Constitution says about religion, of their knowledge of recent court decisions about religion in schools, and their knowledge of religion in the curriculum, concludes teachers are either uninformed or misinformed about the appropriate role of religion in schools (Sisemore, 1994).

The Des Moines committee suggests this situation exists because 'almost no policies in schools governing the role of religion in the curriculum' are to be found and that 'supplementary volumes and curricula in these areas are rarely readily available in school libraries and other teacher support networks and, in most cases, do not exist'. In reviewing the teaching about religion in the state of Iowa it noted there were only four elective courses on religion across the state (one of these, Religion in Human Culture, it commended) and that in schools where it was taught by inclusion in other subject areas it invariably lacked clear educational objectives. In redressing this situation the committee sets out a short but sound policy with the following highlights. Firstly, in contrast with the UK, it gives no preference to any one religion over another and, more significantly, to any religion over non-religion or vice versa. Secondly, while the policy is neutral regarding religion it does not imply indifference, recommending that 'teachers honestly, fairly and forthrightly teach about religion'. Thirdly, the policy recommends both separate courses for the study of religion as well as teaching about the role and influence of religion in subjects such as history, literature, art, music, science, or other relevant areas where religion has played a part. Fourthly, the teaching methodology should be one which exposes students to a variety of religious views, it should be academic and not devotional in approach, and encourage tolerance of various religious beliefs and 'an understanding about religion as an important cornerstone of a pluralistic and democratic society' (Haynes, 1994, Appendix B). These policy objectives would certainly be consistent with the criteria outlined in this book. The major objection against them is that the policy seems to imply a descriptive approach – historical, sociological, and so on – rather than an analytic and evaluative one.

The Des Moines, Iowa, policy contrasts strongly, for example, with those of the Wicomico County Board of Education in Salisbury, Maryland, or the St Louis Park public schools in Minneapolis, Minnesota, which opt for teaching about religion within the context of other curricula subjects, such as literature, music, drama, and the arts, rather than as a study in its own right. Yet, like the Iowa policy, they stress the need for strong educational objectives to underpin its inclusion in the curriculum.

One of the outcomes of this protracted debate about the place of religion in public schools is the close consideration given to the educational justification and methodology for such courses. In setting out the rationale and guidelines for teaching about religion, Charles Haynes gives the following useful six principles:

1. The schools approach to religion is academic, not devotional.
2. The school strives for student *awareness* of religions, but does not press for student *acceptance* of any one religion.
3. The school sponsors *study* about religion, not the *practice* of religion.
4. The school *exposes* students to a diversity of religious views; it does not *impose* any particular view.
5. The school *educates* about all religions; it does not *promote* or *denigrate* any religion.
6. The school *informs* students about various beliefs; it does not seek to *conform* students to any particular belief. (Haynes, 1994)

Haynes sees these six principles as built on the '"Three Rs" of religious liberty' which he cites as rights, responsibilities, and respect. This commitment to an open-ended study of religion which respects the right of the individual to develop her or his own belief system is good as far as it goes, but it has one serious shortcoming – it avoids dealing with the truth status or validity of those beliefs. Not to be concerned about whether another's beliefs are true or false might in fact be construed as not respecting that person at all. To allow another to persist in error seems to be inconsistent with respecting that person. Haynes has two problems here. The first is that to assess beliefs as true or false might be seen to conflict with his fifth principle above which avoids denigrating another's beliefs. But, not to do so gives rise to possible conflict between his first and fifth principles in that academic discourse (Principle 1) rightly concerns itself about the validity of claims. A way out for Haynes is to adopt a comparative, rather than evaluative, approach to the study of religion, which is what he suggests, '[s]tructural parallels ... may be a helpful way to organise the class discussion. It is appropriate to compare and contrast the different perspectives different religious groups might have...' (Haynes, 1994). But he cautions against any 'qualitative comparisons between religions' or claims that one religion is superior to another.

This reluctance to assess the validity of truth claims is a general weakness of many studies of religion courses, here as elsewhere, as we have pointed out. Haynes, however, is aware of this and warns of the ensuing dangers of relativism and reductionism, but ultimately his hands are tied. The second and more serious problem Haynes confronts in any attempt to assess the truth status of religious beliefs is that it leaves the teacher or school open to legal action from parents as an infringement of their right to the free exercise of religion. Nord seems to adopt a stronger position in regard to Haynes' first problem. He comments:

> [w]e cannot help but be aware of many different, often conflicting ways of making sense of the world. And we have come to believe – in most fields, if not always in religion – that it is through a self-conscious, critical consideration of the alternatives that we are most likely to acquire truth. (1995, p. 200)

Nord acknowledges the pluralist and multi-faith nature of societies which confront pupils today and the need for approaching this welter of competing truth claims through critical reflection and evaluation. He contends, consistent with the position adopted in this book, that the appropriate context for religious education is within the liberal education tradition which 'initiate[s] students into a self-conscious search for better, more reasonable, more humane ways of thinking and acting ... [and which] *liberates* students from parochialism by enabling them to see and feel the world in new ways' (Nord, 1995, p. 200). Nord's position, however, seems to be well ahead of much of the general debate on this issue. He would in fact like to see religious studies as a core part of the education of all school students.

In conclusion, we can note the following aspects of the US situation. The general tendency is to teach studies of religion within the context of other subjects such as history, social studies, art, and music, and not as a study in its own right; studies of religion is not part of a national curriculum as in the UK, rather some states require the study of religion in the curriculum, others permit it as an elective within certain policy guidelines, others again have no formal position. On the whole, the debate about the role of studies of religion as a subject in its own right seems to be hindered by concerns of legal action by parents who can take the school and teachers to court. Perhaps the way ahead is for some test cases to be heard on the right of schools as academic institutions to assess the validity of the propositions studied in religious education courses. The overall progress of US schools towards the adoption of studies of religion programmes in schools seems at present to be considerably behind that of the UK or Australia, but there is a growing interest in attempting to improve the situation.

AUSTRALIA

Government Policies on Religious Education

From the beginning of white settlement in 1788 up to the 1870s the provision for education of any sort was generally unsystematic and inadequate. As late as the 1870s only about half of the children of school age attended school at all. Both public schools and church schools existed and were supported in varying degrees by the state colonial governments with there being a good deal of rivalry and hostilities between the two sectors.

A growing movement towards free, compulsory, and secular education culminated in a series of Education Acts in all states between 1872 and 1893 which established government school systems with compulsory attendance to about age 12 and withdrew financial aid to church schools. As a result of the Acts the number of Anglican schools declined significantly, while the number of Catholic schools greatly expanded. This dual system of private and public schools has survived to the present day with between 25 per cent and 30 per cent of all students presently educated in private schools.

In recent years there has been a rise in the number of Anglican and some other Protestant schools as well as significant growth in Christian fundamentalist schools but the Catholic system remains by far the largest in the private schools sector. In the 1960s, political, social, and economic changes in Australia led to the reintroduction of State aid to church schools in all states and this remains to the present day.

Religious education in government schools was allowed to the extent of weekly denominational classes held by visiting ministers from various churches. The major development of recent years has been the introduction in all states of studies of religion programmes which, as discussed earlier in this book, are designed to provide education in religion rather than education in faith.[4]

Programmes in Religious Education

We will now examine studies of religion programmes in the three largest Australian states, New South Wales, Victoria, and Queensland, as these provide a representative sample and cover almost three-quarters of the Australian population. We are focusing on the studies of religion syllabuses, as these reflect the major current development in the teaching of religion in schools, and provide an educational model for all those involved in the teaching of religion. Increasingly, such syllabuses are taking the place of the more traditional education in faith syllabuses in church schools and provide a new curriculum area in state schools. The reason for their growth in popularity is partly due to the fact that they are given status as a part of the official curriculum and can be counted for matriculation purposes. Another significant reason is that they are specifically designed to be relevant to pupils living in a multicultural society and are more open-ended in their approach to teaching religion. We will restrict our discussion to the syllabuses available in the final two years of the secondary school as they represent the most in-depth educational development of the subject. By 1992, all Australian states offered studies of religion as an elective matriculation course. Because these three syllabuses have had such a major impact on thinking about religious education in Australia and are attracting increasing numbers of students annually, we will analyse them in some detail.

Queensland's Study of Religion Senior Syllabus

We will begin by examining the programme in Queensland as, of any of the Australian syllabuses, this seems to meet our criteria for a desirable studies of religion programme the best. The course is set out in the Queensland Board of Secondary School Studies document, *Study of Religion: Senior Syllabus*, 1995 (henceforth referred to as Qld). The course was officially approved in 1989 but, up to this point, has been used only in a limited number of schools, mainly those with a church affiliation.

The aims of the syllabus include such goals as helping students understand their own patterns of belief and how these shape their experiences, how various aspects of human experience prompt a religious interpretation of life, and the various roles that religions play in society.

The course is designed to last over the two final high school years and is composed of four semester units. Unit 1, entitled Religion and Human Experience, has two sections: the first covers the nature of religion, the second examines religions of the world and at least three religions are studied. Unit 2, Religion in Society, is devoted to an analysis of religion in Australian society and is followed by an elective chosen from topics such as Ritual, Religion/State relations, Sacred Writings, and Ethics. Unit 3 looks at Religion in a Pluralistic World and involves a field study of a religion in the local community and the choice of a second elective study. Unit 4, The Search for Meaning, aims to draw together insights gained from the previous three units and relate these to the students' personal search for meaning and is organised around six themes which are origins, purpose, destiny, identity, values, and authority (Qld, 1995, pp. 13–17).

Let us now see how the programme meets some of the criteria for religious education in a multi-faith, pluralist society listed above. In the first place, the liberal education criterion of critical rationality is given prominence in the syllabus where factors such as openness, the avoidance of proselytising, and the encouragement of such abilities as distinguishing between factual statements and value judgements, testing hypotheses against available evidence, and clarifying and justifying personal value positions are stressed (Qld, 1995, pp. 3–5). These factors also reflect a commitment to an ethics of belief as discussed in Chapter 5.

Secondly, the Queensland syllabus realises well the need to relate the study of religion to the students' own search for meaning (what we have called personal transcendence). In this regard the following important statement in the document is indicative:

> Studying religion can assist in the development of an understanding of the ways in which a particular cultural context has influenced and continues to influence the formation in individuals of a world view and a framework of beliefs in the light of which experience is interpreted. (Qld, 1995, p. 1)

A range of affective objectives are spelt out which include 'a desire to advance both self-knowledge and an understanding of the contextual factors contributing to the shaping of one's own life' (Qld, 1995, p. 6).

Unit 4 of the programme is particularly valuable in helping children work out their own position on issues of ultimate concern. The six key areas examined all raise very interesting issues that would have particular relevance for adolescents. Some examples of the questions included under these headings are: Where do I come from? Does life have a purpose? Must there be suffering? Is this life all there is? Am I free or only a puppet? What is worthwhile? In whom or what does authority lie? These and similar issues would all be of interest to students whether they hold religious views in the traditional sense or not. Such topics are similar to those listed in the 'Third Perspective' syllabus in the UK.

The criterion of epistemological coherence as discussed above has both an internal and an external dimension. The internal dimension relates to the internal consistency of the programme, and the Queensland syllabus is again strong here. The various elements of the course support each other in a meaningful way and there is a consistent overall philosophy of an open-ended educational study of religion guiding all aspects of the syllabus. The external dimension relates to relationships with other subjects in the curriculum. The key thing to watch for here is that children are not presented with contradictory epistemological messages in different areas of their studies. This has happened in the past, for example, with religious education based on an education in faith perspective, where children may be taught that in the event of a conflict between religious and scientific accounts of say, creation, they should accept the religious account. Alternatively, in science they may be taught the opposite order of priority should obtain. Given the attention in this syllabus to factors such as rationality, openness, and justification, there does not seem much danger in this regard. Reference is made in Unit 4 of the syllabus to drawing on other subject areas as well as religion in exploring basic questions of meaning and purpose:

> In exploring these questions, reference can be made to some ways in which people engage in the continual search for answers to life's questions, including reference to literature, the arts, the sciences and popular culture. By linking these to the doctrines and teachings of belief systems, the students can gain some skill in recognising and, if necessary, in dealing with such questions and the faith responses which they might elicit. (Qld, 1995, 17)

This is a promising suggestion and is enhanced by a list of useful resources such as print and electronic media which may be helpful in this regard (Qld, 1995, p. 55).

In terms of breadth of coverage, the Queensland syllabus is also reasonably strong. In Unit 1, Section 2, at least three religions must be studied as indicated above. In Unit 4 a range of different religious beliefs about such things as human suffering, death, personal identity, morality, and authority are explored. There is also some examination of non-religious responses to such issues but this is one aspect that seems underemphasised and could have been developed more to bring out the full range of possible responses.

Two particularly valuable elements of the Queensland syllabus are the elective on ethics in Unit 2 and the introduction to philosophy of religion contained in Unit 4 (where, for example, some of the traditional arguments for the existence of God are explored, along with the problem of evil). While both of these would perhaps be rather intellectually demanding for some students, they provide a very useful introduction to philosophical issues in ethics and religion and could develop in students a desire to pursue these subjects at tertiary level. These units dealing with philosophical issues in ethics and religion will also have the added advantage of helping to develop the ability to evaluate critically and assess the merits of conflicting religious propositions. This will also promote the values of an ethics of belief.

The Queensland course also accords well with the extended pluralist approach to the teaching of religion discussed in Chapter 3, as is evident from the following stated objective:

> All students and teachers participating in these courses bring their own beliefs, understandings and values to the study. Within the educational approach, no assumption is made about the teacher and students sharing a common set of beliefs, understandings and traditions ... The commitment to an educational approach ensures that Study of Religion is available to all schools throughout Queensland and units developed are relevant to all students. (Qld, 1995, p. 3)

Finally, the comprehensive liberal values criterion (from Chapter 6) which stresses the importance of developing positive tolerance in pupils towards others religions and communities is recognised explicitly in the rationale for the syllabus:

> The study of a range of religions and the understanding of alternative ways of viewing reality can make a valuable contribution to cross-cultural harmony and mutual enrichment. Ignorance of the integrity of the world view of others can lead to rejection or prejudice against them, sometimes to the point of violence. (Qld, 1995, p. 1)

We may conclude that the Queensland programme is a very useful one and, with a few exceptions, satisfies well our basic criteria for religious education in a pluralist society.

The NSW Studies of Religion Course

The NSW studies of religion course (NSW Board of Studies [henceforth NSW], 1994, 1996) was introduced in 1992 and is one of the fastest growing subjects at Higher School Certificate (HSC) level, increasing in pupil numbers at 30 per cent per annum and currently representing over 10 per cent of the HSC candidature. It is mainly studied in church schools where it is sometimes made a compulsory unit. The course has a wide variety of options which is one of its strongest features. This wide choice even extends to the option of undertaking the course as either a one-unit or two-unit course. If we consider the two-unit course, the student spends 20 per cent of course time on Foundation Studies, which involves a brief study of the five core religions of Buddhism, Christianity, Hinduism, Islam, and Judaism; a study of Aboriginal beliefs, spiritualities, and some current related problems; an examination of an individual's general search

150

for meaning – both religious and non-religious; a study of the characteristics of religion; the history of Australian Christianity and its flashpoints; and the modern tendency towards religious pluralism. The next 60 per cent of the course is labelled Depth Studies and requires a total of four units to be studied from two major groups. Two units are to be chosen from the first group of Depth Studies of the individual core religions mentioned above. Similarly, two units are to be chosen from the second group of Depth Studies comprising six cross-religion studies analysed from the perspective of at least two religious traditions, in any of the following: Rites of Passage, Sacred Writings and Stories, Teachers and Interpreters, Religion and Ethics, Ways of Holiness, and Women and Religion. The final 20 per cent of the course is accounted for by two Interest Studies chosen from 13 possible units: eight cover the areas of religious biography, architecture, visual arts, literature, music, ecology, the media, and the topic of religion and non-religion; four units investigate the Asian religions of Confucianism, Shinto, Sikhism, and Taoism; the final option is a school-developed unit.

There is plenty of variety in this course and much to sustain the interest of students. The Foundation Studies provide breadth of coverage of religion and of its various characteristics, while the first set of Depth Studies allow a range of religions to be examined more closely to assess critically both the differences between religions and their underlying unity in respect of six components. The second set of Depth Studies allows a detailed analysis of specific aspects of religion. Thus, at least in principle, the course provides an adequate balance between breadth and depth of study. In fact, although it is possible to obtain an in-depth acquaintance of five different religions, in practice (given the present state of teacher preparation to teach such a course) most schools will probably choose to study only two by doubling up on the religions studied in the various components in the course, and hence not achieve sufficient breadth. It is even possible to concentrate mainly on just one religion. This would most likely be Christianity which is the major focus in the Foundation Studies and could also be taken as the Group 1 Depth Study and as the major perspective from which the Group 2 cross-religion studies and the Interest Studies are pursued.

In regard to problems generated by religious diversity, the syllabus introduction contends that encountering such diversity is good as it allows students to 'develop confidence in investigating religion and [to] gain an understanding of the diversity of religion in Australia' (NSW, 1996, p. 5). More generally, the course aims at an 'engagement which will allow students to increase their understanding of religion as a living and pervasive element of human existence' (NSW, 1996, p. 5). To facilitate the analysis of such diversity, the syllabus valuably employs a range of methodologies including theology, history, phenomenology, and sociology (but omits philosophy). This use of multiple methodologies is an attractive feature of the course and as such dictates some of the content selection. For example, in the Foundation Studies, the history of Christianity in Australia and its points of crisis is studied; also, a sociological analysis of religious pluralism in modern Australia is undertaken and students are encouraged to investigate the beliefs and practices of a significant religious group in the Australian context, such as the Greek Orthodox Church (NSW, 1994, pp. 51–3). This is good as far as it goes but one is left with the impression that much of this course is largely descriptive and one wonders to what extent it satisfies the syllabus aim of presenting 'a religious tradition as an integrated belief system [providing] a distinctive answer to the enduring questions of human existence' (NSW, 1996, p. 29). This would seem to be an excellent point at which to introduce students to the long history of philosophical discussion on these 'enduring questions of human existence'. Certainly, the Queensland syllabus very creditably does this in its fourth unit on personal belief systems.

As commented upon in our liberal education model, there is a need for courses to promote critical rationality, personal transcendence, and epistemological coherence. The NSW syllabus reflects a commitment to the first two of these outcomes in its objectives, and states that there is a need for students to develop the 'ability to judge religious issues rationally and with confidence', with the desired outcome being that students would 'value their own critical appreciation of different religions as they seek to establish their own set of religious beliefs and moral and ethical judgments' (NSW, 1996, p. 15).

Yet, although this commitment is clearly stated, there remains the problem that while historical and sociological analysis might well examine the consequences of holding particular beliefs, it leaves untouched the question of their validity. This testing of validity is essential if students are to assess their own religious and ethical beliefs, which is a prerequisite for their achieving the goal of personal transcendence. In fact, the NSW document is ambivalent on this point and cautions teachers that '[students] may have a series of assumptions about their own religion related to their own identity and self-esteem and may feel threatened by critical analysis' (NSW, 1996, p. 6). While this sensitivity is important, still, as the Queensland syllabus shows, the requirements of both sensitivity and critical analysis can be met. That the latter should be included is perhaps confirmed by a recent survey, conducted by the Australian Institute of Biology, of 4,225 first-year university students at 17 Australian universities which showed that one in eight (12.6 per cent) students accepted the creationist view that 'God created man pretty much in his present form at one time within the last 10,000 years' (Pockley, 1992). Clearly, this view conflicts with the evolutionary biology taught in high-school science and represents a significant failure of the criterion of epistemological coherence. One way of responding to such conflicts is to examine explicitly the broad philosophical questions of scepticism, exclusivity, and relativism and the implications that flow from them in relation to religious belief systems. The syllabus document does at least acknowledge one of these issues, that is, exclusivity, in remarking that the 'study [of diverse religious traditions] should demonstrate to students that people who share a religious view of reality have much in common' (NSW, 1991, p. 17).

A related problem is the question of whether this course is designed particularly for believers, that is, only for those who already have a commitment to a specific religion. One might ask what it offers to those students who are sceptical about religious claims but who would like to examine them further with the possibility of incorporating religious beliefs into an integrated belief system embracing a transcendental dimension, or what it offers to those students with doubts about some of their religious beliefs and are looking for clarification? In other words, how can it be improved to meet our criterion of extended pluralism? One possible remedy here would be to add a unit on the philosophy of religion which analyses some of these questions. The Interest Study elective, religion and non-religion, is a step in this direction but there needs to be a broader analysis of philosophical questions arising in religion which could become a compulsory unit. Perceived in this light, the syllabus could more confidently tackle questions of justification and validity of religious belief structures, as well as questions about their diversity, ubiquity, prevalence, and tenacity.

Victoria's Religion and Society Course

In the Victorian studies of religion programme there are two courses: Religion and Society (Victorian Board of Studies, 1994a; Victorian Curriculum and Assessment Board, 1990a [henceforth Victoria 1994a, 1990a]) and Texts and Traditions [henceforth Victoria, 1994b, 1990b]. We will deal here only with the former of these courses which is the one taken by the majority of students studying religion.[5] Religion and Society is made up of four units: Religion and Identity, Ethics, The Search for Meaning, and Challenge and Response. Within each unit, religious traditions are analysed through one or more of the following phenomena: beliefs, myths and stories, texts and sacred literature, rituals, symbols, social structure, codes of behaviour, and religious experience. The influence of the phenomenological approach is evident here and this is acknowledged in the *Course Development Support Material* (Victoria, 1990a, p. 1).

Units 1 and 2 are to be studied through two or more selected religious traditions. Units 3 and 4 may be studied through a single selected religious tradition. Each unit consists of approximately 50 hours of study. Units 1 and 2 are normally taken in Year 11, and Units 3 and 4 in Year 12. Many church schools have introduced this syllabus into their curriculum, many even making the study of at least one unit compulsory. At this stage, however, very few state schools are using the syllabus, which mirrors the trend in the other two states.

The first general impression that one gains on reading the *Study Design* is that it is a rather bland document compared to the Queensland and NSW syllabuses. The units are described in quite general terms and make little reference to specific religious traditions or to how religion can assist in one's personal search for meaning. However, the generality of description does have the advantage of allowing a good deal of flexibility to individual schools to develop programmes to suit their own particular needs. Also, on reading the *Support Material*, the course takes on a lot more vitality and many interesting issues emerge as possible areas for study. But, as with NSW, the course tends to underplay the philosophical dimension and to concentrate on the more descriptive, sociological aspects of religious study. The liberal education criterion of critical rationality is therefore insufficiently developed in most aspects of the course. It does, however, receive some attention in the unit on Ethics, where one of the objectives is that students 'learn the skills of research, analysis and discussion appropriate to the study of ethical issues and decision-making' (Victoria, 1994a, p. 16). And, in their compulsory essay, they are encouraged to 'develop the skill of presenting a reasoned, balanced and coherent position on an ethical issue studied in depth' (Victoria, 1994a, p. 20). Also in Unit 3, The Search for Meaning, one of the objectives is for students to develop 'the skills of investigation, description, analysis and interpretation appropriate to the study of beliefs in human thought and experience' (Victoria, 1994a, p. 22). This is fine as far as it goes but even here, and to a certain extent in the Ethics unit, the emphasis is on describing and understanding arguments that may be made, instead of actually assessing them to see whether they are valid or not.

In relation to our criterion of personal transcendence, the conclusion is similar. There is some attention to this area (mainly in Unit 3, The Search for Meaning) but as with the NSW syllabus it is insufficient to achieve this goal to its proper extent. The role of the course in helping the students develop their own considered position on ultimate issues could be given more stress (but as indicated above, there is at least scope for individual schools to emphasise this aspect more if they so wish). The general emphasis, even in Unit 3, is on understanding and appreciating the experience of others and the role religion plays in society, rather than on seeing what significance all this has for the individual student's own life. This is where Unit 4 of the Queensland syllabus would serve as a useful model.

The Religion and Society syllabus is generally satisfactory as regards internal epistemological consistency with the phenomemological approach at least, giving it a clear and consistent framework. There is a genuine attempt to be fair to all points of view (perhaps too fair, in not giving enough critical evaluation of the merits or otherwise of the range of beliefs surveyed) and to treat religion as a valid area of educational enquiry. In terms of its links with other subjects in the curriculum there is little attention given.

There is a problem with breadth of coverage. As indicated above, students will emerge from the course having studied only two traditions in Units 1 and 2 and generally one tradition in Units 3 and 4. The fact that the *Study Design* points out that there are benefits to be gained (Victoria, 1994a, p. 6) from a wider study does not go far enough to ensure that students really do look at a sufficient range of religions. Our preference stated in Chapter 1 was for a minimum of three, and only the Queensland syllabus ensures this.

In regard to how the Religion and Society syllabus deals with the philosophical issues of scepticism, exclusivity, and relativism in relation to religion, the general lack of emphasis on philosophical modes of investigation (except in the Ethics unit) means that these aspects of religion receive minor attention. Because there is little attempt to assess the validity of religious claims, students may wrongly gain the impression that religious beliefs are unproblematic in terms of epistemological status and are not in many cases mutually exclusive. At the same time they may infer that the religious (or non-religious) beliefs one comes to accept are basically just a matter of how and where you are brought up. All of these matters should be explicitly addressed and students made aware of some of the complex issues involved, if the liberal education and ethics of belief criteria for such a programme alluded to earlier are to be satisfied. In terms of these criteria, the strongest of the four units is the Ethics one, which, interestingly, has the least to do with religious questions *per se*. It would stand in its own right as a useful introduction to moral education for secondary school students, as we have argued elsewhere (Hobson and Edwards, 1992, p. 57). This, in fact, is an area of the total school curriculum in all three states that is presently very underdeveloped as a separate area of study.

The course seems to reflect the key elements of the extended pluralist methodology advocated in Chapter 2 in that it provides 'open inquiry without bias towards any tradition in particular' (Victoria, 1994a, p. 5) and allows for the study of a non-religious tradition in Unit 2.

Mention is made of the use of myths and stories in analysing religious traditions across the four units. However, their function as models and their fruitfulness, both in religion and in other knowledge domains, is not sufficiently developed nor an adequate treatment given to the complex role of myths in religious discourse.

Having now examined the new studies of religion syllabuses in the three states of Queensland, NSW, and Victoria, it is evident that they represent a significant advance in the study of religion at the senior secondary level in Australia and have established religion as a valid matriculation subject. The major step forward lies in the fact that religion is now studied from an educational point of view and has a multi-faith orientation appropriate for current society. These new developments at this stage have been confined largely to church schools but, as the merits of these new courses become more widely known, it is hoped that they will be adopted more generally.

However, as we have argued, all of these new courses leave room for further improvement. Generally, in all three states the syllabuses pay insufficient attention to philosophical approaches to the study of religion, which must be present if the subject is to meet the criteria for religious education in a multi-faith, pluralist democracy outlined at the beginning of this chapter. Religion by its very nature raises fundamental philosophical questions, such as the validity of religious statements, the ethical acceptability of religious moral codes, and the role of the transcendent in informing the pupil's personal search for meaning. The preferred model of religious education argued for throughout this book tries to encapsulate these issues and describes how religious studies should be taught if it is to fully meet such criteria.

The different syllabuses vary in how well they respond to these criteria, with the Queensland one generally the strongest, particularly in terms of personal transcendence and breadth. The NSW syllabus, while in theory catering for a good balance between breadth and depth of study, in practice too easily allows schools to concentrate on just two religious traditions across all of the course (and even here to focus particularly on one of them). The Victorian Religion and Society syllabus has some useful elements, particularly its unit on Ethics, but tends overall to take a largely descriptive approach to religion.

One useful way of addressing some of the common shortcomings of these courses would be to include in all of them a specific unit on the philosophy of religion which would explicitly address the sorts of philosophical issues mentioned above. Unit 4 of the Queensland syllabus is a useful step in this direction but needs further development to realise this goal more fully. Such a unit could include, for example, an examination of the history and articulation of the grounds for religious belief, possible responses to the problem of evil, and evaluation of the debate between the scientific and religious world views. Naturally, these topics could not be pursued in the same depth as at tertiary level, but nevertheless students could be introduced to these in a stimulating and intelligible way.

CONCLUSION

We may conclude this survey of government policies and programmes in religious education in the UK, the USA, and Australia by noting that of the three countries, the programmes are significantly more developed and widely adopted in the UK and Australia than in the USA. However, the only country where religious education is taken by all pupils is the UK (which also offers the possibility of an additional elective course in the subject). In Australia, the subject is an elective taken by a minority of pupils but the numbers are growing significantly each year in most states. In the USA, as yet only a small number of states provide separate courses in religious studies but there is now a growing interest in the subject and those planning further development in the area could profitably look to British and Australian models for useful ideas.

In all three countries there has been a recognition of the need to make religious education multi-faith and non-confessional if it is to play its proper role in a liberal, democratic, pluralist society. Religious education has become an educationally valid subject which can make an important contribution to the liberal education of all students. However, in most existing programmes there is one aspect that requires further development. This is the need for more stress on the subject's role in assisting the pupils' own search for meaning and the associated requirement for more attention to issues of truth status, validity, and moral acceptability of the religious beliefs under examination, especially in the senior years of study.

NOTES

1. Apart from the model syllabuses there have been a range of other influences on the construction of agreed syllabuses. Among these are a number of research projects in religious education centred in universities that focus more specifically on curriculum development and teaching methodology in the subject. Two of the most interesting and influential of these are the University of Birmingham's 'Gift to the Child Approach' (Hull, 1996b) and the University of Warwick's 'Warwick RE Project' (Jackson, 1996, 1997).

   In the Birmingham model a religious item is chosen for presentation to the pupil (this might be a word, sound, story, page, statue, or even a person), the aim being to convey its educational and religious gifts to the children. Pupils are encouraged to interact with the religious phenomenon at an imaginative level and to reflect on their experience of it and thus deepen their understanding of their own and other people's religious experience.

   The Warwick model involves ethnographic studies of various religious communities in Britain, focusing on the transmission of religious culture to the young. The data are then used to generate religious education materials which reflect the richness and internal diversity of the various religious traditions.

2. The key stages are the periods in each pupil's schooling to which the National Curriculum applies. There are four such stages, normally related to the age of the majority of the pupils in the teaching group: Stage 1, 5–7; Stage 2, 7–11; Stage 3, 11–14; Stage 4, 14–16.

3. The factual information reported in this section is based on material in the following references (from which more detailed information may be gained): Boyer (1992), Lines (1988), Nord (1995), Provenzo (1990), and Tavel (1979).

4. The factual information reported in this section is based on material in the following references (from which more detailed information may be gained): Barcan (1980), Jones (1974), and Partridge (1968).

5. For a discussion of the Victorian Text and Traditions course, see Hobson and Edwards (1994), pp. 294–7.

REFERENCES

Barcan, A. (1980). *A History of Australian Education*, Melbourne, Oxford University Press.

Bowness, C. (1995). 'Keeping the RE Debate Open: The "3rd" Perspective Syllabus', in V. Barnett et al., *World Religions in Education 1995–6: From Syllabuses to Schemes – Planning and Teaching Religious Education*, London, Shap Working Party on World Religions in Education.

Boyer, E. (1992). 'Teaching Religion in the Public Schools and Elsewhere', *Journal of the American Academy of Religion*, 60, 515–24.

Great Britain: Public General Acts (1988). *Education Reform Act*, London, HMSO.

Haynes, C.C. (1994). *Finding Common Ground: A First Amendment Guide to Religion and Public Education*, Nashville, TN, Vanderbilt University Press.

Hobson, P. and Edwards, J. (1992). 'Moral and Religious Education in Secondary Schools: The Need for an Independent Program in Moral Education and Some Suggestions for its Implementation', *Australian Religious Studies Review*, 5, 1, 55–62.

Hobson, P. and Edwards, J. (1994). 'A Liberal Education Rationale for Studies of Religion Programs and Its Application to Courses in Three Australian States', *Australian Journal of Education*, 38, 3, 282–99.

Hull, J.M. (1995). 'Religion as a Series of Religions: A Comment on the SCAA Model Syllabuses', in V. Barnett et al., *World Religions in Education 1995-6: From Syllabuses to Schemes – Planning and Teaching Religious Education*, London, Shap Working Party on World Religions in Education.

Hull, J.M. (1996a). 'A Critique of Christian Religionism in Recent British Education', in J. Astley and L.J. Francis (eds), *Christian Theology and Religious Education*, London, SPCK.

Hull, J.M. (1996b). 'A Gift to the Child: A New Pedagogy For Teaching Religion to Young Children', *Religious Education*, 91, 2, 172–88.

Jackson, R. (1996). 'Ethnographic Research and Curriculum Development' in L.J. Francis, W.K. Kay, and W.S. Campbell (eds), *Research in Religious Education*, Leominster, Gracewing (Fowler Wright Books).

Jackson, R. (1997). *Religious Education: An Interpretive Approach*, London, Hodder & Stoughton.

Jones, P.E. (1974). *Education in Australia*, Melbourne, Nelson.

Lines, P.M. (1988). 'Treatment of Religion in Public Schools and the Impact on Private Education', in T. James and H. Levin (eds), *Comparing Public and Private Schools*, Philadelphia, PA, Falmer Press.

Mann, H. (1957 [1837]). 'First Annual Report 1837', in L.A. Cremin, *The Republic and the School: Horace Mann on the Education of Free Men*, New York, Teachers College Press, Columbia University.

Nord, W.A. (1995). *Religion and American Education: Rethinking a National Dilemma*, Chapel Hill, University of North Carolina Press.

NSW Board of Studies (1994). *Studies of Religion: Preliminary and HSC Courses: Draft Support Document*, Sydney, Board of Studies.

NSW Board of Studies (1996). *Studies of Religion Syllabus Years 11–12*, Sydney, Board of Studies.

Partridge, P.H. (1968). *Society, Schools and Progress in Australia*, Oxford, Pergamon Press.

Pockley, P. (1992). 'Creationism Alive and Well in Unis', *Weekend Australian*, 13–14 June.

Provenzo, E.F. Jr. (1990). *Religious Fundamentalism and American Education: The Battle for the Public Schools*, Albany, State University of New York Press.

Queensland [Qld] Board of Secondary School Studies (1995). *Study of Religion: Senior Syllabus*, Brisbane, Board of Secondary School Studies.

Religious Education Council of England and Wales (1991). *RE, Attainment and National Curriculum*, London, RE Council.

SCAA (School Curriculum and Assessment Authority) (1994a). *Model Syllabuses for Religious Education*, London, SCAA.

SCAA (1994b). *Faith Communities Working Group Reports*, London, SCAA.

Sisemore, P. (1994). 'Elementary Teacher Attitudes and Beliefs Regarding Religion and Education Compared with the American Population as a Whole, and Related Legal Decisions', Manoa, Master's Thesis, University of Hawaii.

Smart, N. (1968). *Secular Education and the Logic of Religion*, London, Faber & Faber.

Tavel, D. (1979). *Church–State Issues in Education*, Bloomington, IN, Phi Delta Kappa Educational Foundation.

Victorian Board of Studies (1994a). *Religion and Society: Study Design*, Carlton, Board of Studies.

Victorian Board of Studies (1994b). *Texts and Traditions: Study Design*, Carlton, Board of Studies.

Victorian Curriculum and Assessment Board (1990a). *Religion and Society: Course Development Support Material*, Melbourne, VCAB.

Victorian Curriculum and Assessment Board (1990b). *Texts and Traditions: Course Development Support Material*, Melbourne, VCAB.

8

The Teaching of Religious Education:
Recommendations and a Charter
for the Teacher

In this final chapter we will draw out the implications of the conclusions reached in the previous seven chapters for religious education programmes in schools and universities. We will begin with some suggestions for the teaching of the subject and then look at what these recommendations mean for the actual teacher.

Aims

As argued in Chapter 1, we see the rationale for the teaching of religious education to be found in a contemporary model of liberal education which includes elements of the holistic approach to education. This model stresses the three characteristic liberal education values of critical rationality, personal transcendence, and epistemological coherence which are concerned respectively with the manner in which we reach our beliefs, how we relate them to our own life, and how we understand the interrelationships between the beliefs we hold. The holistic paradigm corrects the traditional liberal education model's overemphasis on the cognitive aspects of learning by bringing out the importance of affective goals and also supplements its individualistic focus with attention to communitarian values.

When we apply the liberal education criteria to religious education, the approach in which they are best realised is one involving an *open-ended exploration of world views or philosophies of life* rather than one aiming at *education for commitment* or at mere *education about religion* (the three approaches discussed in Chapter 1). *Education for commitment* (also known as education in faith) may have a place within a faith community which wishes to pass on its religious beliefs and doctrines to succeeding generations. However, we have argued that in the public school system in a liberal, pluralist, multicultural society, the more open-ended and educationally-oriented approach is preferable.

Such an approach has, in fact, been gaining ground steadily in most western countries and is often called studies of religion or religious studies. In the UK, where the teaching of religion is compulsory, the subject is still called religious education but, as we have seen in the last chapter, is nevertheless closer to our open-ended model than to education in faith. Studies of religion courses are equally appropriate in both public and private schools and in countries such as Australia are widely taught in the latter (sometimes in addition to or alongside education in faith courses).

The sharp distinction that we have drawn between education in faith and studies of religion courses sometimes breaks down in practice where, for example, education in faith programmes examine other religions and encourage a degree of critical inquiry, or where studies in religion programmes concentrate particular attention on the home religion or the one held by most pupils. Our general position throughout the book has been to promote the values of the open-ended approach to religious education and we would see important aspects of this as also applicable to education in faith programmes.

In regard to the approach of *education about religion* discussed in Chapter 1, we see this as educationally valuable but not as utilising all the resources that religious education offers in terms of making a contribution to the pupil's own search for meaning in life. This is where our third model of *open-ended exploration of world views or philosophies of life* has much to offer to contemporary students living in western post-industrial societies. It is the one subject they can study at school (and among a limited number at university) that is particularly equipped to explore the deeper issues of life, something that many are harking for in an age of materialism and economic rationalism. It does this, not by providing any one ready-made answer, but by encouraging the pupil's own search in a rational and well-informed way, covering most of the major possibilities, whether these are religious in the traditional sense or not. Such a course is more likely to evoke a positive response from contemporary youth than one that they sense does not respect or promote their capacity for autonomous decision-making.

Methods

The question of how to teach studies of religion is a challenging one for both the novice and the experienced teacher of religious studies, and represents one of the more contentious issues within the literature of the subject. The difficulty arises from the need in a pluralist society to teach about a range of different religions which, for their respective adherents, represent a cherished way of life, a repository of moral and religious truths, and a touchstone for directing their lives, while at the same time reconciling those values with the values of a liberal, postmodern, and democratic society – and also the teacher's own values and beliefs. The subject thus presents a host of competing truth and value claims which need to be adjudicated. A wide range of possible teaching methodologies for dealing with these problems are in evidence. Among the most popular are the phenomenological, sociological, historical, and theological approaches.

The phenomenological approach studies religion from the point of view of the adherent and attempts to get on the 'inside' of what is it like to follow a particular religion. Questions of truth are put on hold and questions about the validity of the beliefs being studied are avoided. The sociological approach endeavours to study the role of religion in human society, while the historical approach examines the important role religion has played in human history. All of these methodologies are part of the so-called social sciences and bring to the study of religion an objective, empirical, and 'scientific' character. Theological methodologies, on the other hand, cover conceptual and doctrinal issues from within the framework of a faith perspective, examining their role, coherence with the central tenets, and their conceptual power to elucidate the faith message. However, all the above approaches generally avoid the fact that different religions make different truth claims and they therefore avoid the philosophical problems posed by pluralism. For this, a philosophical methodology, as argued for in this book, is recommended.

One such philosophical approach, outlined in Chapter 3, is extended pluralism. This sets out a methodology for teaching studies of religion in a way which does not prejudge, either implicitly or explicitly, the truth status of the various beliefs being taught – nor does it simply put the questions of truth on hold as phenomenology does. Extended pluralism considers the truth status of religious beliefs to be a core property of such beliefs and it considers that any attempt to study them without considering their truth status leads to problems such as reductionism (discussed in Chapter 2) which fails to represent religious discourse adequately or misrepresents it as an alternative discourse such as psychology or morality. Extended pluralism stands in contrast to exclusivism (which treats one religion as true and all others as false) or inclusivism (which treats all other religions through the perspective of one religion) and studies religion in an educational way: it values what can be gained from alternative perspectives and uses them as a measure for testing the validity of one's own beliefs. In this way, teachers can comfortably present their own view as one among many, having imparted to their students the various criteria by which they might arrive at their own answer. This approach reflects the emphasis on critical rationality as one of the features of liberal education which we see as the appropriate context for studies of religion. Extended pluralism, then, is consistent with the values of a liberal democracy with its emphasis on tolerance, freedom, and the pursuit of truth in a non-dogmatic and open-minded way.

A complementary philosophical approach to studying religion within the context of a modern, post-industrial society is that of critical realism which includes the examination of the role of models, myths, and metaphors in science and religion (see Chapter 4). Rather than setting science and religion in opposition to each other as alternative explanatory systems for interpreting one's experience of the world, this approach shows how each draws upon the use of models, myth, and metaphor to harness a powerful tool for articulating and elucidating different aspects of that experience. Science and religion are not seen as opponents but as partners in a shared endeavour to articulate the complexities and mysteries of an evolving universe. And just as our scientific understanding evolves to adapt new discoveries and theories to better and more comprehensive interpretations of the world around us, so too our religious understanding must draw upon new insights and models to articulate and interpret our modern cultural, political, and religious experience. This interrelationship between science and religion captures the notion of epistemological coherence which is one of the hallmarks of the model of liberal education developed in Chapter 1.

In responding to the modern cultural and multicultural context, the teaching of studies of religion should incorporate such modern cultural genres as film, video, and drama. These media represent an important avenue through which today's generation articulates its key concerns and central values. Whereas ritual and sacred text may have been used in the past to convey core values, one may look today for their counterparts in film, video, and drama. This emphasises the continuity of core values in religious traditions while seeing them articulated in a modern form. Similarly, studies of religion should interact with contemporary technologies such as the Internet, with its diversity of religious-oriented World Wide Web (www) sites; use computer-based multi-media resources (such as CD-ROMS showing sacred art, or maps of ancient lands and cities); and avail itself of computer software which allows for textual analysis and searches of sacred literature.

Finally, given the fact that religions are a way of life with their own rituals and symbols, there should be the opportunity for students to observe and experience these. Visiting synagogues and mosques allows students to see how sacred texts and traditions often culminate in centres of complex symbol, ritual, and rites. In the absence of this, studies of religion can become too academic a pursuit rather than be seen as an investigation of, and dialogue with, contemporary culture and practice. However, a clear line should be drawn between observing and participating in such ceremonies and rituals.

Content

If we consider religious education in terms of the open-ended approach as exemplified in religious studies courses, the first thing to note is that it needs to be taught as a course in its own right, not by mere inclusion in other subjects such as history or social studies. This is the only way that a coherent, structured understanding of religion and religious issues is possible, rather than the ad hoc and possibly disjointed information that may be picked up through other subjects.

How many religions should be covered in the course? In Chapter 1 we argued for a minimum of three (and preferably more) in order to guarantee sufficient breadth of understanding of the variety of forms that religion can take and to provide sufficient scope for comparison. Which religions should be studied? In most western countries Christianity should certainly be on the list and perhaps required because of its relevance to an understanding of western culture and history. The others could be chosen from Judaism, Buddhism, Hinduism, Islam, Sikhism, or any others that may be significant in the particular community of the school.

As well as conventional religious systems, students should also be able to study alternative world views such as humanism and existentialism in order to be able to contrast religious with non-religious approaches to the basic questions of meaning and purpose in life. In this way, students can feel confident that whatever commitment they come to make, they have at least explored the major alternatives and have a rational basis for preferring the one they do. Mill's marketplace of ideas argument, referred to in Chapter 6, whereby an opinion is strengthened if it is subjected to testing against competing viewpoints, is very relevant in this context.

With regard to what topics, themes, and issues should be covered in the course, this would depend on the particular needs and interests of the school and community and some useful and relevant topics have been mentioned in our examination of the programmes in the UK, the USA, and Australia in the previous chapter. In the light of the position taken in this book, we would like to see topics such as The Search for Meaning, Ethical Issues Arising in Religion, and Varieties of Religious Experience and Understanding covered. Similarly, in the light of our argument in Chapter 1 about the importance of epistemological coherence, we would like to see appropriate links drawn with other subjects in the curriculum where relevant. For example, links could be drawn with what students learn in science about the creation of the universe, or what they learn in history about Biblical times and the role of religion in important political events. Finally, there would need to be appropriate content related to the methodologies discussed in the previous section (for example, philosophy, history, and sociology of religion).

Overall the content needs to reflect the aims of teaching religious education in a pluralist, multicultural, liberal society as set out above, and combining sufficient breadth and depth of study to encourage the development in students of religious autonomy as described in Chapter 1.

Issues

While each of the above three sections deals with key topics in the teaching of studies of religion, such as why it should be taught, how it should be taught and what should be taught, there are still a host of other significant issues which the teacher must address. Among these are the following: Should studies of religion be a compulsory or elective subject? What differences of approach should be adopted between primary and secondary schooling, or, at the secondary level, between compulsory and post-compulsory schooling? In a multi-faith classroom how can a student's belief system be realistically addressed while avoiding superficiality or some form of syncretism or reductionism? In a multi-faith classroom is there a likelihood of students drawing a relativist or sceptical conclusion about religion? In the light of such questions how should we proceed? Finally, should studies of religion be evaluated – is it possible to evaluate someone's search for meaning?

The question of compulsory versus elective courses in studies of religion has been answered differently in different countries. In the UK it is compulsory for all students up to the sixth form but does not form part of the National Curriculum for publicly supported schools. In Australia it is an elective subject in public schools but a compulsory subject in many private church-related schools. In the US studies of religion has very little place as a separate subject and its presence in schools runs into significant barriers arising from the Establishment Clause and the Free Exercise Clause in the Constitution (refer to Chapter 7). However, if the aim of education is to help students achieve critical rationality, personal transcendence, and epistemological coherence then it is difficult to see how this can be achieved unless the structure of their personal belief system, which has a central role in helping students orient themselves within the context of a pluralist, liberal democracy, is examined. In this respect, we see studies of religion having a central role through to the end of secondary education, and while there are strong arguments for making it compulsory throughout, we recognise the constraints placed on students by matriculation exams and the need for flexibility in subject choice at this level. We therefore suggest it be made compulsory only in primary school and in the compulsory secondary school years and made an elective subject in the senior years.

The issue of how to approach studies of religion in primary and secondary schools is an important one. For primary students in religious education (as in moral education) there is a need for students to appropriate their home religion first and to develop some awareness of other religions before they can begin to subject it to closer scrutiny. This would imply the teaching approach would be predominantly descriptive. As argued in Chapter 6, there is perhaps also some justification for an education in faith approach in primary schools as students explore the boundaries of their own faith perspective. However, it is difficult to see how this can be easily achieved in public schools where there is a diversity of faiths within the classroom. At the secondary level, the focus should move, firstly, towards the goal of achieving personal transcendence, critical rationality, and epistemological coherence in the life of the student. Secondly, it should now also promote the community goal of initiating students into a liberal, pluralist, postmodern society. Even at the secondary level this move will be gradual, keeping pace with the students' stage of development. At the secondary level, too, there must be a corresponding shift in the responsibility of parents from initiating their children into the family faith to developing their children's civic responsibilities as members of a liberal pluralist democracy (see Chapter 6 for a fuller discussion).

The multi-faith nature of the classroom presents considerable challenges to implementing a studies of religion course and may even lead some to question whether such programmes should go ahead at all. The first set of challenges refers to the selection of which faiths should be examined and the level of prominence given to Christianity. In the UK and elsewhere the emphasis on studying Christianity has evoked considerable debate. However, the previous section of this chapter on content has given some support for its inclusion, but not for its dominance. The other challenges refer to the dangers of superficiality, syncretism, or reductionism which can result from studying too wide a range of faiths. To this may be added the risk of putting students in a position to draw negative inferences about religion such as scepticism, relativism, or exclusivism. However, we would argue that the challenges can be overcome and that far from reducing the problems by not offering the subject, the problems would in fact be exacerbated by not doing so. Religious intolerance and conflict are serious problems in pluralist societies and must be addressed. But, more importantly, students have a right to expect assistance in helping them to fashion a belief system which will equip them to flourish in modern western societies.

This last point highlights the importance of considering both the role and context of education. Education must help students not merely to survive but to flourish in complex technological societies. A key ingredient for this is for students to develop autonomy, an ability adapting them as Raz says 'to cope with changing technological, economic and social conditions' and which helps them 'to adjust, to acquire new skills, to move from one sub-culture to another, to come to terms with new scientific and moral views' (1986, pp. 369–70). What is important to realise here is that, for both children and adults alike, religious belief systems have the potential to entrap rather than liberate, to limit possibilities for change rather than enhance them, and to lock their adherents into narrow cultural perspectives rather than expand their vision. The type of society in which children need to flourish is liberal, pluralist, multi-faith, democratic, postmodern, post-industrial, and cybernetic and this requires a commitment to a comprehensive set of liberal values as argued in Chapter 6. Hence, some critical understanding of the role and nature of religion is essential.

Finally, there is the question of evaluation in studies of religion. Can you in fact evaluate a student's search for meaning? The answer turns on drawing a clear distinction between adopting an educational rather than confessional approach to teaching studies of religion. If the course is taught as a matriculation subject then it will have the same assessment procedures as other subjects. More importantly, as studies of religion utilises such methodologies as the phenomenological, sociological, historical, theological, and philosophical then surely the student's mastery of these different approaches and their content can be assessed and reported on. Students are not being asked whether they have the answers to the complex questions raised by religion, but whether they have the skills needed to begin to analyse the questions. In assessing students' work in this area, then, the aim is not to see whether they have the 'right' answers but whether they have developed the capacity to explore these issues in a fruitful and rational way for themselves.

Knowledge Required by Teachers

One of the more daunting prospects for the teacher of studies of religion is the breadth of knowledge required to understand in any significant way the major world religions such as Christianity, Judaism, Buddhism, Islam, Hinduism, and Sikhism. Each of these major religions has many traditions within them, such as the Protestant and Catholic traditions within Christianity, and each of these traditions further divide, for example, the Roman and Orthodox rites within Catholicism, which also further subdivide, such as the Orthodox rites splitting into Russian, Greek, and Coptic, and so. On top of this complexity of classification is the diversity of methodologies for studying religion, such as history of religion, phenomenology of religion, philosophy of religion, psychology of religion, and sociology of religion. To this may be added theology with its own many areas of specialisation. How should a teacher respond when confronted with this complexity of detail and multiple modes of enquiry?

Clearly, a teacher cannot be expected to be an expert in all of these areas or to have a detailed competency in each. It is more important for the teacher to understand the range of methodologies available for studying religion and to appreciate the broad spectrum of world religions, together with a more detailed understanding of how a religious or non-religious world view informs a personal belief system and provides the infrastructure for a way of life. As with all subjects within the curriculum, it is important for the teacher to have a working knowledge of the studies of religion syllabus and be prepared to work collaboratively with other teachers to ensure the subject is lively and challenging to students. In this way, students will begin to appreciate the importance of developing a coherent philosophy of life which allows them to weigh up responsibly the pros and cons for the various actions and decisions they need to make in today's complex societies.

Skills Necessary for the Teacher

It is clear from the previous section that the studies of religion teacher requires a broader range of skills than is necessary for many other subjects, even though the approach to teaching the subject has a similar educational orientation as other subjects. Firstly, the teacher needs to have good communication skills which allow her or him to interact clearly with students as they endeavour to construct or reconstruct their personal belief systems. Often this requires the teacher to be able to articulate and clarify the many complex issues which students are grappling with. Secondly, it requires a sympathetic approach on the part of the teacher. In many cases students are putting forward personal views informed by their own religious and moral values, values held dear by their families. The teacher needs to be able to examine the concepts within the framework of criteria established within the course and allow the students to see how their views can be assessed against those criteria. If the teacher has the capacity to articulate and analyse her or his own views within this framework this gives the lead to how the students might also proceed.

Another important skill for the teacher of studies of religion is to be able to convey to students the importance of the quest for truth and meaning. This allows students to see that religious belief systems are attempts to encapsulate various values and truth-claims within a rich matrix of symbol, rite, ritual, practice, and textual tradition. In this way, the teacher conveys to students the value and regard for religious belief systems as significant attempts to articulate a vision of truth and meaning. At the same time, the teacher needs to convey an attitude of openness to alternative attempts to explain the nature of reality.

Finally, teachers will need some skills in philosophical reasoning. More often than not this will express itself in the ability to be able to set aside commitment to a set of views or principles so as to judge their coherence, consistency, and adequacy within a broader epistemological and logical framework. More importantly, the teacher should be able to distinguish those views which have good justification and cohere with views from other religions and other subject areas from those views which find little support either internally or from other subjects. In such cases teachers should be able to express more confidence in the former set of views and hold the latter as more speculative or less well established.

Attitudes Appropriate for the Teacher

What are the desirable attitudes for a teacher of religious studies? First of all one would expect such a teacher to have a deep and abiding interest in questions of meaning and purpose in life and in those issues to do with understanding the ultimate nature of reality that religion seeks to answer. In regard to education, a commitment to the key liberal educational values of critical rationality, personal transcendence, and epistemological coherence as well as the more affective and communitarian goals of the holistic paradigm would obviously be important. Perhaps the most essential attitude would be one of openness to new perspectives and an ongoing interest in the search for truth (rather than a conviction that one already has all the answers). At the same time, a desire to assist others in the same search and to share one's doubts and questions would be highly desirable.

We have spelt out in Chapters 3, 4, 5, and 6 in terms of the notions of extended pluralism, critical realism, the ethics of belief, and comprehensive liberalism, what we see as the underlying philosophical assumptions involved in the teaching of studies of religion. While obviously not every teacher will necessarily share every detail of our preferred perspectives, we believe that they together represent the most appropriate values position for a teacher of studies of religion. At the very least all teachers of the subject should consider where they stand in relation to these perspectives and be able to respond to the sorts of issues they raise about the teaching of religion in liberal, pluralist societies.

Issues

Apart from the types of knowledge, skills, and attitudes that a teacher of the subject, studies of religion (or of religious education as conceived in a liberal multi-faith manner) should have, there are a number of other significant issues relevant to the role of such a teacher that need to be considered. Because of the complexity of this role, it is highly desirable that specialist teachers be available, those who have been specifically prepared for the task. Teacher education programmes in this area are now being updated and improved in most western countries to meet the needs of teaching religion in a pluralist society, but further developments in this area are necessary in most cases.

The switch in focus to teaching religion as an educational rather than faith-oriented subject needs continual reinforcement at all levels where relevant. One aspect of this is to recruit potential teachers with appropriate attitudes to the subject as discussed in the above section. Students with fundamentalist views, for example, would not be well suited to teaching religious studies, and if they have any place at all in education it would be in education in faith programmes. There is a danger that such students may be attracted to teaching religion because of their conviction that they have the answer and wish to make sure that others come to share this great 'truth'. An important part of teacher education in studies of religion would be to try to show the inappropriateness of such attitudes.

This is not to say that religious education teachers should not have strong views of their own on the subject. This is perfectly normal – the point is that they should not see these as the only possible views nor their task as convincing others to share them. As we said in Chapter 1, it is better for teachers to reveal their own views to their pupils but make clear that these do not carry any special validity or authority. If the three criteria of objectivity, fairness, and balance mentioned there are implemented, this will go a long way towards ensuring that no undue indoctrination of pupils takes place.

There are a number of ways studies of religion teachers can keep their courses relevant, up-to-date, and educationally valid in a pluralist society. One is to work closely with other teachers who have an interest in religion or basic philosophical issues or who teach in related areas. In this way the various courses taken by the students can be mutually reinforcing and exhibit epistemological coherence. Another way is to make contact with relevant professional associations such as Studies of Religion and Religious Education societies and to read where possible some of the contemporary research in the area as found in the relevant academic and professional journals or recently published books. There are a lot of interesting and exciting new developments in the area (both at the academic and school level) across the western world and it would be both professionally valuable and invigorating for the teachers of religion to tap into this ferment of ideas.

This is an appropriate point on which to end this chapter and this book, as it highlights the enormous challenges and excitement of the subject at the present time – something to which this book has attempted to make a contribution.

REFERENCE

Raz, J. (1986). *The Morality of Freedom*, Oxford, Clarendon Press.

Glossary

axiology, the branch of philosophy which studies questions of value, especially in the areas of ethics and aesthetics.

autonomy, the state of being independent and self-determining, having control over one's choices or destiny. Three forms of autonomy are intellectual, moral, and religious autonomy. **Intellectual autonomy** is the ability to reason independently in assessing one's beliefs in any realm. **Moral autonomy** refers to an independent selection and assessment of the principles which guide moral choices. **Religious autonomy** refers to a reasoned commitment to a personal philosophy of life with a justifiable position on the place of the transcendent realm within it.

correspondence theory of truth, an epistemological theory that judges the truth of a proposition by its correspondence with reality. **A holistic correspondence theory of truth** is an extension of the correspondence theory of truth to include elements of a coherence theory of truth (q.v.).

coherence theory of truth, judges the truth of a proposition in terms of its consistency or coherence with other propositions within a belief system.

critical rationality, the ability to critically evaluate evidence and forms of justification in order to arrive at rationally acceptable conclusions.

critical realism, see realism.

degrees of belief, holds that propositions are not simply true or false but that they have an epistemic confidence level ranging from 0 to 1 according to the evidence or justification supporting them.

deontological, the view that some acts are morally obligatory regardless of their consequences.

education in faith, aims to bring about commitment to a particular faith.

education in religion, aims to bring about knowledge and understanding of religion as a sphere of human thought and action in general rather than commitment to any specific faith.

epistemic community, a model of a community which resolves disputes by rational means. This involves four epistemological commitments: realism (q.v.), fallibilism (q.v.), rationalism (q.v.), and respect for others' points of view.

epistemic liberalism, see liberalism.

epistemic primitives, basic axioms of any belief system expressing fundamental assumptions about the nature of reality.

epistemological coherence, refers to the consistency between different propositions within a subject (**internal coherence**) as well as to the consistency between propositions in different subjects (**external coherence**).

epistemology, a branch of philosophy dealing with theories of knowledge, e.g. what can be known and how it can be justified.

ethics of belief, deals with our moral responsibility to acquire beliefs in a rational way and to be aware of the moral consequences of the beliefs we hold.

exclusivism, treats one religion as true and all others as false.

extended pluralism, an underlying epistemological methodology for religious studies programmes based on the view that all significant attempts to answer issues of ultimate concern deserve careful and open consideration.

fallacy of tolerance, the failure to draw the conclusion that others' beliefs are false when that is logically entailed by your own set of beliefs.

fallibilism, acknowledges the possibility that one's beliefs are false.

fundamentalism, involves, in the religious context, strict adherence to certain dogmatic beliefs taken to be revealed unambiguously in relevant sacred texts.

global scepticism, see scepticism.

holistic education, is concerned with relationships and connections between all parts of human experience, both in the social and natural environments, and aims to produce a fully rounded and balanced individual.

ideological liberalism, see liberalism.

inclusivism, judges all other religions by the standards of one religion.

indirect voluntarism, see voluntarism.

instrumentalism, see realism.

liberal education, a form of education which promotes the values of critical rationality (q.v.), personal transcendence (q.v.), and epistemological coherence (q.v.) and in the contemporary form developed in this book incorporates key elements of the holistic education paradigm (q.v.).

liberalism, a position that involves a commitment to the moral and intellectual freedom of the individual achieved through adherence to rational procedures, and in the political sphere to settling disputes by public debate and consensus rather than conflict. This in turn entails a commitment to the values of tolerance, respect for others, and equality of all citizens.

Comprehensive liberalism promotes the substantive liberal values of critical rationality, autonomy, holding beliefs in an open and flexible way, and being exposed to a wide range of points of view. It may be distinguished from **political liberalism**, which is a more restricted form confining itself to procedural values necessary for democratic citizenship such as tolerance, respect for others, freedom of opinion, freedom of religion, and the rule of law.

Epistemic liberalism is a commitment to liberal values without desiring to impose these on others against their will whereas **ideological liberalism** involves a commitment to liberalism as a total belief system and political policy which should be promoted as widely as possible.

Also, comprehensive liberalism can be distinguished from epistemic liberalism, in that the former focuses more on the political context of liberalism whereas the latter focuses more on the epistemological and educational context. Similarly, comprehensive liberalism can be distinguished from ideological liberalism in that it does not necessarily involve the imposition of secular, humanist, global values and allows a degree of freedom for people to choose alternative world views.

local scepticism, see scepticism.

logical positivism, see positivism.

metaphysics, that branch of philosophy which attempts to explain the ultimate nature of reality.

model, a way of representing one area of knowledge by expressing it in terms of another. A model can be grasped as a whole and gives a vivid summary of complex relationships.

naive realism, see realism.

naive relativism, see relativism.

naturalism, used by John Hick to refer to a non-religious interpretation of the universe.

negative tolerance, see tolerance.

noumenal, see phenomenal.

ontology, that branch of philosophy which studies the assumptions about existence underlying any belief system.

paradigm, a set of conceptual and methodological assumptions that provide a theoretical framework within which scientific theories can be tested and revised.

personal transcendence, the educational goal of moving beyond a particular state of knowledge and awareness to a broader and deeper perspective. This may or may not involve a commitment to a spiritual realm.

phenomenal, used by Kant to distinguish between the phenomenal and the noumenal realms. Noumena are things in themselves which cannot be directly experienced but can only be inferred from phenomena, which are things as perceived by us.

phenomenological, an approach which studies religion from the point of view of the adherent and attempts to view religion from the insider's perspective. Questions of truth are put on hold.

pluralism, the existence of multiple competing belief systems and practices in any one society.

positive tolerance, see tolerance.

positivism, is the view that all genuine knowledge is based on sense experience and that metaphysical or speculative knowledge is invalid. **Logical positivism** holds that only empirical or analytic propositions are meaningful and hence may be valid.

rationalism, a commitment to deciding the truth of a proposition on the basis of the best available reasons.

realism, the view that physical objects exist independently of being perceived. **Naive realism** is the view that the external world exactly corresponds with our theories. **Instrumentalism** is the view that theories are merely convenient instruments for helping us to explain our experiences and have no necessary relationship to objects in the world. **Critical realism** is a mid-position between these two extremes which holds that theories are not just merely convenient instruments or explanatory devices but track or represent objects existing in the world while not necessarily exactly representing reality.

relativism, the view that there are no universal standards by which to determine the truth of a proposition. **Naive relativism** asserts that each person's view is as good as another's. **Sophisticated relativism** asserts that conflicting views between two belief systems represent different judgements about highly complex matters. This lack of certainty should be reflected in the degree of belief accorded to such conflicting propositions, which should remain open for ongoing appraisal and critical analysis.

reductionism, collapses one domain of knowledge into another. In the case of religion, it may involve, for example, interpreting religious propositions as moral or psychological statements.

scepticism, a position that doubts the truth status of propositions. **Global scepticism** applies to all areas of knowledge and **local scepticism** applies to specific areas of knowledge such as religion and ethics.

sophisticated relativism, see relativism.

tolerance, a fundamental value of liberalism. **Positive tolerance** involves not merely 'putting up with the ideas of others' (what may be termed **negative tolerance**) but an openness to learning form others with different points of view.

voluntarism, the view that we can totally control or will the beliefs we come to hold. **Indirect voluntarism** asserts that although we cannot directly will our beliefs as true we can control to some extent the manner in which we arrive at our beliefs.

Further Reading

The following recent books cover similar themes to the present book and are recommended for further reading:

Astley, J. (1994). *The Philosophy of Christian Religious Education*, Birmingham, AL, Religious Education Press.
Astley, J. and Francis, L.J. (1996). *Christian Theology and Religious Education*, London, SPCK.
Astley, J. and Francis, L.J. (1994). *Critical Perspectives on Christian Education*, Leominster, Gracewing (Fowler Wright Books).
Cooling, T. (1994). *A Christian Vision for State Education*, London, SPCK.
Noddings, N. (1993). *Education for Intelligent Belief or Unbelief*, New York, Teachers College Press.
Theissen, E.J. (1993). *Teaching for Commitment*, Leominster, Gracewing (Fowler Wright Books).
Wright, A. (1993). *Religious Education in the Secondary School*, London, David Fulton.

Index

abortion 17,95,98
ACE (Accelerated Christian Education) 100–1, 120
Ackerman, Bruce 39
agnosticism 56–7
Amish religion 108, 117
Anglican schools 117, 146
anti-realism, *see* realism
Aristotle 37, 86, 87
atheism 56, 136
Australia, *see* religious education
autonomy 5–8, 10, 12, 14, 15, 39, 85, 86, 87, 91, 97, 106–17, 119, 122, 125, 162, 168; intellectual 5–6, 12, 14, 15, 96, 103, 109; moral 5–6, 12, 15, 96, 109; religious 6, 15, 16, 103, 166
axiological, *see* methodologies in RE

Baha'i faith 14
Baier, K. 6
Bailey, Charles 3–12, 17, 96–7, 109
Banner, M.C. 69
Barbour, I.G. 67, 68, 70, 71, 72–3, 78, 79, 80
Birmingham's 'Gift to Child Approach' in RE 158
birth control 89, 101
Braithwaite, R.B. 41
Bridges, D. 105
Burtonwood, N. 106, 121, 125
Burwood, L. 106, 122–3, 125

Callan, E. 105, 114
Catholic Church 50, 101, 110, 140, 169
Catholic schools 117, 140, 146
causality, law of 29, 30
children's rights, *see* rights
Christianity 20–1, 48, 50–1, 53, 68, 75, 76–7, 81, 94, 110, 134, 135, 151, 152, 165, 167, 169
church schools 21, 97–8, 117, 119, 121, 125, 146, 147, 150, 156, 162, 166
Clifford, William 86–7, 91
coherence theory of truth, *see* truth
comparative religion 19, 102–3, 144–5

correspondence theory of truth, *see* truth
Crawford, M. 20
creation science 99, 141, 166
Creation Theology 14
Cresswell, R. 106, 116
critical rationality 3, 14–15, 16, 57, 62, 105, 106, 107, 108, 109, 111, 113, 125, 131, 138, 148, 152, 154, 161, 164, 167, 171
critical realism, *see* realism
Crittenden, B. 105, 122, 123–5
Cupitt, Don 41–2

D'Agostino, F. 89–91, 97
Darwin, Charles 100–1
Davies, Paul 60, 74
Dearden, R.F. 4, 11, 87–8
Degenhardt, M.A.B. 87–8
degrees of belief 31–6, 40, 59, 73, 93, 94
democratic community, *see* society
democratic values, *see* values
deontological argument 86, 110
Dewey, John 139
dogmatism 90, 98, 99, 114, 121, 164
Donovan, Peter 55, 61–3
doxastic responsibility 86–7
Duke, David 110

economic rationalism 13, 162
'education in faith' 18, 97–8, 102–3, 115, 146, 161, 162, 167, 171
Edwards, J.S. 156, 158
Ellis, Brian 33–4
emancipation 7, 11
empowerment 10–11
epistemic community 9, 85, 89–91, 93, 94–5, 97, 99
epistemic ethos 89,90
epistemic liberalism, *see* liberalism
epistemic primitives 28–31,40
epistemic responsibilities 27,85,89
epistemological coherence 3, 14–17, 29, 57, 105, 131, 138, 148, 152, 153, 155, 161, 164, 166, 167, 171, 172
equality 7, 124

ethics 26, 41, 136, 147, 149, 151, 154, 155, 156, 157
ethics of belief 9, 27, 85–103, 110, 120, 122, 132, 138, 148, 156, 171
euthanasia 17, 89, 95, 98
Evers, C. 16
evolution 141, 153, 164
exclusivism 14, 26, 31–6, 43, 47, 48–9, 55, 58, 62, 64, 66, 79, 93, 131, 137, 153, 155, 163, 168
existentialism 19, 58, 165
extended pluralism, *see* pluralism

fallacy of tolerance 31–6
fallibilism 9, 59, 89–91, 93, 95
Feinberg, J. 108
Feuerbach, Ludwig 41
Flew, Antony 41
forms of knowledge 4, 9–10, 16
Forrest, Peter 16, 33–6, 40, 67–8, 71–2
Fox, Matthew 14
freedom 5–8, 106, 107, 114, 124, 164
Freud, Sigmund 41
fundamentalism 66, 78, 79, 95, 98, 99–101, 111, 117, 120, 122, 140–1, 171

Gale, Richard 86, 110
Gardner, Peter 31–5, 105, 114
God 75–77, 94, 100, 139, 149, 153
Grimmitt, Michael 62
Gutmann, A. 106, 113

Halstead, M. 106, 107, 109, 119–21
Hanson, Pauline 110
Harvey, V.A. 88, 91, 92, 93
Haynes, Charles 143, 144–5
Hick, John 29, 41, 42, 52–6, 58, 63, 66, 75–6, 80–1, 112
Hill, Brian 99
Hirst, Paul 4, 9–10, 11, 16, 28, 33
Hobson, P.R. 105, 106, 116, 156, 158
holistic correspondence theory of truth, *see* truth
holistic education/paradigm 12–15, 81, 161, 167, 171
'home tradition' 61, 78, 94, 162, 167, *see also* paradigm: primary
Horton, J. 61, 106
Hull, John 135
humanism 19, 58, 61, 110, 136, 141, 165
Hutchins, Robert 11

inclusivism 14, 47, 49–51, 58, 64
indirect voluntarism, *see* voluntarism
indoctrination 90, 96, 99, 114–16, 120, 134, 136, 172
instrumentalism 70, 71, 72, 78, 80, *see also*

relativism
intellectual virtues 86, 88, 92
intolerance: religious 98, 99, 110, 168

Jackson, R. 136, 138
Jehovah's Witness 119
Jonathon, Ruth 6–7
justification 5, 8, 9, 95, 96, 97

Kant, I. 86
knowledge 5, 9, 12, 26, 108, 122, 124; religious 26, 28, 66, 73–8, 164, 166; scientific 13, 29, 66–73, 164, 166
Kuhn, T. 67, 68–9, 70
Kymlicka, W. 61, 106, 109–10, 113, 118–19, 121–2, 125

Lakatos, I. 67, 69, 70, 77
Laura, Ron 28–31, 32, 105
Le Pen, Jean-Marie 110
Leahy, Michael 28–31, 33, 105
Leicester, M. 106
liberal democracy, *see* values, democratic
liberal education 3, 17, 62, 97, 105, 109, 115–16, 121, 124, 131, 145, 148, 151, 154, 156, 158, 161, 164, 170–1
liberal values, *see* liberalism
liberalism 55, 105, 106, 110, 111, 115, 116–25, 168; comprehensive 105–25, 132, 134, 138, 150, 168, 171; epistemic 20, 61–4, 91, 109, 110, 111, 132; ideological 61, 110, 111, 112; political 105, 106, 107, 112, 113, 116, 118, 119, 121, 125
literalism, *see* fundamentalism
logical positivism 41, 78

Macedo, Stephen 106, 111, 113, 121, 122, 125
MacIntyre, A. 40
Mann, Horace 139–40
Marcuse, H. 55
Marx, Karl 41
Marxism 53, 58
materialism 30, 162
McCarthy, G.D. 86
McFague, S. 67, 72, 75
McLaughlin, Terry 33, 39–40, 105, 106, 114
Mendus, S. 61
metaphor 53, 74, 77, 78, 79, 81, 139, 164
methodologies in RE 22–3, 42, 79, 85, 131, 135, 136, 137, 139, 143, 144, 162–5, 166, 168, 169; axiological 23, 85, 91, 92, 98–103; epistemological 20, 32, 131–2; extended pluralism, *see* pluralism: extended; phenomenological 22, 58, 60, 61, 79, 85, 99, 137, 152, 154, 155, 163,

168, 169; philosophical 23, 79, 98, 131, 132, 137, 139, 144, 152, 153, 154, 155, 156, 157, 158, 163, 164, 166, 168, 169, 170; theological 22, 137, 151, 163, 168, 169
Mill, J.S. 32, 61, 91, 109, 113, 116, 165
Miller, Ron 13
minorities, *see* rights
Model Syllabuses for RE (UK) 134–9
models 30, 66–82, 72–3, 132, 138, 146, 156, 164; in religion 68, 74–82, 139; in science 66–75
Moltmann, Jürgen 54–5, 61
multi-faith society, *see* society: pluralist
multicultural society, *see* society: pluralist
Murphy, N. 67, 72
Muslim faith 101, 111, 117, 120
myths 74, 78, 156, 164

'new physics' 74
Newman, J.H. 60
non-interference: rule of 90, 91, 118
non-realism, *see* realism
Nord, Warren 11, 142, 145
noumenal realm 52, 54, 66
Nozick, R. 67, 71

O'Hear, A. 4
objective knowledge 5, 74

paradigm: primary 39, 94, 114–15
paradigms 39, 66–82, 74
parents' rights, *see* rights
Peacocke, A. 67, 72, 78
personal transcendence 3, 10, 14–16, 22, 57, 59, 91, 95, 105, 109, 131, 137, 138, 148, 152, 155, 156, 157, 161, 167, 169, 170, 171
persons 5, 9, 13
Peters, Richard 3, 9, 95
Phenix, P. 4
phenomenal realm 52, 66
phenomenological, *see* methodologies in RE
philosophy of religion 149–50, 153, 157
Plato 26, 37, 86
pluralism 26, 47–8, 51–64, 66, 68; extended pluralism 23, 32, 57–61, 64, 109, 116, 121, 131, 136, 150, 153, 156, 163, 164, 171; Hick's interpretation 52–6, 64; revisitionist pluralism 51–2, 58
pluralist predicament 23, 66–82, 132
pluralist society, *see* society
Pockley, P. 153
Pojman, L. 86, 93–4
Polanyi, Michael 39, 88
Popper, K. 121, 125
postmodernism 5, 55, 66, 163, 167, 168

primary culture/paradigm, *see* paradigm
public schools 18, 21, 115, 117, 120, 125, 131, 139, 140, 141, 142, 146, 147, 162, 166
publicity: rule of 90–1, 93

Quakers, *see* Society of Friends
Quine, W.V. 88
Quinton, Anthony 33

Rahner, Karl 50
rationalism: principle of 9, 89–91, 95
rationality 33–6, 70, 149
Rawls, J. 61, 106–7, 111, 118–19
Raz, J. 7, 17, 15, 61, 107–8, 168
Real, the (in Hick) 52–6, 58, 76, 80
realism: anti-realism 71, 72; critical 5, 13, 23, 37, 66–82, 89, 132, 164, 171; naive 71, 72, 78, 80; non-realism 41–2; principle of 9, 89, 91, 95
reason 5, 8, 95, 96, 97
reductionism 26, 41–3, 53, 67, 131, 137, 145, 163, 166, 168
relativism 26, 36–40, 43, 47, 66–7, 70, 78, 89, 131, 137, 145, 153, 155, 166, 168; naive 37, 80, 123; sophisticated 37, 40, 57, 80, 94; *see also* instrumentalism
religious autonomy, *see* autonomy
religious education (RE) 6, 8, 9, 12, 17–24, 62, 125, 134, 135, 140, 157, 161, 162, 171; in Australia: government policies 18, 131, 146, 157, 166; programmes 20–1, 23, 132, 142, 146–7, 156–7, 166; in NSW (programmes), 99, 137, 146, 150–3, 154, 156, 157; in Queensland (programmes) 146, 147–50, 156, 157; in Victoria (programmes), 146, 153–6, 156, 157; in the UK: government policies 18, 131, 132–4, 145, 157, 166, 167; programmes 20–1, 23, 132, 134–9, 142, 157, 162, 167; in the USA: government policies 18, 131, 139–41, 157, 166; programmes 20–1, 23, 132, 142–5, 156, 157
religious minorities, *see* rights
religious schools, *see* church schools
religious studies 19, 47, 51, 57–61, 63, 79–82, 85, 97–9, 102–3, 115–16, 134, 142–58, 162, 164, 165, 166, 167, 169, 170, 171, 172
Rescher, Nicholas 26–7, 30, 32, 40, 56–7
respect for persons 9, 90, 95, 96, 106, 114, 138, 144
respect for truth 9, 88–91, 95, 96, 106, 114
responsibility: rule of 90, 91, 97
revisability of theories 70, 71, 73
rights: of adults 112–13, 117; of children 96, 105–6, 108–9, 112–16, 117, 120–2, 125,

132, 167; of parents 105–6, 109, 113–25, 132, 167; of religious minorities 105–6, 116–25; of the State 105–6, 109, 110, 111–13, 115–7, 125, 132
Roman Catholic Church, *see* Catholic Church
Rossiter, G. 20

scepticism 26–31, 43, 47, 66–7, 71, 131, 137, 153, 155, 166, 168; global 26–8, 30, 57; local 26, 28, 30;
science 141, 143, 149, 153, 164
scientific research programmes 69, 71, 77
Sisemore, Pamela 143
Smart, N. 137
Smith, Huston 56
Society of Friends (Quakers) 14
society: democratic 94–7, 105, 106, 110, 113, 115, 123, 124, 143, 163, 167; liberal 105, 106, 107, 110, 111, 113, 114, 115, 117, 119, 120, 121, 122, 123, 124, 125, 131, 132, 158, 161, 163, 167, 171; pluralist 3, 7–8, 13–14, 48, 51, 56, 62, 66, 79, 98, 105, 106, 107–10, 111, 112, 113, 115, 116, 119, 120, 122, 123, 125, 131, 132, 133, 139, 143, 145, 148, 156, 158, 161, 164, 166, 167, 168, 171, 172
Socrates 26
Soskice, Janet 73
spirituality 12
state schools, *see* public schools
State's rights, *see* rights
Steiner, Rudolf 14
Stevenson, J.T. 86–7, 91, 110
Stopes-Roe, Harry 22
studies of religion, *see* religious studies
Surin, Kenneth 54, 55, 61

teacher: in RE 21–2, 31, 63, 97, 102–3, 169–72; role of 88, 92, 94–7
'Third Perspective' RE Syllabus (UK) 136–7,

148
tolerance 3, 96, 107, 108, 109–10, 118–19, 121–2, 143, 164; negative 109–10; positive 109–10, 116, 150; religious 109, 118; *see also* fallacy of tolerance
totalistic belief systems 111, 122
transcendence, *see* personal transcendence
transcendent realm 28, 30, 66, 103
truth claims 26, 27, 34, 38, 72, 144, 145, 163, 170
truth: coherence theory of 70, 73; correspondence theory of 67, 70, 71, 72, 73, 79; holistic correspondence theory of 68, 72

UK, *see* religious education
USA, *see* religious education

values: democratic 85, 95–7, 98, 103, 105, 121–3, 164
van Huyssteen, Wentzel 74, 77–8
voluntarism: indirect 87–8, 93
Vroom, H.M. 40

Walker, J. 16
Walzer, M. 106, 121
Ward, Keith 31–2, 37–8, 51–2
Warwick RE Project 138, 158
White, J.P. 4, 12
White, Mr Justice 108, 117
Williams, Bernard 7, 15, 87, 93
Wisconsin *v.* Yoder 108
Wittgenstein, L. 53, 88
women: treatment of 17, 75, 77, 101, 120, 123, 151
Wright, Andrew 59
Wringe, C. 106, 121, 122, 125

Young, G.M. 88
Young, Iris 118

Lightning Source UK Ltd.
Milton Keynes UK
UKOW05f1233101013

218790UK00001B/13/A

9 780713 04039